Japan in the Age of Glol

CW01494654

The multiple and diverse forces of globalization have, indeed, affected Japan significantly over the past decades. But so, it must be said, has Japan influenced a variety of critical global developments – globalization is not a one-way street, particularly for a nation as economically influential and technologically advanced as Japan. The chapters in this collection examine the impact of globalization on Japan and the impact of Japan on the forces of globalization from the various disciplinary perspectives of business, the economy, politics, technology, culture and society. They also explain the manner in which the nation has responded to the economic and cultural liberalization that has been such a profound force for change around the globe. This comprehensive collected works brings the latest research to bear on this important subject and provides evidence of the long history of global influences on Japan – and Japanese impacts on the rest of the world.

This book will be of interest to students and scholars of globalization, Japanese Studies, and Asian Studies.

Carin Holroyd is Associate Professor of Political Science at the University of Waterloo, Canada.

Ken Coates is Professor of History and Dean of the Faculty of Arts at the University of Waterloo, Canada.

Routledge Contemporary Japan Series

Japan in the Age of Globalization

Edited by
Carin Holroyd and Ken Coates

Routledge
Taylor & Francis Group

LONDON AND NEW YORK

First published 2011
by Routledge
2 Park Square, Milton Park, Abingdon, Oxon OX14 4RN

Simultaneously published in the USA and Canada
by Routledge
711 Third Avenue, New York, NY10017

Routledge is an imprint of the Taylor & Francis Group, an informa business

First issued in paperback 2014

British Library Cataloguing in Publication Data
A catalogue record for this book is available from the British Library

Library of Congress Cataloging-in-Publication Data
Japan in the age of globalization / edited by Carin Holroyd and Ken Coates.
     p. cm. – (Routledge contemporary Japan series ; 36)
  Includes bibliographical references and index.
  1. Japan – Economic conditions – 1989– 2. Globalization – Japan.
  3. Japan – Social conditions – 1989– 4. Japan – Foreign relations – 1989–
  I. Holroyd, Carin. II. Coates, Ken.
  HC462.95.J35556 2011
  337.52–dc22   2010052899

ISBN 978-0-415-66584-1 (hbk)
ISBN 978-1-138-01702-3 (pbk)
ISBN 978-0-203-81430-7 (ebk)

Typeset in Times New Roman by
HWA Text and Data Management, London

Contents

Illustrations

Figures

Tables

Contributors

Jeff Alexander is Associate Professor in the Department of History, University of Wisconsin–Parkside. He is the author of *Japan's Motorcycle Wars: An Industry History* (2008) and coauthor (with Joy Dixon) of *The Nelson Guide to Writing in History*. He is currently working on a history of the brewing industry in Japan.

Dick Beason is Professor of Business, University of Alberta. He is the co-author (with Dennis Patterson) of *The Japan that Never Was* (2004). He has worked with the Bank of Japan and several Japan-based companies. His work includes studies of corporate restructuring in Japan.

Janice Brown is Professor and Chair, Department of Asian Languages and Literature, University of Colorado at Boulder. She is the author of *Hayashi Fumiko: I Saw A Pale Horse and Selected Poems from Diary of a Vagabond* (1997), and *Tarnished Words: The Poetry of Ōba Minako* (2005). She is a specialist in the study of modern Japanese women writers.

Ken Coates is Professor of History, University of Waterloo, and President of the Japan Studies Association of Canada. He is the co-author of *Japan and the Internet Revolution* and *Innovation Nation: Science and Technology in 21ˢᵗ Century Japan*. He is working, with Carin Holroyd, on a book on digital media in East Asia.

Jay Goulding is Associate Professor in the Department of Social Science, York University. He has published widely on aspects of East Asian philosophy and edited *China-West Interculture, Toward the Philosophy of World Integration: Essays on Wu Kuang-ming's Thinking* (2008).

Ken Gordon is a venture partner at Chrysalix Energy Venture and President and CEO at Loa Corporation and Loa PowerTools. He previously worked as a business consultant and as Executive Director of Alberta Deal Generator.

Dawn Grimes-McClellan is Assistant Professor of Japanese Studies at Earlham College. She is an ethnographer of Japanese high school experiences and is currently working on a study of the Basic Law for a Gender-Equal Society (1999), focusing on the impact of the legislation of Japanese curriculum.

Kimie Hara is Renison Research Professor of East Asian Studies, Renison University College and the University of Waterloo. She is the author of *Northern Territories, Asia Pacific Regional Conflicts and the Aland Experience* (2009) and editor of *Cold War Frontiers in the Asia-Pacific: Divided Territories in the San Francisco System* (2007).

Carin Holroyd is Associate Professor in the Department of Political Science, University of Waterloo. She is the co-author of *Japan and the Internet Revolution* and *Innovation Nation: Science and Technology in 21st Century Japan*. She is currently working on a study of the politics of environmental technologies in Japan.

Vikas Mehrotra is A.F. (Chip) Collins Chair and Associate Professor of Finance and Department Chair, Finance and Statistical Analysis, School of Business, University of Alberta. His research focuses on corporate restructuring and governance and financial market microstructures.

Masao Nakamura is Konwakai Professor of Japanese Research and Professor for Strategy and Business, Sauder School of Business, University of British Columbia. He is the editor of *Changing Japanese Business, Economy and Society: Globalization of Post-Bubble Japan* (2004) and *Changing Corporate Governance Practices in China and Japan* (2008).

Norio Ota is Coordinator of the Japanese Studies Program, Department of Languages, Literatures and Linguistics at York University. A leading innovator in Japanese language instruction and the use of technology in language teaching, he has developed multi-point language courses and promoted Japanese language studies internationally.

William Tsutsui is the Dean, Dedman College of Humanities and Science, Southern Methodist University. He is a scholar of Japanese business and popular culture and the co-author (with Michiko Ito) of *In Godzilla's Footsteps: Japanese Pop Culture Icons on the Global Stage* (2006) and *Japanese Popular Culture and Globalization* (2010).

Akiko Watanabe is Assistant Professor of Finance, Department of Finance and Management Science, School of Business, University of Alberta. Her research focuses on value and risk in financial markets and investor expectations.

Introduction

Carin Holroyd and Ken Coates

The shocking financial crises of 2008–2009 that the American banking crisis caused around the world lay to rest any lingering questions about the power and reach of modern globalization. In Japan, sweeping lay-offs and massive losses at Toyota headlined a shocking list of financial challenges.[1] The once-vaunted electronics sector followed Toyota's lead, with Sony, Panasonic and Toshiba letting go tens of thousands of workers and shutting plants in the face of collapsing markets in the United States of America and elsewhere. Stock prices fell dramatically, only recently rescued banks teetered on the edge of renewed crisis, unemployment rose to close to 5%, a startling result for the country.[2] The government assembled a US$100 billion stimulus package,[3] unfurled trade development strategies, and sought to reposition Japan internationally. Indeed, the fact that Japan and China played a major role in assisting the International Monetary Fund and the government of the United States signalled the growing twenty-first-century global power of Asia.

Several years ago, when work first began on this collection, globalization meant something very different. In an age of economic expansion and opportunity, globalization referred to Japan's efforts to match its regulatory and business environment with international standards. It spoke to the efforts of Japanese corporations to expand markets and develop trade relations around the world. Globalization was about the impact of the West on Japan and the reach of Japanese popular culture around the globe. Globalization of this type was liberating to some, threatening to others, and was generally viewed as part of a complex, multidimensional reordering of international affairs. For most observers, the integration of world affairs, culture, business and politics was an inevitable and generally positive transformation, one that held the promise of unshackling Japan from its overbearing traditions while sharing the best of Japanese culture and business with the rest of the world.

The multiple and diverse forces of globalization have, indeed, affected Japan significantly over the past decades. But so, it must be said, has Japan influenced a variety of critical global developments. Globalization is not a one-way street, particularly for a nation as economically influential and technologically advanced as Japan. The essays in this collection examine, from various disciplinary perspectives, the impact of globalization on Japan and the impact of Japan on the forces of globalization. They seek to explain the manner in which the nation has responded to the economic and cultural liberalization that has been such a profound force for change around the globe. Readers will quickly see that, in this collection as in the general debate on this issue among Japan specialists, there is no easy consensus on how much has changed, why things have changed, or whether these shifts represent a profound reordering of Japanese society.

Even before the financial crisis hit, the last quarter century had been eventful in Japan. The country rode the "Bubble Economy" to soaring economic heights.[4] Commentators wrote eagerly of the Pacific Century, the Asian Tigers, and of the prospect that Japan's economy would soon overtake the United States in the race for global supremacy.[5] When the bubble burst, the ride down was almost as painful as the surge forward had been spectacular. Companies faced grave economic difficulties, the nation's firms lost their global lustre, and allegations and evidence of corruption, patronage and incompetence plagued both the corporate sector, the political system and the once unimpeachable civil service. Japanese firms closed down factories, opened plants in low wage countries; some even went bankrupt. The economic decay deepened and broadened, to the point where the standard view of Japan's economy was of a nation mired in permanent recession.

The view that Japan is in serious decline does not stand up well to scrutiny, even in the midst of the economic transition sparked by the 2008–2009 financial meltdown. What has been decline is the serious and systematic attempt to understand Japan and to explain Japanese development to Western audiences. Clearly a more balanced appraisal is required. Toyota Corporation, which suffered significantly during the financial crisis, rebounded to profitability quickly but subsequently plunged into disarray in 2009–2010 following a period of over-expansion and quality control issues. Generally, the up tick in the Japanese economy started sooner than most countries hit by the devastating slowdown in global trade. It is easy, particularly in an era of globalization where foreign intrusions are often viewed as signs of national decline, to find fault lines in the Japanese system. Such a view is not consistent with the changes occurring within Japan. The unemployment rate has risen, but it remains comparatively low by international standards. Literacy and reading standards are extremely high (99% across Japan) when judged against other countries.[6] Major indicators of health, from infant mortality rates to life expectancy, suggest that Japan is one of the healthiest countries around (even though smoking remains commonplace). Young Japanese students continue their studies at college or university at a highly competitive rate internationally. And so on and so on. Japan is changing; it shares this reality with all countries. Japan may even be changing faster than many others; the nation certainly has been adapting continuously since the end of World War II to new realities and new opportunities. But the language and rhetoric of decline, however fashionable in Western circles, does not capture the nuances, creativity, complexity and determination of Japan.

The issues associated with globalization have attracted increasing attention; scholars of Japan have contributed significantly to this important international debate. As David Block and Deborah Cameron have written:

Globalization is nothing if not a fashionable term – it pervades contemporary political rhetoric and is a keyword of both academic and popular discourse on economy, society, technology and culture. In languages as diverse as Japanese and Spanish, the word exists in cognate form – as *gurobarizeshon* and *globalizacton*, respectively – and where it does not (e.g. the French term *mondialisation*), it is still understood, in Gidden's terms, as "the intensification of worldwide social relations which link distant localities in such a way that local happenings are shaped by events occurring many miles away and vice versa"; or in Malcolm Water's terms as "a social process in which the constraints of geography on social and cultural arrangements recede and in which people are increasingly aware that they are receding".[7]

Mayumi Itoh's important work, *Globalization of Japan*,[8] examines government support for globalization, and argues that the country's heritage of cultural and political isolation have slowed efforts to open Japan up to international changes. Itoh makes a significant contribution by demonstrating the tensions within the Japanese mindset that created a gap between the official policy of *Kaikoku* (open-door policy) and the long-standing reality of *Saikoku* (secluded nation). This caution has been helpful at times; Japan did not succumb to the frenzy of the dotcom boom and bust, despite being ridiculed by the West for not leaping into the new economy. On other occasions, of course, the *Saikoku* mentality allowed the government and businesses in Japan to erect formidable and unnecessary barriers to international engagement. In many ways, therefore, Japan's struggle with globalization is as much an internal contest as it is a battle with broader international forces. Koichi Iwabuchi's *Recentering Globalization: Popular Culture and Japanese Transnationalism* is one of the most important works in the field, for it illustrates both the impact of popular influences on Japan and the effect that the export of Japanese popular culture has had on other parts of the world. His descriptions of the dramatic receptiveness of other societies to Japanese popular culture helped reverse the long-standing Japanese preoccupation with the manner in which foreign influences were altering conditions within the country.[9]

Other scholars have, of course, contributed to the important work of understanding the influences and impacts of globalization in Japan. *Globalization and Social Change in Contemporary Japan*, edited by J.S. Eades, Tom Gill and Harumi Befu, consists of a series of excellent anthropological and sociological essays on global influences in the country.[10] The individual papers examine such diverse themes as the Yakuza and organized crime, consumerism and the global role of Japanese managers and demonstrate, as do the papers in this collection, the complex interplay between Japanese and internal influences. At a more detailed level, the edited collection *Globalization and Language Teaching*, by David Block and Deborah Cameron, demonstrates that the complexities being experienced in Japan are being felt internationally, as languages – and language teachers – struggle with the growing overlap and interconnections between national languages, English and international cultural content.[11] Ryuko Kobata's excellent chapter on language teaching in Japan, in particular, documents the strong Japanese reaction to Anglicization, the concomitant rise in Japanese nationalism, and the manner in which these factors effect language instruction.[12] On a broader political and economic front, *The Internationalization of Japan*, edited by Glenn Hook and Michael Weiner,[13] examines the growing global engagements of Japan, with individual contributions considering the manner in which Japan's economic, political culture, education system and values reflect international influences. The papers in these collections, and several others including this one,[14] seek to provide crucial building blocks in the broader understanding of globalization in Japan. Clearly the process of *kokusaika* (internationalization) is destined to be both a formidable force within Japan, between Japan and the rest of the world, and within the scholarly community that seeks to understand twenty-first-century Japan.

Globalization has many facets and implications. A collection of twelve essays can only begin to review the impact and implications of this powerful and influential force for change, one that has been an important part of Japan's evolution over many centuries. Indeed, if the current debate about globalization has had any lasting impact, it is likely the strong understanding of the complexity, reach and effect that global and international forces have had at multiple levels within all societies, even those like Japan that have traditionally been seen as comparatively closed to global influences. The essays that follow have been organized into four sections. The first, "The history of globalization in Japan", uses three very different themes – philosophical influences, corporate histories and concepts of childhood – to demonstrate some of the complexities of globalization in the past. The section entitled "Globalization and the Japanese economy and business environment" tackles one of the dominant issues of our time – the economic impact of international commercial entanglements – and examines how Japan has responded to these influences and pressures. The third section – "Cool Japan and the global age" – reveals that Japan is an active player in contemporary global culture and, equally, that global influences have had a profound impact on Japan's internal cultural dynamics. In the final section, "Globalization and Japan's place in the world", two essays examine the manner in which global forces have altered Japan's security situation and environmental awareness, provoking internal debate about national vulnerability and Japan's global responsibilities. The final contribution, an essay entitled "Japan in the age of twenty-first-century globalization", reflects on future prospects and identifies a possible research agenda that capitalizes on the interdisciplinary perspectives and ideas raised in this collection.

The recent debates about globalization and its multiplicity of influences have obscured the degree to which the effects of globalization have long been a part of Japanese realities. Generations before Western industrial nations intruded into Japanese space in the mid-nineteenth century, the people of Japan lived with a variety of external, largely Asian, influences. Jay Goulding, in his contribution, asserts that philosophical developments in the Tokugawa era created mental structures and conceptual frameworks within which Japanese intellectuals could understand their culture and, therefore, their place within a broader, more complicated world. In Japan as elsewhere, the effort to understand one's world within a broader, global context has long been a key element in national cultures and in the development of intellectual concepts of both place and "others". These cultural roots, in turn, provided the social cohesion which subsequently played – and plays – a crucial role in Japan's reaction to the rest of the world.

Japan's rise to economic prominence and subsequent decline played out against a rapidly changing global environment. Of course, World War II brought prominence to Japan – and left a bitter international legacy that influenced the world's understanding of the country to the present day. As Jeff Alexander documents in his original paper on the "missing" war-time corporate history of Japan, this period of time remains extremely sensitive and is often suppressed. The country's economic successes in the 1960s and 1970s created a striking mythology about Japan Inc. and the seemingly infallible combination of Japanese business and government. Beginning in the early 1980s, trade liberalization and the adoption of free market policies by several leading nations encouraged increased international trade. Investment patterns shifted dramatically, as industries once protected by a veil of tariff barriers crumpled in the face of developing world competition. Economic globalization proceeded, it seemed, hand in glove with cultural and social integration. Increased international travel and communications – cheaper and faster than before – bridged cultural barriers and brought people closer together. The power and thrust of Western (particularly American) mass culture made global icons out of mediocre Hollywood stars, NBA basketball players, and the corporate leaders of the "new economy". This new economic order was more than just international in scope. It was fuelled by the technological and commercial revolution, one tied to the spread of the personal computer and the stunning development and expansion of the Internet.

Commentators, overly enthusiastic in their assumption that the trends of the day foreshadowed major and permanent transformations in the near and mid-term, spoke prematurely of the collapse of the nation-state and the weakening of national governments.[15] They argued that the Japanese government's developmental state approach, deemed responsible for the growth of the 1960s and 1970s, had become an anachronism. Analysts assumed the ascendancy of the United States, driven by its seemingly insurmountable lead in the digital economy and its culture of aggressive entrepreneurship. Japan's staid and efficient commercial order seemed destined to crumble in the face of the American juggernaut. English, it was also assumed at least by Western commentators, would dominate all global endeavours. In a provocative assessment of Japanese restructuring efforts – understood to be one of the central manifestations of commercial globalization – Dick Beason and his colleagues argue in their contribution that the restructuring efforts arising out of the economic distress of the 1990s generated weak returns for companies and shareholders, suggesting that Japanese managers and investors remained sceptical about the extent of change that was needed and about expectations regarding responsiveness to market realities. Masao Nakamura reaches similar conclusions through his analysis of corporate governance reforms, suggesting that Japanese firms proved selective in their adoption of American-style governance systems while holding on to key Japanese elements. Western popular culture would prove attractive in Japan, driven by the technology of the Internet and the wealth and push of American media outlets, but the business community remained resistant to change. Japan, all but the most optimistic analysts agreed, was destined to suffer grievously in the new order unless it abandoned traditional values and practices, adapted to global forces, and prepared itself for a technology-driven transformation.

Few, if any, however, would have suggested that very little has shifted in Japan through this most recent era of globalization. The nation's economy has been affected markedly, due to a variety of competitive and structured pressures. Lifetime employment, long the hallmark of the Japanese enterprise system, has been in decline (as it has in other nations). For decades, Japanese firms purchased the loyalty and commitment of their employees through the promise of guaranteed work for life. Competitive pressures and changing international realities make such promises increasingly difficult to keep. There are numerous signs of Japanese firms abandoning their nation-specific approach to management and adopting international/Western techniques. Some major companies now hire throughout the year, and not just once a year in April as was almost always the case in the past.[16] Firms like Matsushita and Fujitsu have adopted merit (as opposed to seniority) based pay. Some companies have allowed female office staff to dress as they wish, no longer requiring the use of uniforms. In a direct illustration of the influence of foreign practices, Seiyu, which merged with Walmart, has changed its job titles into English. Japanese–foreign mergers, once extremely rare, have become more commonplace. And global competitive pressures (and the shortcomings of the national banking system) have driven several major Japanese companies to join forces. At the same time, some firms attempted the changes motivated by international models and then reversed directions, re-implementing Japanese practices.

Changes at the company level are reflected in a wide-ranging series of national debates about the future of the Japanese "system." The long-celebrated, and often-criticized, Japanese education system is being challenged to adapt to the new work-place realities and to explore Western models for ideas on how to prepare students. As Dawn Grimes-McClellan argues in her contribution, Japanese attempts to understand the domestic impact of globalization have resulted in a reinterpretation of childhood and the emergence of a new, globalized language to describe the experience and challenges of young people. This, in turn, has caused strain within families and contributed to substantial shifts in expectations about the behaviour and aspirations of youth. More broadly, criticism of the Japanese financial and political structures have resulted in major efforts to deregulate the Japanese economy, and to bring national practices in line with widely accepted global standards. Sweeping changes in securities trading, banking, telecommunications, domestic investment and other areas are indicative of the Japanese efforts to align their practices with the free market, more laissez-faire model that has become increasingly common throughout the industrial world.

Japanese politicians and bureaucrats responded to changing global conditions because the sluggish domestic economy demanded new approaches. Significant shifts have occurred. Deregulation led to soaring levels of foreign investment in Japan, from US$5.5 billion in 1997 to over US$28 billion in 2000. Foreign investment in Japan has increased steadily in recent years, from ¥5.8 trillion in 2000 to ¥12.8 trillion in 2006. Major firms from the United States, Germany and France sought opportunities in the once-closed Japanese market. Companies like Carrefour, Costco, Manulife, Walmart, Goldman Sachs and Merrill Lynch invested in Japan. Foreign acquisitions of Japanese firms soared as well, doubling between 1998 and 1999, with most of the investment coming in finance, transportation and telecommunications. Several high profile investments – Renault's acquisition of Nissan, Daimler-Chrysler's purchase of Mitsubishi Motors, British Telecom and AT&T's investment into Japan Telecom – provided graphic evidence of the degree to which Japan's commercial environment had changed.[17]

In the midst of these sweeping economic changes, Japan has joined with other countries in the search for the commercial foundations of the "new economy", an order many believe will be dominated by the products and services derived from cutting edge scientific and technological discoveries. As Ken Coates and Carin Holroyd argue in their paper, major investments in science and technology and a commitment to the innovation economy sit at the foreground of Japanese attempts to adapt to the new global realities. In this instance, the important confluence of investment, competitiveness and Japanese cultural loyalty has given the country an important lead in the development of the high technology economy. Ironically, commitment to country, cultural homogeneity and Japanese model of scientific and commercial collaboration may well be crucial factors in economic success in a globalized world.

The changes associated with globalization reached far beyond the commercial sector. As Janice Brown argues in a provocative paper on the impact of globalization on aspects of Japanese literature, the preoccupation of analysts with the economic effects of globalization has marginalized the study of cultural changes and responses. This, in turn, has resulted in an obscuring or narrowing of the assessment of the cultural influences and reactions associated with the multifaceted influences of globalization. Western television programs, movies, music and other elements of mass popular culture became increasingly evident across the country. An increasing number of Western companies, from Starbucks Coffee to Toys R Us, have become commonplace in major cities. (Starbucks now has over 700 shops in Japan and Toys R Us has over 150 outlets.) The study of English, typically with young Western instructors, became something of a national preoccupation. The Japanese government's JET (Japan Exchange and Teaching) program sees thousands of young foreigners (mainly Australian, American, British, Canadian and New Zealanders) assisting with teaching in Japanese junior and senior high schools.[18] As Norio Ota points out in his paper, the infusion of English and its accompanying values has resulted in sociolinguistic changes to the Japanese language and to an increase in the use of foreign loan words. Globalization, then, has a documented influence on the most fundamental instrument of Japanese culture – the national language.

The influences are not entirely Western or North American. Many of the Japanese traveling abroad are going to Asia; after the United States, the next most popular destinations for Japanese tourists are South Korea, China, Thailand, Taiwan and Hong Kong. Chinese and other language classes have increased in popularity. Changing demographic conditions resulted in a marked labour shortage which, in turn, led to a loosening of immigration regulations and an effort to recruit workers of Japanese ancestry from Brazil and Peru. Foreigners, as a result, became increasingly common in the country's larger cities, many working either as labourers or scientific and technical professionals. The economic downturn resulted in efforts to reverse the flow of immigrants, changing at least temporarily the force of the incoming population. However, despite this foreign onslaught, Japanese culture has held its own. In fact, many Japanese commentators point to a revival of interest in Japanese traditional art forms even among young people. Kabuki and Noh theatre continue to attract large crowds[19] and even imported television programs like *Lost*, *Prison Break* and *24* cannot dislodge the ever-popular Japanese adult soap operas, sumo matches, high school baseball and very unusual game shows from the television schedule.

Globalization works in multiple directions, as it does for Japan. The same quarter century that has witnessed profound changes due to global influences in Japan has seen Japan have an increasingly prominent global role. The emergence of Japanese automakers as world leaders in terms of both product quality and market share provided the best example until the crisis that hit Toyota in 2009–2010, matched in some ways by the importance of major technology firms, including Sony, Matsushita, Toshiba, NEC and others. The sales strength of PlayStation (Sony) and Wii (Nintendo) is but one example of the global reach of Japanese technology and commerce. At the other extreme, the gradual expansion of sushi as a food of middle-class, professional choice in countries around the world reveals a growing appreciation for Japanese culinary traditions. Japanese baseball, once carefully sprinkled with a handful of foreign (largely American) players, began exporting its stars to North American teams, creating a frenzy of interest on both sides of the Pacific.[20] Japanese travellers are now familiar around the world, with over 16.6 million Japanese visiting other countries in 2010. They do more than travel. In some areas like Hawaii and Australia, Japanese travel firms have dominated major portions of the local market. In others (Italy, Thailand, Canada, the United Kingdom), Japanese travel companies send thousands of big spending Japanese tourists on high priced overseas trips. Some Japanese choose to marry abroad – Hawaii is the most popular destination but Vancouver has attracted a fair number of couples also – and recently a number of Japanese seniors have chosen to retire overseas in countries like Thailand.[21]

The global impact of Japan can be seen in other areas. Japanese designers and developers have had a profound influence on the video game industry.[22] Although less widely acknowledged than the role played by Sony, Sega and others in the production of the hardware, the global software industry for video games has a decidedly Japanese character. In a related area, Japanese *manga* (cartoons) and *anime* (animation) have become increasingly popular, both among children and adults. Sailor Moon, Dragon Ball, Gundam and Princess (Hime) Mononoke are among the best liked. Other Japanese commercial campaigns, such as Pokémon, Hello Kitty, dancing flowers and tamagotchis have all enjoyed global success. There are elements of Japanese fashion (although not the oddly coloured hair of teenagers and the baggy white socks) that have found favour internationally, particularly in Asia. Japanese popular music, particularly by female singers like Utada Hikaru, Amuro Namie and Hamasaki Ayumi, is almost completely ignored in North America and Europe, but is extremely popular throughout Asia. A few Japanese authors like Yoshimoto Banana and Murakami Haruki have also become popular outside Japan as have a number of Japanese films (most recently, *Shall We Dance?*, remade with Richard Gere) and in Asia, television dramas. William Tsutsui's analysis of the globalization of Japanese popular culture documents the spread of such iconic marketing items as Hello Kitty while wondering if the acceptance of Japanese cultural artifacts really translates into meaningful political or economic power.

Japan is, long-term economic slowdown and occasional recessions notwithstanding, still a major global player. Japan's influence can be seen on every continent on the globe but again especially in Asia. Within Asia, Japan is the largest foreign investor, the largest exporter, and the primary provider of technology and foreign aid. Japan is one of the largest provider of foreign aid in the world, with much of the money directed toward East Asia, largely to support telecommunications and energy projects.[23] Japan remains a major foreign investor on a truly global scale, contributing over 20% of global foreign investment in 1990. The value of Japanese investments and their percentage of total world foreign direct investment fell after the collapse of the bubble economy (from US$50 billion in 1990 to slightly more than US$30 billion in 2000), but the cumulative investment overseas of close to US$600 billion (2008) placed Japan ninth in the world.[24] Nonetheless, Japan's auto plants can be found in dozens of countries, including six locations in Europe, four in the United Kingdom, eleven in North America and an astonishing 110 plants throughout Asia. Each plant supports numerous affiliated parts companies. The electronics section has a similar profile, with over 142 Japanese plants in Europe, 210 in North America, more than 850 in Asia, 41 in Central and South America, six in Oceania and three in Africa. These numbers, pre-dating the economic crisis of 2008–2009, may dip in the coming years as Japanese firms, like their counterparts elsewhere, look to protect corporate and national interests.

In several sectors, Japan remains a technological innovator – notwithstanding the long-standing refrain that the country is more imitative than original. On a pragmatic level, Japanese firms have set a global standard for the development of industrial robotics operations (over 54% of the industrial robots in use in the world are in Japan); no other nation comes close in this potentially critical area.[25] Japan's robotics industry has expanded in other areas – producing service, rescue and humanoid robots and seeking to redefine the sector on a national and international level. Led by NTT DoCoMo, Japan has the world's most successful mobile Internet and mobile commerce implementations. The company and the country have been in the middle of the global debate about the potential of the 3-G mobile phones. Continuing strengths in such important fields as computers, cameras, and consumer electronics have served to solidify Japan's global presence. Research and development currently underway hold considerable promise for the future prominence of Japan. This is particularly true for such areas as biotechnology and nanotechnology.

Japan's role in international security has also changed in the last decade, continuing a post-World War II pattern that has challenged Japan's ability to maintain its international diplomatic authority without the ability or willingness to establish a military presence. Kimie Hara's assessment of the Japan–Soviet Union–China security issues in recent decades demonstrates the manner in which historical events and processes continue to influence contemporary affairs. Drawing on multilateral examples, Hara suggests, could produce workable solutions in the region and reduce tensions considerably. Of course, Japan continues to struggle with its relationship with the military and international conflicts. In 1992, Japan expanded the role of its Self Defense forces (SDF) and began participating in United Nations sponsored peace-keeping activities and helping with disaster relief. Post September 11, also saw the passage of the Anti Terrorism Special Law allowing Japanese forces to offer logistical support to US ships, an issue that remained very contentious in Japan in subsequent years. Japan's role in Asia has also been evolving, with the ascendancy of China and continuing tensions on the Korean peninsula. While it is likely that Japan will have a crucial role in helping to maintain stability in the region – with worry about North Korea's intentions topping the list of concerns – the depth and nature of the country's role in international peace-keeping and conflict resolution remains very much in question.

Concern about globalization has, in the aftermath of the Kyoto Accord and the 2009 gathering in Copenhagen, increasingly focused on environmental concerns. Even before the economic meltdown took full hold, the world was debating the impact of, and response to, global climate change. The demonstrable environmental interconnections had forced most world leaders to rethink the relationship between domestic and international politics, to consider radical changes in environmental management, and to better understand the manner in which economies and societies the world over were tied to each other. Japan's role in the environmental debate, symbolically entrenched in the hosting of the meetings leading to the Kyoto Accord, elevated the country's engagement with global affairs and established Japan as a player in the international politics of globalization. Carin Holroyd's study of the relationship between global environmental concerns and Japanese political and corporate actions demonstrates the manner in which global affairs can influence domestic policy and business environments and vice versa.

Scholars continue to debate the meaning, impact and origins of contemporary globalization. Analysts have noted that globalization is not a new phenomenon.

Trade, for example, was extensively global before World War I. Developments, including the 9/11 attacks and its aftermath, the prolonged and largely unsuccessful "War on Terror" highlighted by conflicts in Afghanistan and Iraq, resulted in the reassurance of national sovereignty and a return to concern about economic protectionism and internal security.[26] Globalization is not inevitable, nor is it unidirectional. It is not entirely Western, nor are its impacts irreversible. The very complexity of the globalization phenomenon makes it particularly worthy of careful evaluation and extended debate. Japan's economic difficulties have diminished North American coverage of Japan and have left many people with the impression that Japan is no longer of importance on the world scene. Nothing could be further from the truth. From business to culture to international relations, Japan has and will continue to play a vital role. In some areas, Japan's impact is more profound in Asia than it may be in North America but that renders the impact no less important.

For several generations, scholars have wrestled with questions about Japanese exceptionalism and uniqueness; the same issue arises in the study of globalization. In general, Japan's record with globalization is not particularly unusual. Other countries, particularly dominant powers like the United States, China and Western Europe, seek to expand their global influence and reach while mitigating the impact of international forces on their own citizens. Emerging powers – India, Brazil, Russia and the Middle East – are particularly concerned about the dual influences of external economic control and cultural transformation through global forces, although the economic equation appears to be tipping somewhat in their favour. Japan is not in the contest over globalization by itself, nor is the country any better or worse than many other nations in coping with the new realities. Similarly, Japan has a long history of struggling with the balance between nation and world, between defending national interests and participating in the broader economy and society. The contemporary debate about globalization had earlier manifestations in the Tokugawa period of prolonged and deliberate isolation, proved pivotal during the Meiji Restoration, and have dominated Japan's discussion about its present and future state since the early 1900s. The record from the past, particularly the country's considerable success with protectionism and cultural isolation, remains a powerful influence within Japan as the nation seeks to respond to an even more profound level of external change and influence.

Japan, of course, plays another crucial international role in the twenty-first century. From the mid-nineteenth century on, if not earlier, issues of globalization focused on the preponderant power of Anglo-American axis, demonstrated through a powerful combination of colonization, military strength and economic reach. Scholars such as Koichi Iwabuchi and Ronald Dore, among others, have demonstrated that Japan has increasingly played a countervailing role, contesting the Anglo-American dominance through trade, industry and now popular culture, and providing an offsetting globalization force.[27] Indeed, until the post-World War II period, globalization was synonymous with the steadily increasing power of Great Britain and the United States. Since that time, led by Japan, globalization became a more multicentred phenomenon, with the Japanese node of international prominence competing with the Anglo-American influences and with other nodes, particularly China, emerging to contest the long-standing British-American hegemony. Understanding Japan's experiences with globalization – both as a recipient of global forces for change and as a worldwide exporter of Japanese influences – is therefore a critical element in coming to terms with the most important international phenomenon of the twenty-first century.

Work on this volume began with the 15th annual Japan Studies Association of Canada (JSAC) conference, held in October 2001 at the University of Saskatchewan in Saskatoon. JSAC affords scholars of Japan in a wide range of disciplines an opportunity to get together, share their research and keep abreast of economic, political and social changes taking place in Japan. The theme for the 15th JSAC was *Japan in the Age of Globalization*. In a series of lively presentations and discussions, participants examined numerous aspects of the impact of globalization on Japan and Japan's impact on the rest of the world. Over time, we came to the realization that several of the core papers at the conferences provided a solid foundation for a collection on Japan's experience with globalization. We solicited additional papers that allowed us to broaden the range of topics covered. With the passage of time, the original papers required updating and the contributors graciously agreed to do adapt their essays to recent literature and contemporary developments. Indeed, with the economic turmoil of the past few years, the very nature of the questions of globalization shifted dramatically. The result is a collection, we believe, that is very current and comprehensive and that brings the latest research to bear on this important subject. Together, the various contributions provide evidence of the long history of global influences on Japan – and Japanese impacts on the rest of the world – and of the social, economic, cultural and political dimensions of this complex and multifaceted issue. We know now that the years to come will bring more and perhaps even faster change, albeit in a very different direction from what we anticipated only a short while again. Understanding the nature, extent and impact of globalization, it seems, is an essential element in knowing how Japan will be changed by the fasting moving, worldwide, winds of change.

Notes

1 "Toyota 2010 Forecast: 500,000 Lost Sales, CEO Resignation, 40,000 Layoffs", *MarketWatch*, 3 February 2010 (http://www.marketwatch.com/story/toyota-2010-forecast-500000-lost-sales-ceo-resignation-40000-layoffs-2010-02-03).

2 The volatility of the Japanese market continues. See, for example, "Nikkei 225, Topix Fall the Most in 14 Months on U.S. Jobs, Euro", *Bloomberg Businessweek*, 7 June 2010 (http://www.businessweek.com/news/2010-06-07/nikkei-225-topix-fall-the-most-in-14-months-on-u-s-jobs-euro.html).

3 "Japan Announces $100bn Stimulus Package to Curb Recession: Facing the Worst Economic Crisis Since the Second World War, Japan's Financial Plans Outstrip Those of the UK and US", *Guardian.co.uk*, 9 April 2009 (http://www.guardian.co.uk/business/2009/apr/06/japan-financial-stimulus-curb-recession).

4 Christopher Wood, *The Bubble Economy: Japan's Extraordinary Speculative Boom of the '80s and the Dramatic Bust of the '90s* (New York: Atlantic Monthly Press, 1992);

Gary Saxonhouse and Robert Stern, eds, *Japan's Lost Decade: Origins, Consequences and Prospects for Recovery* (London: Wiley Blackwell, 2004).

5 Frank Gibney, *The Pacific Century: America and Asia in a Changing World* (New York: Scribner, 1994); Fun Mee Kim, *The Four Asian Tigers: Economic Development and the Global Political Economy* (New York: Academic Press, 1998).

6 Index MundiL Japan Literacy, citing evidence from the *CIA Fact-Book*, (http://www.indexmundi.com/japan/literacy.html).

7 David Block and Deborah Cameron, *Globalization and Language Teaching* (New York: Routledge, 2002), 1. Imbedded references removed from the quote.

8 Mayumi Itoh, *Globalization of Japan* (New York: St. Martin's Press, 1998).

9 Koichi Iwabuchi's *Recentering Globalization: Popular Culture and Japanese Transnationalism* (Durham, NC: Duke University Press, 2002).

10 J.S. Eades, Tom Gill and Harumi Befu, *Globalization and Social Change in Contemporary Japan* (Melbourne: Trans Pacific Press, 2000).

11 David Block and Deborah Cameron, eds., *Globalization and Language Teaching* (New York: Routledge, 2002).

12 Ibid.,13–28.

13 Glenn Hook and Michael Weiner, eds, *The Internationalization of Japan* (New York: Routledge, 2001).

14 See, for example, a series of Canadian publications, including Keizo Nagatani and David Edgington (eds), *Japan and the West: The Perception Gap* (London: Agate, 1998), Masao Nakamura, Ed., *Japan in the Global Age* (UBC: Centre for Japanese Research, 2001), and Joseph Kess and Helen Lansdowne, *Why Japan Matters!*, 2 vols (Victoria: Centre for Japanese Research, 2005). See also Patrick Heenan, ed., *The Japan Handbook* (New York: Routledge, 1998).

15 Kenichi Ohmae, *The End of the Nation State: The Rise of Regional Economies* (New York: Free Pres, 1996).

16 Pacific Bridge, "Japan Recruiting Update", provides a useful overview of the transitions underway in the Japanese workplace (http://www.pacificbridge.com/publication.asp?id=22).

17 Ralph Paprzycki, "The Impact of Foreign Direct Investment in Japan: Case Studies of the Automobile, Finance, and Health Care Industries", Institute of Economic Research, Hitotsubashi University, HI-STat Discussion Paper Series, No. d05–141.

18 David McConnell, *Importing Diversity: Inside Japan's JET Program* (Los Angeles: University of California Press, 2000).

19 Martin Banham, *The Cambridge Guide to Theatre* (Cambridge: Cambridge University press, 1995), 569.

20 The classic book on Japanese baseball is Robert Whiting, *You Gotta Have Wa.* 2nd edition (New York: Vintage, 2009). The arrival of Ichiro, a star outfielder with the Seattle Mariners, changed global understanding of Japanese baseball.

21 Marcia Sakai, Jeffrey Brown and James Mak, "Population Aging and Japanese International Travel in the 21st Century", *Journal of Travel Research*, Vol. 38, No. 3, 212–220 (2000).

22 Yuko Aoyama and Hiro Izushi, "Hardware Gimmick or Cultural Innovation? Technological, Cultural, and Social Foundations of the Japanese Video Game Industry", *Research Policy*, Vol. 32, Issue 3 (March 2003), 423–444.

23 David Arase, ed., *Japan's Foreign Aid: Old Continuities and New Directions* (London: Routledge, 2005).

24 Pradyumna Prasad Karan, *Japan in the 21st Century: Environment, Economy, and Society* (Lexington: University of Kentucky Press, 2005), 313–315.

25 Timothy Hornyak, *Loving the Machine: The Art and Science of Japanese Robots* (Tokyo: Kodansha, 2006).

26 Yutaka Kawashima, *Japanese Foreign Policy at the Crossroads: Challenges and Options for the 21st Century* (Washington, DC: Brookings Institute Press, 2005).

27 Koichi Iwabuchi, *Recentering Globalization: Popular Culture and Japanese Transnationalism* (Durham, NC: Duke University Press, 2002); Ronald Dore, *Stock Market Capitalism: Welfare Capitalism: Japan and Germany versus the Anglo-Saxons* (Oxford: Oxford University Press, 2000).

1 Pioneers of globalization

Tokugawa's cross-cultural communications

Jay Goulding

Introduction

In the last forty years, the issue of globalization has become a hot topic in the West. Ever since Marshall McLuhan characterized the world as a "global village," the buzzword "globalization" has entered everyday vocabulary (McLuhan, 1964; Benedetti and DeHart, 1996). For McLuhan, the age of electronic media created a global village "as wide as the planet and as small as the little town where everybody is maliciously engaged in poking his nose into everybody else's life" (Benedetti and DeHart, 1996: 40). The contradiction of large and small indicates there is no standard definition of globalization. Subsequently, no one discipline owns the discourse on globalization. Philosophy, history, politics and sociology, to name a few, have invested considerable time in debating both the meaning of globalization and its consequences (Morley and Robins, 1995; Wilson and Dissanayake, 1996; Jameson and Miyoshi, 1998). Although the multidisciplinary aspect of the debate is desirable, the consequences need some thought and explanation.

In a generalized way, globalization promises to open gateways to communication and culture by relaxing the ridged barriers of national borderlines and the conceptual identities that accompany them. This can be advantageous for all nations if it addresses some reciprocities of communication. What is assumed from Western society is that each nation wishes to communicate and on some level, implicitly or otherwise shares some common goals such as advancing technology or other knowledge and increasing trade. From historical and philosophical points of view, globalization might threaten already established worldviews and societies that respond to them. From a political and sociological point of view, the consequences of globalization might depend on different political systems or value systems used to support those governments. In other words, globalization and its consequences are relative to the philosophical assumptions of different societies. What is good for one is not necessarily good for another. To use a popular political example, from a liberal point of view, globalization might be good for advancing the agenda of freedom, equality and human rights; from a Marxist point of view, globalization might be another name for hegemony that seeks to create further systems of dependency. These ideological differences do not, however, preclude that some interactions between diametrically opposite societies would be mutually beneficial by fostering alternative conceptions of self, culture and society. The world today hopes for some such interactions in a climate of clashing ideologies.

Rob Wilson and Wimal Dissanayake characterize globalization as a two-part problem: "a new world-space of cultural production and national representation which is simultaneously becoming more *globalized* (unified around dynamics of capitalogic moving across borders) and more *localized* (fragmented into contestatory enclaves of difference, coalition, and resistance)" (1996: 1). Hence, the logic of capitalism comes up against the logic of traditional non-Western societies and developing societies. The nation-state tries to hold its own by collecting itself into an "imagined community" under the *aegis* of "warfare, religion, blood, patriotic symbology, and language" (Wilson and Dissanayake, 1996: 2). The picture that Wilson and Dissanayake paint is one of great concern for the preservation of local cultures alongside the overwhelming forces of global power.

How does the complex mesh of issues known as globalization apply to Japan? Norio Ota argues that: "The whole world, and human beings, have been experiencing globalization since ancient times. Human history can be perceived as the process of globalization from its inception" (2001). None of the above modern Western considerations are particularly new to the Eastern world. Japan faced all of these hurdles and more in its past history. It does so over the entire period of the Tokugawa Shogunate (1603–1868), which is the sole topic of this chapter. The Edo Period is the first to engage fully with European culture and trade. Ironically, Tokugawa is also an era of *sakoku* (鎖国 "national isolation") that seemingly would promote the opposite of globalized values and practices. In respect to this, part of the misunderstanding of Tokugawa falls on the shoulders of Western scholarship. Those of a more narrow-minded opinion often stereotype Japan as an isolationist civilization, which keeps to itself for thousands of years as a group of islands protected by high seas and winds. On the contrary, this chapter argues that Tokugawa is the wellspring of cross-cultural communications or "world interculture," a cornerstone of the positive attributes of global thought, especially in respect to language and culture (Goulding, 2001, 2005a, 2005b, 2008). Tokugawa is not one-dimensional but multi-dimensional, drawing strength from many cultures including Korea and China. This multiculturalism is readily visible, extending throughout the language and culture of the Japanese Floating World (*ukiyo* 浮世).

Tokugawa globalization?

The idea of Tokugawa globalization might at first appear quite contradictory. In historical context, this chapter offers an alternative view. Japan of the Edo Period is not completely isolationist. Its philosophy is one of innovation, openness and accommodation to many cultures. *Sakoku* is a brilliant strategy which restricts the flow of foreigners and foreign trading centres in Japan but does not close off Japan to the world. Its purpose is to preserve traditions of Japanese civilization while engaging with European and Asian cultures. By 1700, the Dutch and

Chinese are allowed to trade exclusively at the port of Nagasaki. The impact of this policy results in increasing the volume of trade. The restricted flow enhances interest in Japan and at the same time slows the political and religious positions of Europeans (Jansen, 1992: 35–41). The internal struggles in Japan over strategies for dealing with the rest of the world are not without heated debate. At the end of the Ashikaga Shogun, many *samurai* (侍), weary from long periods of clan warfare are opposed to the development of any types of global policies. As to the fate of the newly constructed towns, folklore has it that the famous warlord Oda Nobunaga (織田信長 1534–1582) announced: "If the canary does not sing, kill him." By this, he means that if the towns are to fail, stop them up immediately. Toyotomi Hideyoshi (豊臣秀吉 1536–1598) responds: "If the canary does not sing, make him." By this, he means that the towns would need martial law in order to survive. Tokugawa Ieyasu (徳川家康 1543–1616) concludes: "If the canary does not sing, wait until he does." By this, he means to give the towns a chance over a period of time. By the end of the sixteenth century Tokugawa's words of tolerance and delay become the blueprint for the Edo Period that is much in need of new commercial interactions.

The town cultures of Edo, Osaka and Kyoto see an influx of European and Asian traders. This culture is known as *ukiyo* (The Floating World) that includes teahouses, baths, brothels and theatres. Generating out of the Floating World towns are paintings, poetry, literature, *bunraku* (文楽 puppet plays) and *kabuki* (歌舞伎) theatre that are both popular amongst the townsfolk and in turn exported to an inquisitive Europe. Despite *sakoku*, Chinese junks continue to arrive at a welcoming Nagasaki port. Smuggling and offshore unloading are common. Marius Jansen, a renowned historian, argues against Tokugawa's false image of isolation while instead concentrating on its true indebtedness to global relations. He writes: "Chinese influence rose to a peak in the Tokugawa years. The rising tide of literacy meant that more Japanese could read and write Chinese. The production of poetry in Chinese, something expected of every educated person, was so great that it may have exceeded the amount of verse composed in Japanese" (Jansen, 1992: 4). Various Chinatowns populate the coast from the Kii peninsula to Kyushu and in Yamaguchi, Matsuyama, Kawagoe and Odawara (Jansen, 1992: 7). In 1853, Matthew Perry's "black ships" arrive in Japan from the United States of America, followed in 1856 by Townsend Harris, the first American consul. The resulting trade treaties seem to end Tokugawa's official seclusion policy.

The Tokugawa Peace is a watershed for Japanese civilization as one of its most creative periods and indeed, a progenitor of global philosophy. It is the beginning of an era of "brush-talk" (*hitsuwa* 筆話) with China in which a free exchange of ideas flows back and forth amongst scholars. It is an era of the opening of towns where traders from several continents exchange goods and cultural customs. It is an era where *samurai*, peasants, artisans and merchants intertwine their cultures with dozens of others. Thus, it is a time when borders, boundaries and customs are changing and adapting to a new globally conscious world. The Japanese *psyche* of Tokugawa is one of the first to shape and be shaped by a global perspective. Although Japan has outward physical boundaries of mountain and sea, its inner strength is boundless. Hence, its heart is already globally oriented. At the same time, it cautiously accepts strangers while nurturing the recovery and preservation of its own heritage.

The preceding discussion acts as a contextual backdrop to Motoori Norinaga (本居宣長 1730–1801), who is an important precursor of a philosophy of globalization. He fosters the crossing of conceptual borders and the dissolution of barriers to communication. The language of Tokugawa, as illustrated by Motoori, forms the backbone of a Japanese civilization that would prove resilient in a changing global world order. The key to global adaptation is the idea of rebounding and adjusting to new times, new perspectives and new challenges. Tokugawa becomes a leader in respect to checks and balances of its own moral stature and perceptions. Its biggest rebound is maintaining peace after a period of a thousand years of internal clan warfare. Its most concrete contribution is a reshaping of language at a fundamental level through Motoori and the resuscitation of an ancient cultural heritage.

Motoori Norinaga's *kotodama* (言霊)

Japanese language and culture in the Edo Period (1603–1868) demonstrate a self-correcting resilience, itself a strategy of globalization. The combination of cultural relations and linguistic prowess affords scholars such as Motoori the opportunity to bring to shape the floating and fragmented images of both Japanese and Chinese heritages. In this era, Japanese language owes much to the tradition of *kotodama* (言霊 "word soul/spirit"). Language acquires a bodily metaphor or "corporealization." Words become the receptacles of ancient essences. The word literally "houses" the wisdom of the classical world. The form of the word is filled with the spirit of Shinto gods. Thus bodies of literature and bodies of knowledge revolve around the spiritual essence of words. This word spirit is a grass roots aspect of Shinto. As a proponent of such word spirit nativism, Motoori resurrects the *Kojiki* (古事記 *Record of Ancient Matters*) of 712 (Philippi, 1968). In doing so, he revitalizes both Shinto principles and the uniqueness of the Japanese language in its invocation of *kami* (神 Shinto Gods) through the reunion of humans and gods. Words become *shintai* (神体 "bodies" of *kami*). Motoori's stimulus for such thought came in the wake of Japan's interaction with other East Asian countries and with Europe, especially in the quickly growing cultural milieu of the Floating World towns. In this influential multicultural environment, Motoori senses the need for Japan to re-establish its own cultural and linguistic heritage by turning his gaze backward to the Nara Period (645–794).

The checks and balances of Japanese language and culture find a doubling back of depth to surface in the philosophy, literature and poetry of the period. Motoori's work is not a reactionary nostalgia of an isolationist civilization. It is the exact opposite. It is the bread and butter of a society preparing to meet the world by collecting the best of its past for the future. The Edo Period is not simply a Chinese dominated cultural era. It exemplifies unique combinations of both Chinese and Japanese philosophies.

It would be easy enough to characterize the Tokugawa Shogunate as an ideational preamble to modern Imperial Japan of the two World Wars. It would be easy enough to stereotype *Chushingura* (忠臣藏 "Treasury of Loyal Retainers") as simply a re-awakening of warrior spirit for that purpose. Motoori's resuscitation of Shinto-laden imagery could be seen as a fanciful legitimation for the re-politicization of Japanese life (Konoshi, 2000). Through this way of thinking, Japan's only attempt at globalization would be imperialism. And consequently, Kuki Shuzo's (九鬼周造 1888–1941) re-invention of a Japanese past could be easily dismissed as the ruminations of an unwitting ideologue caught in the fervor of a new wave of "Japaneseness" (Pincus, 1996). There is much to be said for the cogency of these arguments from historical and political perspectives. However, John Brownlee's most balanced account offers another view. He sees Motoori and his "National Learning" (*kokugaku* 国学) colleagues as reinstating "the literal truth of the ancient myths" (Brownlee, 1997: 6). Although Brownlee accurately explicates Motoori's "historical fallacy" of Japan's independent emergence, it is clear to him that "with the work of Norinaga, *Kojiki* also became a source of religious, ethical, social, and political values unique to Japan" (1997: 63). These constellations of values emerged because of Tokugawa's increasing interaction with the world. They would not have been possible or even necessary if Tokugawa were simply shut off.

On that note, it is important to address some of the educational elements of Motoori's *Kojiki-den* (古事記傳 "commentary on *Kojiki*") completed in 1798, in respect to language and global philosophy. Rather than dismiss Tokugawa's inventive thinkers and commentators as deluded with nostalgic hallucinations of mythic pasts that never existed, we can applaud them as proponents of emancipatory recollections in the face of contact with the rest of the world. In other words, we can see Tokugawa thinkers as recovering the past (recollection) in a way that frees thought for present and future use. In this sense, the past is not its own prison house. It is a vibrant, living entity. The past is not a form of self-incarceration but of liberation. We can free past images from their murky, twilight tombs and animate them for present use. This is a goal of Tokugawa's finest linguistic, literary and philosophical thinkers. If we embrace this perspective, Motoori can be praised as a linguistic innovator. The linguistic innovator reshapes the history of language for modern use. These possibilities seem to be forgotten in the overriding presence of arguments revolving around *samurai* politics. The temptation of Motoori's time is to forget the past altogether and move forward with the flow of technology. He resists this by reinventing the Japanese language and thereby rescuing it for the future. Without Motoori, Japanese might well have disappeared as an archaic language after the Second World War. The adaptability of Japanese language to incorporate foreign words through the *katakana* (片假名) holds its own by way of checks and balances. Motoori has a double impact on language and culture. It is Motoori who makes language flexible and it is Motoori who explains its functioning through *Kojiki*.

He kills two birds with one stone by reinventing simultaneously a focus on language and culture. As stated above, his motivation comes from Japan's new "global" status.

In respect to Tokugawa, much has appeared on the neo-Confucian debates of Ogyu Sorai (荻生徂徠 1666–1728) and Ito Jinsai (伊藤仁斎 1627–1705) that fill libraries around the world. Much has appeared on the innovations of Tokugawa culture from the love stories of Chikamatsu Monzaemon (近松門左衛門 1653–1725) to the townsfolk tales of Saikaku Ihara (井原西鶴 1642–1693) to the poetry of Basho (松尾芭蕉 1644–1694) (Hume, 1995; Nishiyama, 1997). Yet not much has appeared on Tokugawa language. In the past few years, Sakai Naoki remedies this with a seminal study of 18th-century language in Japan (1991). His argument is anything but an isolationist view of a society with a frozen social structure. He sees Tokugawa as a creative time period enhanced by contact with the rest of the world. He argues that an imaginary space opens in which many aspects of traditionally Chinese-inspired society are transformed. Language breaks free from the obligations of Chinese imitation. Ironically, the more contact Japan has with China, the less obligated it feels to copy Chinese linguistic, cultural and philosophical forms.

In an intriguing section entitled "Anteriority of Voice," Sakai in his book *Voices of the Past* (1991) explicates the scholarships of Kamo no Mabuchi (賀茂真淵 1697–1769), Motoori and Fujitani Nariakira (富士谷成章 1738–1779). All three are National Learning authors. Parallel to Ogyu Sorai's *kobunjigaku* (古文辞学 learning of ancient text and word), Sakai sees Motoori attempting "to decipher archaic Japanese ... by the cognition that one could envisage Japanese antiquity through its language" (1991: 257). Sakai goes on to argue that Motoori's efforts to make the *Kojiki* readable should not be forgotten, even though his reductions of Chinese characters to phonetic *kana* (假名) are "largely arbitrary" (1991: 257). In terms of interpretation theory, reading generally carries a "posterior" voice. The voice is second to the writing itself. The more readers there are of the text, the more voices there are in interpretation. Motoori's view is the exact opposite of this. It relies on the "anterior" voice. For him, *Kojiki* is an occasion to recall a primordial (originary) voice that transports us immediately to the ancient world (Sakai, 1991: 258–259) or double folds ancient time into the present. In this case, the speaking is more important than the writing: speaking first, writing second. Ancient "divine words" as *kotodama* are portals to the ancient past. Hence, we understand Motoori's interest in *kotodama* as *kami* bodies or divine word repositories of the spirit of Shinto gods. According to legend, the Otomo and Okume clans at the Yamato court were "experts" in interpreting *kotodama* within songs (Bocking, 1997: 107).

There are several methods by which Chinese characters are deciphered in ancient Japan. The first is *kanbun* (漢文), a form of Classical Chinese. As Donald Philippi suggests, we do not know if ancient Japanese readers spoke the words in Chinese imitation or in translation. In any case, systems of Japanese inflections and word orders were developed by the Nara period. The second method is employing Chinese ideographs phonetically "completely divorced from lexical meaning to represent Japanese sounds" (Philippi, 1968: 27). *Manyogana* (万葉假名) from the revered poetry collection *Manyoshu* (万葉集 *Ten Thousand Leaves*) of the 8th-century Nara Period, and later *hiragana* (平假名) and *katakana*, are examples. The third method is most difficult: "Chinese ideographs used in a modified or hybrid *kanbun* style and read in pure Japanese. In this system words were read phonetically or ideographically in their Chinese equivalents but were read in Japanese, much as we might read the Latin abbreviation *i.e.* in English, calling it 'that is'" (Philippi, 1968: 27). On top of these great ambiguities, we must understand that there are no spaces between words, so it is frightfully difficult to decipher the text. Hence, any readings of *Kojiki* are "conjectural" and give rise to the creation of "crude inventions" such as the *shindai moji* or *zindai mozi* (神代文字 "Age of the Gods script") of the Tokugawa era. "Graphic substitution" is widespread in *Kojiki*. A single ideograph has multiple meanings. Philippi's famous examples include the same Chinese character used to represent "jewel" or "bead" and "spirit" or "soul" and all pronounced *tama* (玉). The character for "comb" also carries the adjectival meaning "wondrous" with either pronounced *kusi* (櫛) or *kushi* (Philippi, 1968: 29).

Meaning, event, word

For the most part of his adult life, Motoori elaborates on the above methods with an eye to a wholesale *kun* (訓) gloss that is a Japanese reading of Chinese characters. Hence, the more familiar expression *kanseki no gakumon* (漢籍の学問 study of Chinese classics) becomes *kara-bumi no manabi* (Wehmeyer, 1997: 10). The more familiar *kogo* (古語 ancient language) is glossed as *hurukoto* (Wehmeyer, 1997: 28) or *furukoto* (Konoshi, 2000: 62). In this way, Motoori distances Japanese language from the "ornaments" of Chinese. The closer that Japan moves to China in trade, the farther away Japan moves in language and culture. In an effort to preserve Japanese language in a quickly developing global age, Motoori concentrates on the sound as uniquely Japanese rather than the graph as uniquely Chinese. He writes:

> [I]f one is to speak of the superior features of the *Kojiki*, one would first of all note that in ancient times, books did not exist, and the things which people must have conveyed via the mouths of people were not necessarily like the decorative language (文) of the *Nihonshoki* [日本書紀 *Chronicles of Japan*, 720]; rather, they were probably like the words (詞) of the *Kojiki*. The *Nihonshoki* strives to resemble the Chinese, and ornaments its figures of speech (文章, *aya*), while the *Kojiki* pays no attention to the Chinese and merely aims at not losing the words (語言, *kotoba*) of ancient times … Meaning (意, *kokoro*), event (事, *koto*), and word (言, *kotoba*) are all things which are consistent with one another. In the world of the ancients, there were the meanings, events and words of the ancients, and so, too, in the later ages, there exist the meanings, events, and words of the later ages. China, too, has its own meanings, events, and words. The *Nihonshoki* uses the meaning of

the later ages to record the events of the ancient age, and because it uses the language of China to record the meaning of our imperial country, there are many things which are not in correspondence with one another.

(Wehmeyer, 1997: 21–22)

With such a strategy, Motoori moves "meaning," "event" and "word" into the same interpretive space. The previously Chinese influenced system is thus shifted toward a more Japanese-styled space. As Sakai recalls: "[C]haracters were permitted to shift their ideological register fairly freely and could float, so to say, from the status of phonetic signifier to that of ideographic signifier, to that of illustrative symbol" (Sakai, 1997: xiv). Thus, Motoori disrupts and deconstructs (fundamentally disassembles) what Sakai dubs the "regimes" of reading, writing, narrating and reciting built around the Chinese character. He replaces these with the primacy of recitation. The calligraphy disappears as it is spoken; the logocentric disappears into the phonocentric; the Chinese characters disappear into elemental Japanese native sounds. The stimulus of multi-languages and multi-cultures in the Floating World results in a re-inauguration of distinct, local, Japanese folk culture with visible links to its ancient past.

Through this most inventive process, Motoori utilizes different styles for deciphering *Kojiki* as a main text for preserving Japanese life through inventive use of *kanji* (漢字 "Chinese characters"). The first style is writing everything in *kana* (假名) or *karina* (假字 "provisional letters"). For example, *sakura* (桜 cherry blossom) is written as three arbitrarily chosen *kanji* (*sa* 佐 assist, *ku* 久 long time, *ra* 羅 bird net). *Yuki* (雪 snow) is written with two arbitrarily chosen characters (*yu* 由 reason, *ki* 伎 deed) (Wehmeyer, 1997: 78). The second style is called *masamozi* or *masamoji* (正字 "correct graphs"). Motoori uses the example of the sounds for *ame* (*a* 阿 flatter, *me* [*mai*] 米 rice) written as "heaven" (*ten* 天) and the sounds for *tuti* (*tu* 都 metropolis, *ti* 知 know) written as "earth" (*chi* 地) (Wehmeyer, 1997: 82). Hence, "heaven and earth" is pronounced *ametuti* but written with correct Chinese graphs (*tenchi* 天地). Wehmeyer explains: "*Masamozi*, a term coined by Motoori, is the method whereby Chinese graphs are used as logograms to write down native Japanese words. It is now customary to refer to this method as *kun*" (Wehmeyer, 1997: 93). It is also referred to as a "*kun* gloss." *Masamozi* includes using graphs not found in China or graphs with partial radicals or graphs assigned different meanings altogether from the Chinese.

The third style is called *karimozi* or *karimoji* (借字 "borrowed graphs") in which, as Motoori explains, "no attention is paid to the meaning of a word, and the reading of a graph is simply 'borrowed' to represent a word with a different meaning" (Wehmeyer, 1997: 83). For example, the Chinese graph for garden (*niwa* 庭) might be used to represent the particle sequence *ni wa* (には) (Wehmeyer, 1997: 94). This style is common in names of deities, persons and places. In addition to working with *teniwoha* (辭 diction, particle system), a vague system of particle and inflectional endings for assigning Japanese readings to Chinese texts, Motoori discovers two different sets of phonograms used for vowels (Wehmeyer, 1997: 113–114).

The fourth style is a hodgepodge of all of the above, often used in names. Example, the *kanji* for the river name *Asuka* (飛鳥) come from its "pillow word" *tobu tori* (飛鳥 flying birds) from the *Manyoshu* (Wehmeyer, 1997: 113–114). A pillow word (*makura kotoba* 枕詞) is a filler in classical poetry that acts to check and balance accent and number of feet, although it has no specific meaning. James Hepburn describes pillow words as "words without meaning for ornament" (1983: 255). Fashioned by Motoori, the shape-shifting ability of the Japanese language reflects the mutability of the Castle Towns in Tokugawa as they face new challenges from both Eastern and Western interactions.

The core and the tip

Alongside Motoori's work, Fujitani reveals a body metaphor for language in Tokugawa. Chinese nouns were no longer the hub of meaning. They only meant something when animated by Japanese adverbials, adjectivals, particles and verb forms. For Fujitani, the Chinese noun was like the thorax; it could only be mobilized with Japanese nonnominals, the "legs," "hats," and "clothes" of language (Sakai, 1991: 268). The "intention" of words is more important than its meaning. For Motoori and associates, the "fixed centre" is animated by the "flexible periphery" (Sakai, 1991: 269). Sakai writes:

> This association explains why Motoori so often talked about *kotodama* (spirit of language) in reference to *kakari musubi* [係り結び], a traditional term denoting syntactical rules that govern the relationship between the conjugation of a verb, an adjectival or an adverbial, and particles located in the preposition. Possibly the obsolescence of these rules by the eighteenth century encouraged Motoori to attribute the spirit of language to this grammatical trait of old Japanese.
>
> (Sakai, 1991: 269)

Thus, 18th-century scholars look to the in-between of what Motoori calls the "core" and the "tip" of language (Sakai, 1991: 269) as checks and balances. Motoori elaborates: "[Y]ou must make the intention of ancient people's usage of the word evident rather than seek for its original meaning. Once you understand the intention of its use, you can do without understanding the original meaning" (quoted in Sakai, 1991: 269). Although Motoori distrusts the tradition of Chinese sages, he does have some reverence for Daoist "naturalism" (Wehmeyer, 1997: 237). In the above instance, his argument might be fueled by Zhuangzi's (莊子 fourth century BCE) parable of the net. Once you have caught the fish, you can forget the net. If you have the image, you can forget the words and their images (Watson, 1968: 302). This is a Daoist principle of *yan wuyan* (言無言 words without words). Of course, if you lose the net, you lose the fish. When Zhuangzi releases the earthly net, he can rely on Laozi's (老子 sixth century BCE) "heaven's net" (*tian wang* 天網): "Though its meshes are coarse, nothing slips through" (Feng and English, 1972: Poem 73).

While the Chinese Daoists strive to forget, the Tokugawa Japanese strive to remember. Motoori can rely on the in-between of Heaven and Earth as the "core" of Japanese civilization, while the checks and balances of language and culture are its "tip." Once again, the word becomes a housing for *kami*. Motoori relies on the Shinto Way of the Gods rather than the Daoist Way of the Water. For him, the Chinese had a rather confusing image of "the way" (Goulding, 2002). In Motoori's view, the Japanese way is "derived from the august spirit of the wondrous God Taka-mi-musubi" (Wehmeyer, 1997: 245). For Motoori, *musubi* (産霊) is "generative spirit" in this instance. We also recall the homonymic relationship with *kakari musubi* (係り結び). As the *kanji* suggests, you are bound (tied) to your duty by the rules of language. The spirit, the name and the grammatical rules are all in accord as meaning, event and word. Do as you say and say as you do. These linguistically ethical checks and balances shine forth in both Fujitani's and Motoori's body metaphors:

> His [Fujitani's] morphological classification of the syntactical functions of words was counterbalanced by equating the integrity of an utterance to the integrity of the attitude in a corporeal action … Similarly, Motoori Norinaga recognized in *kakari musubi* (conjugational rules of old Japanese) the manifestation of an integrity comparable to the bodily attitude into which a gesture of a part of the body is always coordinated and subordinated.
>
> (Sakai, 1991: 302)

Iki (いき)[1]

With such a diverse and widespread achievement in language, culture and philosophy, it is clear that the Edo Period was not standing still in isolation but quite vibrant in relation to other cultures as exemplified in the Floating World contacts. These budding global interactions motivate Motoori to revitalize a past for the sake of the present and future of Tokugawa, especially after the wakeup call of *Chushingura* where the stillness of the Shogunate and the movement of *samurai* and *chonin* (町人 merchants, townsfolk) were at stake.

Parallel to Motoori, Kuki Shuzo's 20th-century blending of phenomenology and pinpoint cultural analysis helps situate Tokugawa in terms of openness rather than isolation (1981, 1987a, 1987b, 1987c, 1997). Kuki himself is a pioneer in global thought. He is one of the first Japanese philosophers to engage with European thinkers, living in Europe for many years and bringing back much of Western thought to Japan. His achievement is recognized in both Europe and Japan. In this sense, he truly practices what he preaches as a philosopher in-between East and West. Having studied for seven years with prominent phenomenologists Martin Heidegger and Edmund Husserl, Kuki brings much to the table (Light, 1987; Goulding 2005b).

In an uncanny way, Kuki's methodology mimics Motoori's by studying the phenomenon of everyday language, especially in Tokugawa. Both thinkers aim to recover a primordial beginning through language. Through a study of their origins, words become portals to the ancient past that can be recovered in the present (Heidegger, 1962, Heidegger and Fink, 1979: 29). In his idea of *iki* (いき), Kuki reveals the spirit that embraces both Motoori and himself in this task of recovery. *Iki* is a "refinement" of behaviours and attitudes stratified throughout language and culture. Similar to Motoori, Kuki's method of explanation involves bringing things far away close to hand. Since language is the horizon of our being-in-the-world, words are an occasion to begin asking fundamental questions about life. The words or their meaning are not ultimately important but their directions toward conditions and possibilities of life are essential. As Kuki states: "The question of the validity of meaning cannot invalidate the question of the being of meaning" (1997: 28). In other words, questions of truth or falsehood are secondary to questions of ontology (the study of Being). To this end, Kuki and Motoori attend to "the authenticity" of being and language through "hermeneutics" (Kuki, 1997: 34; Heidegger, 1962). This involves moving from surface to deep analysis. Both thinkers are responding to the collision of Eastern and Western cultures through globalization.

Attesting to its shapeless shape, *iki* (いき) is written in *hiragana*. Like the language of Motoori's *Kojiki-den*, many meanings and accurate *kanji* are assigned to *iki* including "live" (*iki* 生), "breath" (*iki* 息), "go" (*iki* 行) and "chic" (*iki* 意気) (Kuki, 1981: 23; 1997: 162). Kuki reserves *sui* (粋 essence) for a special distinction. He uses the old Chinese character composed of two parts, the radical for "uncooked grains of rice" (*mai* 米) and "the soldier" or in ancient Chinese etymology, "the soldier's mantle" (*sotsu* 卒). The modern version of the character carries the mnemonic (memory instruction) "ninety grains of uncooked rice" (*iki* 粋). For Kuki, the difference of *iki* and *sui* seems to hinge on the divergence between Edo and Home Provincial speech, although they share "the same semantic content on the horizon we regard as the problem" (Kuki, 1997: 133).

Part of Kuki's checks and balances of Japanese life involves stratifying *iki* throughout the social structure of the Edo Period. He is not just talking about the courtesan's floating world morality of Saikaku Ihara; he is not just talking about *samurai* politics of *Chushingura*; he is not just talking about merchant ethics of Ishida Baigan (石田梅岩 1685–1744); he is not just talking about Buddhist resolve of Basho. Admirably, he speaks of all these layerings simultaneously. Courtesans, *samurai*, merchants and Buddhists are all part of *iki*. They flow in and out of each other. How does the courtesan behave in fallen times? How does the *samurai* behave in times of peace when he lays down his sword? How do merchants and Buddhists behave in a globally engaging world that challenges their daily habits? In a global context, the flexibility of Kuki's argument is most beneficial for explaining Tokugawa's stratifications as it adjusts to commerce with the rest of Asia and Europe.

With these questions in mind, Kuki triangulates on *iki*; it manifests three components: *bitai* (媚態 coquetry, "erotic allure" [Pincus, 1996: 127]), *ikiji* or *ikuji* (意気地 brave composure) and *akirame* (諦め resignation) (Kuki, 1997: 37–46). He also describes these three in terms of *iropossa* (色っぽさ amorousness), *hari* (張 pluck, "cool galantry" [Nishiyama, 1997: 54]) and *akanuke shita* (垢抜けした urbaneness, "with the grime removed") (Kuki, 1981: 23; 1997: 46, 130). Although *bitai* is derived from courtesan culture, *ikiji* from *samurai* culture and *akirame* from both Buddhist and merchant culture, they are not limited to their origins. They seamlessly blend throughout Tokugawa society as a whole. For example, Kuki explains: "The ideal of the *geisha*, at once moral and aesthetic, that which is called *iki*, is a harmonious union of voluptuousness and nobility" (1987c: 87). For Tokugawa Buddhists, *nirvana* (*nehan* 涅槃) is the extinguishing of desire, and abolition of the will or negation of the will; for *samurai*, *bushido* (武士道 way of the warrior) is the purity of the will, "the negation of the negation, in a sense, the abolition of nirvana" (1987a: 50). Both Buddhist resignation and *samurai* pluck are oppositely linked pairings which are ultimately held together by overlapping aspects of *iki*. Each is a check and balance of the other. Similarly, merchants can resist the overwhelming lure of fortune and lovers can curtail lust (Light, 1987: 29). None of these forms would have emerged without Tokugawa's increasing interaction with the outside world. *Iki* is a type of moral gyroscope that assists Tokugawa in adapting to a quickly emerging global environment.

Kuki becomes Motoori

For Kuki, Tokugawa exemplifies both a "horizontal" phenomenology of everyday experiences and a "vertical" phenomenology of spiritual experiences. In a variety of ways, both Kuki's and Motoori's goal is to bring to shape what appears in daily life through a rigorous examination of the unspoken assumptions of the mundane life-world. *Genshogaku* (現象学 phenomenology) in Japanese or *xianxiangxue* in Chinese is the study of that which manifests or represents appearance or presence. Both Kuki and Motoori study time as a horizon of experiences, hence a horizontal phenomenology. For them, the world is composed of rings of perception or what Husserl calls the "*co-present* margin" (1962: 92). Philosophical, linguistic, cultural, social and psychological assumptions wind ring after ring of perceptions around experiences and thereby create a horizon through which we judge the world. These rings exist simultaneously in a co-present. The more rings, the thicker the perception (Goulding, 2005b).

Motoori implicitly utilizes this understanding as he relates ancient myths to the language of the present. For Motoori, this is the *kotodama* of ancient languages. The equilibrium of Tokugawa society finds a harmony in the crossings of language and culture through both their visibility (materiality) and invisibility (spirituality). If the study of the visible life-world is a horizontal phenomenology, then the study of the invisible world is a vertical phenomenology. Both Motoori and Kuki recognize that Tokugawa balances daily experiences (materiality) with the harmonization of the three teachings of Confucianism, Buddhism and Shinto (spirituality). In its global framing, it manages intercourse between and amongst other Asian and European cultures. Not only is the Japanese language and culture of the Edo Period a blending of multicultural elements, as both Motoori and Sakai demonstrate, but also a harmonization of the three teachings. Kuki understands what motivates Motoori. Part of what gives Tokugawa its global resilience is this balance of materiality and spirituality. Not only the external appearance of balance but also the internal manifestation of harmony operate as twin generators of *iki* as a purity of cultural style or chicness in the Edo Period.

Kuki further elaborates on vertical phenomenology as a "mystical ecstasis," "each instant, each present, is an identical moment of different times" (Kuki, 1987a: 45–46). This is very similar to Motoori's *kotodama*. In a strange sort of way, Kuki *becomes* Motoori Norinaga. Word, event and meaning are synchronous; the ancient past folds into the now. Without the gesticulations of Tokugawa's pioneering global challenge and response, the understanding of the world that motivates both Motoori and Kuki could not have happened. Pressures from the outside world suggest to Motoori how to blend word, event and meaning with the mythologies of the past and the street sensibilities of the present. Similar to Motoori, Kuki asks: "What is the relationship between meaning, which is the content of words, and the being of a people? … meaning or language is nothing but the self-manifestation of the past and present mode of being of a people, and the self-unfolding of a specific culture endowed with history" (1997: 27–28). We can say the same for Tokugawa language and culture in a global context: "the self-manifestation of the past and present."

Akin to Motoori's notion of *kotodama*, Kuki's concept of time is a *kairos*, a revelatory moment of eternal nows. Being and time are not separate but are linked, something like the Buddhist monk Dogen Zenji's (道元禅師 1200–1253) *uji* (有時 "being-time") (Cleary, 1986: 102–110) or something like the Buddhist *ma* (間) or *aida* (間), an interval between life and death, between heaven and earth, between this and that, like the pause of a *no* (能) theatre performer between movements. The same creative space that opens upon Kuki at the time of writing *Iki no kozo* (いきの構造 *The Structure of Iki*) also opens for Motoori at the time of writing *Kojiki-den*. Neither Kuki nor Motoori rely simply on one layer of Japanese culture but on the phenomenological intertwinings (chiasms) of many layers (Merleau-Ponty, 1968: 130–155), especially in their respective elaborations on Tokugawa. Their discussions of daily language and culture weave together the fabric of Edo culture as it relates to the religious and philosophical stuffing of the age. In his interrogation of the Japanese soul, Kuki quotes Motoori's poem:

> If one asks
> What is the Japanese soul?
> It is the mountain cherry blossom
> Exhaling its perfume in the morning light.
>
> (Kuki, 1987b: 79)

Here we have multiple layerings of meaning – religious, philosophical, aesthetic – all coinciding with *sabi* (さび [寂] loneliness), "the rust on a sword," combining the elegance of dew at dawn and the *samurai*'s duty, both the horizontal phenomena (everyday decisions) and their vertical implications (the fate of the soul). All these images emerge from a Tokugawa society that actively engages with both East Asia and Europe – not in isolation but in openness.

Conclusion

Much of what Motoori and Kuki say is poetic, fanciful and inventive. Nonetheless, it is extremely provocative. It provides a horizon for the manifestation of an uncertain language and culture of the past that engages Tokugawa's changing global culture. As Kuki maintains: "*Iki* ignores a facile supposition of reality and boldly brackets real life. Whilst detachedly breathing neutral air, *iki* purposely and disinterestedly engages in self-disciplined play" (1997: 44). Indeed, Motoori is equally engaging. He brings the muteness of the ancient world to speech in an age replete with the interplay of Eastern and European languages and culture. As Kuki aptly expresses:

> The secret of success in the understanding of a cultural state of being is to grasp it in living form, just as it is, without damaging its concrete facticity. [Henri] Bergson says that when we recall the past in scenting the fragrance of the rose, we do not associate ideas with the fragrance of the rose. We scent the recollection of the past.
>
> (Kuki, 1997: 33)

Motoori and Kuki continue to "scent the recollection of the past" through our interpretations. Motoori's innovations helped shape Tokugawa language in an era of increasing interaction with other countries. Ironically, Tokugawa's official isolation policies result in a bubbling Floating World life of multiculturalism that encourages Motoori to achieve his most creative work. His scholarly contributions are a result of global interactions rather than simply a nostalgic turn to the past. As a pioneer in East–West intellectual relations, Kuki and his idea of *iki* as a phenomenological topic benefit from the remarkable cultural developments of Tokugawa. Kuki understands these developments, including Motoori's, as a response to Japan's developing global position of the eighteenth century. As precursors of global philosophy, these thinkers illuminate cross-cultural communications or world interculture. Japan's philosophy of mutability, adaptability and flexibility in language and culture owes much to Motoori Norinaga's invention and Kuki Shuzo's interpretation. Together, they reveal the forgotten Tokugawa sources of a global/local nexus that remind Japan of its rich historical heritage and innovation in face of constant change.

Note

1 A revised and expanded version of this section and the next appears in Goulding (2005b).

References

Benedetti, Paul and Nancy DeHart eds. (1996) *Reflections On and By Marshall Mc-Luhan: Forward Through the Rearview Mirror* Toronto, ON: Prentice-Hall Canada.

Bocking, Brian (1997) *A Popular Dictionary of Shinto* Chicago, IL: NTC Publishing.

Brownlee, John S. (1997) *Japanese Historians and the National Myths, 1600–1945: The Age of the Gods and Emperor Jinmu* Vancouver, BC: UBC Press.

Cleary, Thomas trans. (1986) "Being Time." pp. 102–110 in *Shobogenzo: Zen Essays by Dogen* Honolulu: University of Hawaii Press.

Feng Gia-Fu and Jane English trans. (1972) *Lao Tsu: Tao Te Ching* New York: Vintage Books.

Goulding, Jay (2001) "Tokugawa Traces in 21st C. Japan." Ch. 12 pp. 159–174 in Masao Nakamura (ed.) *Japan in the Global Age: Cultural, Historical and Political Issues on Asia, Environment, Households and International Communication* Vancouver, BC: The Centre for Japanese Research, University of British Columbia Press.

Goulding, Jay (2002) "'Three Teachings are One': The Ethical Intertwinings of Buddhism, Confucianism and Daoism" in Jiang Xinyan ed. *The Examined Life: Chinese Perspectives, Essays on Chinese Ethical Traditions* Binghamton, NY: Global Publications, Binghamton University.

Goulding, Jay (2005a) "Globalization: Asia" in Maryanne Horowitz ed. *Scribner's New Dictionary of the History of Ideas* vol. 3, pp. 941–947 New York: Charles' Scribner's Sons.

Goulding, Jay (2005b) "Kuki Shuzo and Martin Heidegger: *Iki* and Hermeneutic Phenomenology" pp. 677–690 in Joseph F. Kess and Helen Lansdowne (eds.) *Why Japan Matters!* volume 2, Victoria, BC: Centre for Asia-Pacific Initiatives, University of Victoria.

Goulding, Jay ed. (2008) *China-West Interculture, Toward the Philosophy of World Integration: Essays on Wu Kuang-ming's Thinking* New York: Global Scholarly Publications.

Heidegger, Martin (1962) *Being and Time* New York: Harper & Row.

Heidegger, Martin and Eugen Fink (1979) *Heraclitus Seminar 1966/67* Tuscaloosa: University of Alabama Press.

Hepburn, James Curtis (1983) *A Japanese and English Dictionary with an English and Japanese Index* Tokyo: Charles E. Tuttle.

Hume, Nancy G., ed. (1995) *Japanese Aesthetics and Culture: A Reader* Albany, NY: SUNY Press.

Husserl, Edmund (1962) *Ideas: General Introduction to Pure Phenomenology* New York: Collier Books.

Jameson, Fredric and Masao Miyoshi eds. (1998) *The Cultures of Globalization* Durham, NC: Duke University Press.

Jansen, Marius (1992) *China in the Tokugawa World* Cambridge, MA: Harvard University Press.

Konoshi, Takamitsu (2000) "Constructing Imperial Mythology: Kojiki and Nihon shoki." pp. 51–70 in Haruo Shirane and Tomi Suzuki eds. *Inventing the Classics: Modernity, National Identity, and Japanese Literature* Stanford, CA: Stanford University Press.

Kuki, Shuzo (1981) *Iki no kozo* (いきの構造 *The Structure of Iki*). pp. 1–85 in *Kuki Shuzo Zenshu* (九鬼周造全集 *The Collected Works of Shuzo Kuki*). 11 volumes and supplementary volume. Tokyo: Iwanami Shoten.

Kuki, Shuzo (1987a) "The Notion of Time and Repetition in Oriental Time." pp. 43–50 in Stephen Light *Shuzo Kuki and Jean-Paul Sartre: Influence and Counter-influence in the Early History of Existential Phenomenology* Carbondale, IL: Southern Illinois University Press.

Kuki, Shuzo (1987b) "The Japanese Soul." pp. 79–80 in Stephen Light *Shuzo Kuki and Jean-Paul Sartre: Influence and Counter-influence in the Early History of Existential Phenomenology* Carbondale, IL: Southern Illinois University Press.

Kuki, Shuzo (1987c) "Geisha." pp. 87–88 in Stephen Light. *Shuzo Kuki and Jean-Paul Sartre: Influence and Counter-influence in the Early History of Existential Phenomenology* Carbondale, IL: Southern Illinois University Press.

Kuki, Shuzo (1997) *Reflections on Japanese Taste: The Structure of Iki.* trans. John Clark. Sydney, NSW: Power Publications.

Light, Stephen (1987) *Shuzo Kuki and Jean-Paul Sartre: Influence and Counter-influence in the Early History of Existential Phenomenology* Carbondale, IL: Southern Illinois University Press.

McLuhan, Marshall (1964) *Understanding Media: The Extensions of Man* New York: Signet.

Merleau-Ponty (1968) "The Intertwining – the Chiasm." pp. 130–155 in *The Visible and the Invisible* Evanston, IL: Northwestern University Press.

Morley, David and Kevin Robins (1995) *Spaces of Identity: Global Media, Electronic Landscapes and Cultural Boundaries* London: Routledge.

Motoori, Norinaga (1968–75) *Motoori Norinaga zenshu* 20 volumes compiled by Ono Susumu and Okubo Tadashi. Tokyo: Chikuma Shobo.

Nishiyama, Matsunosuke (1997) *Edo Culture: Daily Life and Diversions in Urban Japan, 1600–1868* Honolulu: University of Hawaii Press.

Ota, Norio (2001) "Impact of Globalization on Japanese Language and Culture," paper presented for the panel "Language and Culture: Checks and Balances" at the 14th Annual Conference, *Japan Studies Association of Canada*, October 12–14, University of Saskatchewan, Saskatoon, Saskatchewan, Canada.

Philippi, Donald L. trans. (1968) *Kojiki* Tokyo: University of Tokyo Press.

Pincus, Leslie (1996) *Authenticating Culture in Imperial Japan: Kuki Shuzo and the Rise of National Aesthetics* Berkeley: University of California Press.

Sakai, Naoki (1991) *Voices of the Past: The Status of Language in Eighteenth-Century Japanese Discourse* Ithaca, NY: Cornell University Press.

Sakai, Naoki (1997) "Preface." pp. vii–xvi in Ann Wehmeyer, trans. *Motoori Norinaga: Kojiki-den Book 1* The Cornell East Asia Series Number 87. Ithaca, NY: East Asia Program Cornell University.

Watson, Burton trans. (1968) *The Complete Works of Chuang Tzu* New York: Columbia University Press.

Wehmeyer, Ann trans. (1997) *Motoori Norinaga: Kojiki-den Book 1* The Cornell East Asia Series Number 87. Ithaca, NY: East Asia Program Cornell University.

Wilson, Rob and Wimal Dissanayake eds. (1996) *Global/Local: Cultural Production and the Transnational Imaginary* Durham, NC: Duke University Press.

2 Mind the gap

Japanese corporate web sites and the missing war years

Jeffrey W. Alexander

Introduction

Since the mid-1990s, nearly every major global corporation has made efforts to showcase its operations online, and Japanese companies too, after an initial delay, have leapt into the digital age. Hosting a global corporate web site has now become standard procedure, and Japan's leading logistics, automotive, electronics, engineering, and food service companies have crafted elaborate and sophisticated online personas reflective of their vast and diverse operations. Powerful firms like Yamaha, Kirin, and Nikon each manage professional and flashy web domains replete with pages of financials, product profiles, annual reports, and links to their numerous international divisions. The common thread that ties these sites together, however, is their single greatest omission: the glaring hole in nearly all of their English-language "corporate history" pages between 1937 and 1945. These skeletal online chronologies almost never fail to skip past this era entirely, leaving an obvious and telling nine-year gap in their operations during the Second Sino-Japanese War (1937–1945) and the Pacific War (1941–1945). They indicate that no products were manufactured, no innovations or anniversaries were celebrated, and no new divisions or subsidiaries were founded – as though Japan's largest, longest-lived, and most significant companies simply ceased to be. Of course, we know this is untrue. During these years, Japan's major manufacturing firms and subcontractors were both engaged in the design, manufacture, and innovation of a wide range of products for both civilian and predominantly military uses. Furthermore, most of these companies have since issued Japanese-language print publications that discuss the era in great detail, and it is to this material that we must turn in order to identify the foundation of their postwar development.

Precisely why these firms are reluctant to discuss the war era is not at issue here. Japanese companies, like many organizations, prefer not to deal with the years 1937–1945 because of the poor publicity that such observations may generate. No company wishes to be seen as proud of its wartime technological accomplishments, or to discuss how it capitalized financially upon those designs in the postwar era. In *English*, that is. In several cases discussed below, the same companies' *Japanese*-language mirror sites deal with the war period in increasing detail. For Japanese firms seeking to expand their business ties with

East and Southeast Asia, such disparities between their online histories may not be surprising. In an increasingly globalized business environment, English web sites serve as a virtual *lingua franca* for clients and investors alike, who rely upon them heavily when researching publicly traded companies. Nevertheless, I argue that such disingenuous omissions in Japanese companies' historical timelines are both historically hazardous and a missed opportunity for Japan. Faced with the globalized nature of online communications, maintaining editorial control over this formerly manageable dimension of any firm's corporate image, its history, has become impossible. I argue that, due to their reticence to discuss the war era in English (and in some cases their very active sanitization of their corporate web sites), many Japanese firms have lost editorial control over their wartime operational histories. They have surrendered them to bloggers, product enthusiasts, and the authors of user-edited wikis – many of whom are fascinated by Japanese culture and technology, but who are armed with dubious and uncorroborated factoids. This corporate preference for prioritizing contemporary PR over historical accuracy has, I argue, the potential to do Japan's leading firms more harm than good.

This chapter explores the histories of companies involved in three of Japan's leading postwar manufacturing sectors – the motorcycle, beer brewing, and optical industries. In each case, I have translated the published Japanese-language print histories of the leading firms that either survived or emerged out of the war era: four motorcycle makers, two beer brewing firms, and the leading optical equipment manufacturer. Given these varying numbers, the three industrial case studies below therefore vary in length, but in each section, I will first outline in brief the wartime operations that enabled the participant firms' postwar development. I will then contrast the details that these companies have published in its Japanese-language print histories with those in their English- and Japanese-language online histories in order to demonstrate how few details about their wartime operations are featured online. In so doing, I will also reveal that their involvement in Japan's prescribed wartime manufacturing regime was both historically important and technologically integral to their postwar development as civilian consumer product manufacturers. Furthermore, I argue that Japan's leading corporations are faced with a unique opportunity to begin to correct the great historical imbalance in the way that Japan has dealt with the war era. Where history textbook revision committees, government ministries, and nationalists have often failed to address the war years squarely, Japan's leading firms have a chance to take back their own histories in precisely the way that the above groups tend to prefer to approach the past – empirically. Japanese history textbooks and similar sources are often criticized for the rote, unproblematized manner in which they build their historical narratives. "This happened, then that happened, and the prime minister said …" Students, naturally, tend to tune out the discussion, for it often provides little chance to think critically about the past. Such empiricism, however, is uniquely suited to the web and is precisely the approach preferred by the authors of online corporate histories. Their sites are generally mechanical and devoid of broad historical analysis. It is online, therefore, that Japan's leading corporations are faced with a clear opportunity to help correct the great historical imbalance in the way that Japan deals with the war era. Indeed, one of the firms explored below, the Honda Motor Company, has begun to seize this opportunity, and I will explore its recent and laudable efforts to take back control of its operational history.

The hazards of historical avoidance in a globalized age

The continuing failure of Japanese firms to make inroads here presents instructors of Japanese history and business at Western colleges and universities with a dilemma; when students propose to write research papers on any of Japan's leading consumer product industries or makers, many of which attract great interest, there is little primary source material worth consulting beyond facile, English-language corporate promotional literature. This is not merely an obstacle for students. Professional business and market writers worldwide often focus upon the histories behind leading Japanese product manufacturers, but those same companies' histories are typically written and produced by their overseas subsidiaries, and almost exclusively for PR and marketing purposes. Japan's leading manufacturers of automobiles, electronics, and so on have made only the most rudimentary efforts to document their own firms' histories in English, and their online corporate histories are often mere bullet-point lists that reveal little about their chronological development. Although firms like Honda have gone much further in the provision of detailed, if rosy, online vignettes that dwell upon their greatest challenges and accomplishments, most manufacturers evidence genuine fear and inhibition when it comes to conveying the details of their companies' histories or prehistories.[1] Faced with such meagre primary sources in English, students and writers are obliged to deal strictly with secondary source material (if it exists), which is often limited to broad monographs and/or exceptionally narrow business case studies. When they turn to the web, however, they soon discover that popular or user-edited sites typically offer *more* information about some of these firms' wartime operations than do the companies themselves. (I will contrast several such examples below.) Although Japan's automobile and occasionally its electronics makers have been the focus of much published scholarship, many other industrial sectors have not been explored in similar depth. This dearth of reliable source material remains true of many other Japanese industries and companies, and in spite of my continuing efforts and the work of other scholars, the availability of online, user-edited material continues to outshine that produced by academics in both scope and accessibility – but not in accuracy.

This global corporate smokescreen is hazardous, I argue, not only for students and market writers around the world, but also for Japanese companies themselves, which become the subject of speculation, supposition, and totally undocumented claims online. For want of the resolve to deal with their wartime operational histories openly, these companies have virtually abandoned them to an uncertain and unknowledgeable internet community. Its anonymous members often have no qualms about enhancing or spinning these narratives in the light of whatever popular interest strikes their fancy – be it weapons design, military strategy, or debates about the styling or performance of various makes and models. These discussions are popular, and often very involved, but they often devolve into historical or technological fetishism, and many firms' activities are misrepresented or focused upon in an inaccurately specific manner. This documentary hazard extends also to many Japanese companies' postwar operations, which are likewise poorly understood and are framed by web authors in virtually no contemporary legal, political, or financial contexts. Seldom do their contributors even acknowledge the real reason why firms are in business in the first place – for profit. The types of products that companies choose to produce are immaterial, beyond their capacity to compete successfully in the marketplace. Companies design, manufacture, and advertise in order to benefit their shareholders – not the enthusiasts who pilot their wares around racetracks or collect their antique lenses. The firms in question, however, have long since lost control over the cataloguing and indexing of their multitudinous product lines, and with the dawn of the web, they have now lost control over their operational histories – to the potential detriment of their brands and their corporate integrity. These firms are and were large, complex, and multifaceted, with extensive market and operational experience, and it is essential to observe the historical contexts in which they struggled with financial and operational challenges and a steady stream of wartime era restrictions, laws, and production directives. Japanese companies and their products – especially their wartime and early postwar products, must not be examined in an operational vacuum, and the reasons behind their manufacture of munitions or postwar goods should not be or remain the sole purview of enthusiasts or collectors of militaria. Only by dealing openly and honestly with these issues of the transwar era will these firms re-establish ownership of their pasts and be in a position to judge, evaluate, or dismiss the claims of others.[2] In a globalized age, corporations, must go further to ensure that their transwar operational histories are neither misunderstood nor misrepresented – as they are presently on enthusiast web sites in many languages. Although no company should be permitted to control the historical narratives of its entire industry, all must act in order to take back control of their own operational pasts in a manner that enables contextualized historical understanding.

The Japanese source material

Online histories are but the tip of the documentary iceberg. Japanese companies also publish broad, often detailed, Japanese-language histories in book form. *Kaisha rekishi* (company histories), or *shashi* for short, are published traditionally by most firms on major corporate anniversaries. A small number are superficial, but the bulk is a respectable blend of corporate development, product manufacturing, and wartime manufacturing operations. My research focuses upon *shashi* often, and although some are arguably promotional in nature, many of them are well written, quite candid, and even critical of their firms' operations, products, and decisions. These handsome volumes are often acquired by or are given as gifts to major North American research libraries, which is an indication of the companies' expectation that someday, Western researchers will read them, discover these firms' wartime histories, and write about them objectively. These *shashi* offer an ideal and uniquely consistent perspective on Japan's political, legal, and even social development because they provide clear, consistent benchmarks for historians. Key events in Japan's history are observed by virtually every senior firm's *shashi*, including the impact of the First Sino–Japanese War (1894–95), the Russo–Japanese War (1904–05), the death of Emperor Meiji (1912), the Great War (1914–18), the Great Kantō Earthquake (1923), Japan's "advance" into Manchuria (1931), the start of the "China Incident" (1937), and the promulgation of the National General Mobilization Law (1938). The last three of these put Japanese industry on a war footing and made many firms into munitions companies (*gunju kaisha*), an issue that is seldom acknowledged in English by the companies themselves. These familiar company turning points, although often referred to in the passive voice, are invaluable signposts for the researcher of Japan's economic, industrial, and technological development, for their advent heralded both significant changes to Japan's corporate environment as well as significant consequences for East Asia and the world.

The historical importance of wartime operations

Wartime experience is the root of most of Japan's major firms' postwar achievements, especially in the lean years of the Occupation era (1945–52) and the recession of the mid-1950s. Fifteen years of concerted state investment in Japan's strategic industries, especially following the destructive Great Kantō Earthquake of 1 September 1923, set many firms on a course for direct participation in Japan's prescribed wartime manufacturing regime.[3] My work aims to shed light on this generally misunderstood dimension of Japan's industrial growth, for most readers are familiar only with the broad rubric that characterizes wartime manufacturing as a product of government direction. As most works that treat this issue note, Japan's civilian product manufacturers were labelled redundant or luxurious and phased out of operations in favour of munitions production by Japan's Ministry of Commerce and Industry (MCI), which became the Ministry of Munitions in 1943.[4] While this rubric is broadly useful, and does reflect the general pattern of industrial transition to wartime production, it offers only limited understanding of the experiences of specific firms. Several authors have focused upon the role of the state's interest in scientific management of industry, especially in the form of Okōchi Masatoshi's *Riken* (Institute for Physical and Chemical Research), which sought to streamline Japan's industrial sectors prior to and during the war in order to maximize efficiency in the manufacture of munitions and related equipment.[5] This was a part of the nation's broader pursuit of self-sufficiency (*jikyūjisoku*) in manufacturing, which characterized the government's popularization of the slogan "Rich Nation, Strong Army" (*fukoku kyōhei*).[6] These campaigns are treated often in the literature, but seldom do scholars press deeper into the histories of smaller firms in seemingly less strategic, but nevertheless vital industries, such as food production, optical glass manufacturing, and the manufacture of a wide variety of component materiel. Behind each of these items lies a series of firms that are often with us even now.

Japan's industrial development was not halted and then born anew in the postwar era – it is characterized by an unbroken continuum of development across the transwar era. The same companies that manufactured aircraft, rifle scopes, and fuel alcohol for the war effort were forced merely to retool, to streamline their workforces, and to identify new or pre-existing designs for the approval of a new developmental master – the General Headquarters (GHQ) of the Supreme Commander of the Allied Powers (SCAP), General Douglas MacArthur (1880–1964). While munitions manufacturing was perhaps forbidden during the early years of the Occupation, this in no way precluded many high-tech firms from sewing their leading designs for missiles, artillery, and optical munitions into new, if perhaps rudimentary, civilian consumer products. During the early months of the Allied Occupation of Japan (1945–1952), the United States Navy conducted a Technical Mission to Japan, aiming to identify the breadth and the capability of Japan's wartime munitions makers, and the results of their extensive and thorough investigation were at once intuitive and surprising.[7] The mission's scientists, technicians, and ordnance experts discovered that much of Japan's wartime technology was inferior to or roughly on par with US designs, but there were a few bright spots that were investigated in depth. Beyond these, the mission found evidence that several leading makers' labs and warehouses were already relieved of their most advanced designs, which were ferreted underground for later use by their creators – or sold simply as scrap. As Takamae Eiji demonstrated in his superb study of GHQ, up to 70 percent of Japan's stockpiles of hardware and munitions went missing during a wave of looting that has few parallels beyond the postwar Soviet effort to pillage Eastern Europe and Manchuria of their industrial and technological riches in late 1945.[8] While most postwar Japanese industrialists and entrepreneurs bided their time during the impoverished early postwar years and produced such rudimentary articles as pots, pans, and cooking utensils, many more developed firms aimed to launch their reformed operations by building tables, suitcases, surgical tools, surveying equipment and even calculating machines. Here is where we see the challenges facing some of Japan's brightest and most capable technicians and engineers at their best; as they aimed to retool high-tech munitions plants to produce cheap civilian consumer products under the watchful eye of Japan's new overlord. The adoption of every design and the use of every scrap of equipment, right down to the last nut and bolt, required GHQ's approval, and here is where these designers, faced with new challenges, applied their skills and experience operating wartime manufacturing plants to a brave new market. This is why the participant firms must better account for their transwar technical development – for the process had no end, and no beginning. To overlook any aspect of their engineering development is to fail to tell the whole story. Importantly, however, I emphasize that Japan's wartime manufacturing operations *need not be celebrated* in order to be studied as the historical roots of the nation's postwar economic and industrial growth and success.

The motorcycle industry

Until recently, very little attention had ever been paid by Western scholarship to the subject of Japan's motorcycle industry.[9] It was for decades, however, one of the crown jewels of Japan's export industries, and Japanese firms were shipping their motorcycles worldwide even by the 1920s. With the advent of the war era, however, Japanese manufacturing was streamlined by the MCI in order to maximize efficiency and to achieve self-sufficiency. Consequently, several motorcycle makers were put out of business or forced into other industries in order to realize Japan's goals of industrial rationalization (*sangyō gōrika*). The four case studies below focus upon Japan's four surviving motorcycle manufacturers, each of which was involved in some aspect of manufacturing, and in munitions manufacturing in particular, during the years 1937–1945. Of these "Big Four" firms, only Honda was actually born anew in the postwar, but its founder, Honda Sōichirō, did manage a wartime munitions company called Tōkai Seiki K.K. (Eastern Sea Precision Machine Company, Inc.), and it is to this firm that Honda does indeed refer today in English. Each of these firms and their published versus online histories will be examined in further depth below.

The Honda Motor Company, Inc.

Honda is a dominant global firm with significant technological roots in Japan's wartime production regime. After apprenticing as an auto mechanic in Tokyo and later opening his own shop in Hamamatsu in 1928, founder Honda Sōichirō focused on the manufacture of piston rings, which in the late 1930s were valued more highly by weight than solid silver.[10] Honda already had some familiarity with the process, and in 1937 he purchased the necessary production machinery and established Tōkai Seiki KK. Named for the Tōkai region in which it was located, Honda repaired cars by day and researched piston ring production at night. His initial efforts at their manufacture, however, were a failure. After further metallurgical study at the Hamamatsu Technical High School, which later became the faculty of engineering at Shizuoka University, Honda at last created a satisfactory piston ring prototype by 1939. Upon assuming the presidency of Tōkai Seiki, Honda toured steel manufacturing plants and universities throughout Japan in order to improve his production systems and to meet Toyota's strict product standards. In 1941, Honda began at last to mass produce piston rings for Toyota as well as Nakajima Aircraft using automated machinery and unskilled wartime labour. His firm became one of the largest firms in Japan's Tōkai region, and Honda soon opened a second plant and expanded his product line to include piston rings and engine parts for merchant and navy ships, trucks, and aircraft. He also stepped up the automation of his production line to accommodate a volunteer-corps workforce composed increasingly of women and schoolgirls.[11] This effort would prove critical to Honda's postwar success in developing an assembly line of inexpert technicians operating largely automated machinery.

With the start of the Pacific War against the United States in December 1941, Tōkai Seiki was placed under the control of MCI, and Toyota made a 40 percent investment in the company in 1942. Soon thereafter, Honda's engineering skills came to the attention of Nippon Gakki (the Japan Musical Instrument Manufacturing Company), the predecessor of the Yamaha Motor Company, and Honda developed a high-speed milling machine to help Nippon Gakki automate its manufacture of aircraft propellers. This initiative earned him a letter of commendation from Japan's military, and he was lauded in the press as a hero.[12] The postwar importance of the relationships that Honda cultivated during his time as a subcontractor for Toyota, Nakajima Aircraft, and the Imperial Japanese Navy simply cannot be underestimated. Although Tōkai Seiki's first plant was bombed by US B-29s in 1944 and its second plant was destroyed by the Mikawa earthquake of 13 January 1945, after the war Toyota purchased the company from Honda for ¥450,000.[13] Nevertheless, the experience earned by Honda while managing the company was invaluable. His efforts to produce high-performance piston rings and to engineer an automated production line that could be operated by unskilled labour corps volunteers was critical to both his company and the war effort, and it was upon this experience that he would later found the Honda Technical Research Institute in 1946 and ultimately the Honda Motor Company, Inc., in 1948.

Honda has opted to document its corporate history online in English with an extensive series of articles, most of which are quite rosy and all of which deal with the firm since the founding of the Honda Technical Research Institute in 1946. Significantly, however, one of these articles actually deals with Honda Sōichirō's tenure as the director of Tōkai Seiki, the wartime piston ring manufacturer, and the experience that he earned developing its automated production systems. The firm's discussion of this important and formative episode reads, in English, as follows:

> Mr. Honda had a contract with Toyota Motor Co., Ltd., but out of fifty piston rings he submitted for quality control only three met the required standards. After nearly two more years of visiting universities and steelmaking companies all over Japan in order to study manufacturing techniques, he was at last in a position to supply mass-produced parts to companies such as Toyota and Nakajima Aircraft. At the height of the company's success it employed more than 2,000 people. However, on December 7, 1941, Japan rushed headlong into the Pacific War. Tokai Seiki was placed under the control of the Ministry of Munitions. The male employees gradually disappeared as they were called up for military service, and both adult women and female students began to work in the factory as members of the "volunteer corps." Mr. Honda would calibrate the machines himself and took pains to ensure that the manufacturing process was made as safe and simple as possible for these inexperienced female workers. It was at this time that he devised ways of automating the production of piston rings. [...] Air raids on Japan

became increasingly intensified and it was clear that the country was headed for defeat. As the air raids continued, Hamamatsu was smashed to rubble and Tokai Seiki's Yamashita Plant also was destroyed. The company suffered a further disaster on January 13, 1945, when the Nankai earthquake struck the Mikawa district and the Iwata Plant collapsed.[14]

The above passage is remarkable and it stands alone among the accounts by Honda's rivals, all of which fail to discuss their wartime operations in English online. This despite the fact that the remaining Big Four motorcycle makers were not newly founded in the postwar as was Honda. Honda's treatment of this episode is candid, accurate, and conveys clearly what Tōkai Seiki was making, for which firms and purposes, the worker inexperience that prompted the automation of its plants, and the dire consequences of the US bombing campaigns. Nothing written here glorifies the war effort, and while it does not state explicitly that its piston rings were installed in war machines, that much is clear. Still, this passage hardly compromises Honda's image, reputation, or share price. In an era of globalized online communication, this initiative on the part of the Honda Motor Company stands as an admirable example of a firm with roots in wartime manufacturing that has taken back editorial control of its founder's role and his historical contribution.

The Suzuki Motor Company, Inc.

Suzuki's history begins with Suzuki Michio, who began constructing weaving looms in 1909 under the company name Suzuki Loom Works, which was established in Hamamatsu in that year. Due to its distance from Tokyo, the company was spared the terrible effects of the Great Kantō Earthquake in September 1923, and it continued to produce weaving machines through the 1930s. The company first attempted building a passenger car in 1937, and its engineers also worked on a motorcycle engine at that time. These efforts were aided by the company's possession of a casting plant and the experience needed to cast parts for looms, which permitted the development of the required dies. In late 1937, Suzuki's engineers managed to finish their first automobile, the "Suzulight," and by 1939, Suzuki's engines were putting out 13 horsepower. However, following Japan's invasion of China on 7 July 1937, automobile production was sidelined by wartime production ordinances, and Suzuki soon became a munitions manufacturer with the passage of the National General Mobilization Law in April 1938. Suzuki was careful, however, to shelve its automobile project for future study.[15]

During the war era, Suzuki manufactured war material for the Imperial Japanese Army and Navy, establishing a permanent arms production division in May 1938. It began by weaving hose, canvas, and tire cord for military use, and in spring 1939 Suzuki erected a massive new arms manufacturing plant at Takatsuka, near Hamamatsu. The extensive complex, completed in summer 1940, boasted 46 buildings for employee use, underlining the scale of the investment and its intended output.[16] At this plant, Suzuki produced hand grenades, machine guns, aircraft sights, mortars, shells, and mobile artillery pieces.[17] In 1940, the manufacture of looms accounted for only 15 percent of Suzuki's business, and finished textiles just 10 percent; thus by that time Suzuki was chiefly an arms manufacturer. Its plants boasted high-precision milling machines and presses and employed a total of 6,500 workers, 400 of whom were women.[18] Just as at Honda Sōichirō's wartime plant, Tōkai Seiki, the involvement of inexperienced volunteer labour prompted the automation of many of Suzuki's manufacturing processes. This experience of erecting, equipping, and managing mass-production munitions plants proved critical to Suzuki's postwar development of automated production lines on which inexpert employees could assemble engines and automobiles. Furthermore, and perhaps most formatively, Suzuki was able to continue its research into automobile production during the war by serving as a parts subcontractor. Suzuki was enlisted by the Tokyo Automobile Industries Company, Inc. (later the Isuzu Motor Company) to manufacture pistons, crankshafts, and other parts for military use engines. Suzuki records that this role offered little opportunity for its engineers to study finished automobile production, but it did enable the firm to keep the dream of automobile production alive.[19] The production of engine parts also enabled Suzuki to learn a great deal about die casting – a critically important technique that would serve the firm well in the postwar.

Production was suddenly interrupted on 7 December 1944 when the Tōnankai earthquake struck, killing 1,339 people in the area, including several Suzuki employees, and toppling several buildings at its Takatsuka plant. Shortly thereafter, the city of Hamamatsu came within reach of American air raids. In all, 27 air raids killed over 3,000 people in Hamamatsu, including 177 Suzuki employees. The attacks demolished Suzuki's head office and manufacturing plant at Aioi Town, but significantly, the firm's newer complex in nearby Takatsuka was not bombed before Japan's surrender on 15 August 1945. Suzuki naturally moved its head office to Takatsuka soon after the end of hostilities.[20] The survival of the latter plant, which was Suzuki's largest and best-equipped, largely enabled the company's foray into motor vehicle production in the early 1950s. The die-casting equipment at Takatsuka in particular served to permit the fabrication of engine parts – an invaluable consequence of state investment in wartime munitions manufacturing that, after a rocky postwar recovery, would soon generate significant postwar returns.

As for Suzuki's discussion of the issue online, this has yet to happen in English or in Japanese.[21] Its Japanese-language online history lists only one detail between 1920 and 1952, that the firm erected a new factory in Hamana county, in Shizuoka prefecture, in 1940 (the Takatsuka plant). Its even more facile English-language history web page omits the point about 1940, skipping directly from 1920 to 1952. The motives for the firm's reluctance to treat the war years in English are obvious, and its silence has resulted in little knowledge of its wartime activities coming to light in English, even on the web. At the time of writing, the most detailed online account that the author can locate in English, from Answers.com, reads as follows:

> By 1937 Suzuki had begun production of a variety of war-related materials, which may have included vehicle parts, gun assemblies, and armor. For its part

in Japan's World War II effort, Suzuki, like thousands of other companies, was requisitioned for war production and probably had no intention of becoming a manufacturer of military implements. Nevertheless, the company continued to manufacture weaving machines for the duration of the war. Fortunately, the Suzuki factory and the city of Hamamatsu escaped the ravages of US bombing campaigns. The company was capable of resuming production after the war, but the economy and supply networks were in ruins.[22]

This passage is incorrect for two reasons. First, Suzuki was unable to manufacture weaving machines for the duration of the war. The firm's *shashi* states that the manufacture of weaving machines fell to just 15 percent of Suzuki's sales already by 1940, and that the shipment of weaving machines continued only through 1941.[23] After that, Suzuki was engaged principally in the production of munitions. Second, while Suzuki's factory at Takatsuka did "escape the ravages of US bombing," both its Aioi plant and the city of Hamamatsu in which it was located most certainly did not. Both were destroyed entirely. Of course, the inaccuracy of user-edited web sources is not surprising, but this is not at issue. What is at issue here is the utter absence of reliable online data in English or in Japanese that might counter this misinformation. Suzuki's continued silence on the issue of its wartime operations is perpetuating these inaccuracies, which benefits neither the firm's nor Japan's history, and serves only to generate further erroneous web accounts and flawed reports by students and unsuspecting market writers. The motorcycle industry attracts a great deal of worldwide interest and enthusiasm, yet Suzuki continues unnecessarily to surrender editorial control over this phase of its operational history.

The Yamaha Motor Company, Inc.

The Yamaha Motor Company is today Japan's second-largest manufacturer of motorcycles, and like Honda and Suzuki, it has an array of prewar and wartime manufacturing experience that netted it significant state investment and developmental assets. Its corporate predecessor, Nippon Gakki K.K. (the Japan Musical Instrument Manufacturing Company, Inc.), was founded by Yamaha Torakusu in 1897 in Hamamatsu, and it succeeded the Yamaha Wind Instrument Works that he founded in 1888.[24] Nippon Gakki began manufacturing pianos in 1899, as well as high-end wooden furniture in 1903, and both occupations enabled the firm to amass a great deal of woodworking expertise. Over the next decade, Yamaha added harmonicas, phonographs, and pipe organs to its product line, but it was the company's skill at carpentry that earned it the attention of the military.[25] In the late 1920s, a time when the Imperial Japanese Army sought to ramp up its orders for aircraft propellers, Nippon Gakki's piano shop was staffed by master carpenters. As propellers were then made of wood, Nippon Gakki was well positioned to diversify and become a propeller supplier for domestic builders of fighter aircraft. Nippon Gakki began to produce metal propellers at the request of the military following Japan's invasion of Manchuria in September

1931. The casting and milling of metal propellers required the acquisition of costly machine tools, and this job soon became a major priority. In 1933, the firm sent a group of its engineers to the United States and Europe to observe the production of propellers there. After Japan's invasion of China on 7 July 1937, Nippon Gakki was faced with increasing orders for propellers, each of which took a week to produce, and it was therefore forced to lower its production of organs and pianos. Following the passage of the National General Mobilization Law in April 1938, piano and organ production ceased and Nippon Gakki's operations were placed under the supervision of the Imperial Japanese Army. The company was designated a munitions factory, its capital stock increased to ¥8.75 million, and its chief task became the production of propellers and auxiliary fuel tanks for military aircraft.

When war with the United States broke out on 8 December 1941 (Tokyo time), the demand for propellers increased and the firm erected a new factory in Iwate prefecture. The company began manufacturing metal Hamilton Standard-type variable-pitch aircraft propellers for large bombers, which were adjustable prior to takeoff.[26] Their manufacture, however, was so time-consuming that by 1943 the firm sought the assistance of Honda Sōichirō with the development of automated milling machines.[27] Though already busy managing Tōkai Seiki, Honda developed cutting machines that were able to mill two propellers in just 30 minutes. Orders for propellers, however, fell by 10 percent in August 1943, and production was interrupted entirely on 7 December 1944 by the Tōnankai earthquake, which killed three workers and injured thirteen. The firm's manufacturing plant at Nakazawa was demolished, but after a massive reconstruction effort, production resumed in January 1945.[28] Through the first half of that year, however, Japan was bombed repeatedly by US B-29s, and Nippon Gakki's music stores in Nagoya, Osaka, and Kobe were destroyed along with those cities in incendiary bombing raids. The firm's factory at Tenryū was bombed on 19 May, as was its Nakazawa plant, burning a total of 33,000 square metres in all. On 29 July, Nippon Gakki's remaining offices and factories at Tenryū and Nakazawa were shelled by US naval artillery. When Japan surrendered on 15 August, the company's manufacturing operations, which had once employed over ten thousand workers, halted.[29] Nevertheless, the die-casting experience earned by Nippon Gakki and its possession of advanced milling machinery would have a huge impact on the firm's postwar operations, thus the company took care to wrap up the milling machines for future use. In 1953, Yamaha's president Kawakami Genichi (1912–2002) steered the company's development toward a future in motorcycle manufacturing, and the parts that his engineers developed were fashioned using those very machines. Their finished prototype, the YA-1, would go on to win Japan's first Mount Asama Ascent Race in Gunma prefecture in 1955 – the firm's industrial endurance race debut.

The Yamaha Motor Company's online histories do not discuss the company's wartime activities in English or in Japanese.[30] However, Yamaha's musical instrument manufacturing division does document its wartime progress on its Japanese web site, but not its parallel English page, which is a clear example of the stark contrast between these two historical arenas.[31] When we turn, therefore, to user-edited online accounts, similar errors and outright falsehoods appear, such as in the following passage from Wikipedia:

> After expanding Yamaha Corporation into the world's biggest piano maker, then Yamaha CEO Genichi Kawakami took Yamaha into the field of motorized vehicles on July 1, 1955. The company's intensive research into metal alloys for use in acoustic pianos had given Yamaha wide knowledge of the making of lightweight, yet sturdy and reliable metal constructions. This knowledge was easily applied to the making of metal frames and motor parts for motorcycles.[32]

Like online accounts concerning Suzuki's wartime operational history, this account too is incorrect for two reasons. First of all, Kawakami Genichi asked his engineers to begin to explore the feasibility of entering Japan's domestic motorcycle industry in 1953, not 1955. Next, and more importantly, Kawakami ordered his engineers to base their initial design upon the best contemporary European motorcycles, for they had long since cultivated their die casting and metalworking skills during the war as producers of aircraft propellers and auxiliary fuel tanks. Interim advances in metal alloys had little bearing upon the company's first motorcycle designs, especially not the critical engine and transmission components. Furthermore, in published online interviews in Japanese, the former CEO of Yamaha, Hasegawa Takehiko, also cites his company's wartime manufacture of metal propellers as the source of its technical growth and postwar manufacturing skill.[33] The above quotation, which has since been deleted from the site altogether, rings rather more like deliberate disinformation than it does history. Once again, however, it is not the inaccuracy of a fleeting Wikipedia entry that is in question – it is the continued unwillingness of Yamaha to publish an official, credible online alternative. Instead, Yamaha continues to surrender editorial control over its operational history in English.

Kawasaki Motors, Inc.

A late entrant to the motorcycle market, Kawasaki's rapid success in the field stemmed from a long history of engine and turbine design and manufacturing. Founder Kawasaki Shōzō (1837–1912) established the Kawasaki Tsukiji Shipyard in Tokyo in 1876, and the firm was incorporated as the Kawasaki Dockyard Company in 1896. From that point through the 1930s, the shipping firm diversified into separate divisions for the manufacture of steam turbines, submarines, locomotives, rolling stock, and aircraft. The firm's aircraft department was established initially within the Kawasaki Rolling Stock Manufacturing Company in 1918, but in 1922 a new plant for aircraft construction was established at what is today Kakamigahara City in Gifu prefecture. Ultimately, the aircraft department was spun off in 1937 as the Kawasaki Aircraft Company Limited.[34] In 1938, Kawasaki sought to expand its operations at Gifu, but there was insufficient space to construct additional manufacturing and aircraft testing facilities. Therefore, the Imperial Japanese Army encouraged Kawasaki to construct a new plant just west of Akashi City in Hyogo prefecture. Sufficient land was available there (1.8 square kilometres) to build a new factory and an aircraft testing ground. As is widely known, Kawasaki Aircraft designed and built a series of fighter and escort aircraft for Japan's military until the end of the Second World War (1939–1945), when the company's engine and assembly plants plant at Hyogo were demolished by B-29s on 22 and 26 June 1945.[35]

With Japan's surrender, Kawasaki's operations were idled until Allied Occupation GHQ ruled which companies were to continue operating and which would be terminated. In September 1945, GHQ forbade absolutely all aircraft design, testing, and production, forcing Kawasaki Aircraft, like Suzuki and Nippon Gakki, to convert its operations, at least temporarily, to the manufacture of other goods.[36] Early after the war, Kawasaki made arrangements to produce such items as firefighting equipment, duralumin suitcases, electric kettles, radio cabinets, typewriters, farm implements, and small engines. As a former manufacturer of its own V-12 aircraft engines, Kawasaki's engineers were a uniquely skilled group, but the production of small engines for agricultural use was a significant shift in both purpose and scale. However, Kawasaki was able to maintain a baseline of technical skills and equipment through its interim role as a service subcontractor for both Douglas Aircraft and Bell Helicopter of the United States.[37]

Meanwhile, Kawasaki's management began laying the groundwork for its foray into motorcycle production in the late 1940s. In 1949, aircraft engineers at the Kawasaki Machine Industries plant began designing the firm's first motorcycle engine, a one-cylinder, four-stroke, 148 cc machine, which they dubbed the KE, for "Kawasaki Engine." Kawasaki began manufacturing the design in 1953 through a new subsidiary called Meihatsu Industries. Although the new Kawasaki brand scooter was priced competitively, the company had no domestic sales network and production ground to a halt after finishing just two hundred units. In February 1954, following the merger of the Kawasaki Aircraft and Kawasaki Machine Industries divisions, Kawasaki decided in July to enter the motorcycle market. Under the joint company name of Kawasaki-Meihatsu, the directors followed Yamaha and developed a 125 cc engine at the Kawasaki Aircraft plant in Kobe in 1955. Kawasaki designed and manufactured the engines, and the finished motorcycles were named Meihatsu. The new machines were well received by industry writers and, satisfied with the performance of its motorcycle division, Kawasaki decided in 1959 to erect a new manufacturing plant at Kawasaki-chō, in Akashi, Hyogo prefecture, dedicated to producing finished machines bearing only the name Kawasaki.

Kawasaki's evolution from a maker of fighter aircraft to a motorcycle producer was a bumpy but logical progression, given the postwar economic, legal, and material conditions facing former munitions firms and given the firm's unique engineering skills. Like its aircraft manufacturing peers Mitsubishi and Nakajima, both of which converted to scooter production in the postwar era, Kawasaki capitalized upon its knowledge of casting and assembly and retooled its operations to satisfy Japan's pressing demand for affordable transportation.

This continuum of technological progress is the foundation of Kawasaki Motors, and the firm's transition from ruined wartime aircraft maker to successful manufacturer of peaceful civilian consumer products is a valuable and cautionary chapter in Kawasaki's history. Company enthusiasts demonstrate knowledge of the motor division's origins, and point out on their web sites that "Japan's Kawasaki Motorcycle Division has been making bikes and other motor-sport craft for over 50 years, since retooling a former aircraft factory in the aftermath of World War II."[38] The firm's continuing failure, however, to document its postwar turnaround in English has not enabled Kawasaki Heavy Industries (KHI) to capitalize upon the cautionary tale that is its postwar conversion to consumer product manufacturing. KHI is a vast corporate conglomerate that was involved even more extensively in shipbuilding than aircraft during the war era, but its extensive coverage of those activities in its Japanese *shashi* histories has yet to receive parallel attention in English. Until it does, KHI will continue to cultivate not the benefits of historical stewardship, but the continued appearance of editorial weakness.

The beer industry

The following section deals principally with case studies of the two Japanese brewers that survived the war, Kirin and Dai Nippon (Great Japan). Just like other manufacturing processes, the brewing of beer requires plants and equipment, access to material resources, a ready labour supply, and effective sales and distribution networks. Japan's commercial beer industry began following the manufacture of beer for commercial sale in Yokohama by the American William Copeland in 1869. His efforts would give rise, after a fashion, to roughly 120 independent brewers with a range of experiences – very few of which would survive Japan's Meiji era (1868–1912). As with many such industries in that era, there were few barriers to entry at the outset, and dozens of companies sprouted up and operated in the Meiji era, with mixed success. Lacking a nationwide transportation network, most firms satisfied smaller, local markets and did not command an especially national level of market share. In time, major brewers like Sakura, Osaka, Nippon, Sapporo, and Kirin Beer came to the fore and through national advertising began to eclipse their rivals and command greater market share. Although their rivals passed on in great numbers or were absorbed by their betters, many of the failed companies left a lasting impression on Japan's commercial and advertising landscape, each having sold their wares for several years before succumbing to the sharp cull of Japan's brewing industry prior to the 1920s. For Kirin and Dai Nippon (the latter of which was the product of a three-way merger of Osaka, Nippon, and Sapporo in 1906), successful marketing also including export sales. At home in the domestic market, however, beer sales were soon hampered by excessive competition and vicious underselling by so-called "locust" retailers (*batta*) – who drove beer prices ever lower through the 1920s.

The brewers, exhausted by rising production rates and falling revenues, met to deal with the situation. On 21 February 1932, representatives of the beer companies, the special contract stores of the Tokyo Alcoholic Beverage

Wholesalers League (*Tokyo yōshu tonya renmeikai*), and the retailers from the Tokyo Alcoholic Beverage Sales Association (*Tokyo shuruisho kumiai*) agreed to form the Tokyo Beer Cooperative Association (*Tokyo bakushu kyōchōkai*).[39] Together, they decided not to ship products to undersellers anymore – such dealers were to be frozen out of the market. When that measure had little influence on the large number of undersellers, the Dai Nippon's new chairman, Ōhashi Shintarō, turned to the conclusion of a comprehensive production and sales agreement with the firm's leading rival, Kirin Beer.[40] Struck on 21 June 1933, the agreement is a remarkable example of market collusion in the name of secure profits. Both companies agreed to invest ¥200,000 in the establishment of a common Cooperative Beer Sales Company (*Kyōdō biiru hanbai kaisha*), which would handle all sales and advertising for both firms. Although shipping costs would be borne individually, and the practical business of sales, such as managing sales networks and taking orders, would be handled individually also, the new firm would serve as an official monitor of sales volume. Their agreed-upon market ratios, which thereafter remain fixed, were to reflect their respective shares of the broader market; a ratio of 70.12 percent for Dai Nippon Beer and 29.88 percent for Kirin Beer. If excess volume was produced by either firm in violation of those levels, compensation would have to be paid to the other party. Furthermore, in an agreement reminiscent of the Laws Pertaining to Military Houses (*Buke shō hatto*) of 1615 – which forbade the construction of new castles or the improvement of existing ones in Japan's Edo-era domains, both Dai Nippon and Kirin agreed not to build new breweries or to improve existing ones without consulting the other party first. This remarkable term effectively fixed the proportions of market share held by these firms relative to those of its competitors – who were not long for this world. This degree of explicit collusion between competing manufacturing firms is seldom seen even in Japan, and it has few parallels in that country's corporate history, yet it was orchestrated in the name of market stability and defending modest, but not excessive, profits. This agreement, reached in 1933, would succeed in raising the price of a box of beer by ¥1, and it succeeded in driving out the locusts.

Meanwhile, beer was often portrayed as part of the civilizing influence of commerce and industry delivered by Japan's expanding imperial presence throughout East Asia in the 1930s, and both Kirin and Dai Nippon would soon establish subsidiary brewing firms in Korea and Manchuria.[41] Kirin had already begun exporting beer to Korea (Chōsen) in the 1910s and 20s, and though it received a rebate for the domestic beer brewing tax owed, an import tax was later imposed by Japan's colonial government in Korea. Still, the production tax in Japan was higher than the import tax liability, so as demand for beer in Korea was rising, shipping beer from Kirin's mainland plants remained profitable. However, in the early 1930s, Dai Nippon Beer inherited part of a large plot of land from Kanebō, Ltd. at Eitōho, in the suburbs of Seoul (then called Keijō), and the brewer began drawing up plans to build a plant there. When Kirin learned of its rival's determination to build a plant in Korea, its managing director, Isono Chōzō, set out for Seoul in December 1932 and began searching for a comparable site. He soon found a vacant brick factory close to a station on the Hikikomi Railway Line, and decided immediately to buy the site. Kirin quickly shipped part of the equipment from its Sendai plant to Seoul and set up operations by December 1933. Dai Nippon Beer's new plant, Chōsen Beer (*Chōsen bakushu*) which had an annual production capacity of 40,000 *koku* (7215.6 kl), was completed in April 1934. Kirin's plant likewise began simply as a part of the parent company, but at the suggestion of the governor general of Korea, a separate company, under a pair of officials, was established as Showa Kirin K.K. in December 1933.[42] These pioneering efforts would be followed later by plant construction in Harbin, Dalian, and elsewhere in the burgeoning Japanese empire – laying the groundwork for a regional beer industry.

During the war era, especially after 1938, beer, like many such commodities, was classified as a luxury item, and its manufacture and distribution was controlled and ultimately rationed very tightly as the hostilities wore on and Japan's access to raw materials grew more pressing. Rather than threaten Japan's brewing capacity, however, the restricted access to ingredients actually prompted the nation's leading brewers to pursue self-sufficiency programs for the cultivation of barley and especially hops, for the latter of which Japan was heavily dependent upon European imports until the outbreak of war in 1939. Driven by the necessity to achieve self-sufficiency in ingredient supply, Kirin and Dai Nippon each acquired several tracts of land in Japan, and especially in Korea and Manchuria, for the establishment of research farms. Likewise, Japan's government prompted the beer producers through MCI, the Ministry of Finance (*Ōkurashō*), and the Ministry of Agriculture and Forests (*Nōrin shō*) to form and maintain strict production and distribution networks that came increasingly to limit sales, but also to promote efficiency in production, shipping, and especially in empty bottle-return programs.

In March 1939, beer became subject to government price controls through Japan's commodity price control system, first in Tokyo in May of that year, and in Osaka in June, and in other prefectures after that. Officially priced products were indicated by a (公) mark appearing in a circle, which was referred to as a "*marukō*." Soon it was decided that the official price for beer would be differentiated for makers, wholesalers, retailers, bars, and restaurants, as well as for Tokyo, 13 other cities, and the various rural areas. However, from 1 April 1943, the price differences between Tokyo and the other regions were abandoned, and a unified official price went into effect nationwide. Likewise, a household-use beer distribution system began in Tokyo, Yokohama, and Kawasaki on 1 June 1940.[43] Naturally, the beer distribution system was itself based upon beer manufacturing restrictions. At the same time, sake production suffered a steep drop in production because its principal ingredient was rice, and because secure food provisions came to be viewed as a priority, sake brewing became virtually impossible by 1940. Offsetting the steep decline in sake production was an increase in the demand for beer, which could still be brewed easily because barley was classified as a B-grade foodstuff. Consequently, more and more beer flowed into the distribution network for commercial sale, and as beer taxes rose, the government came to rely increasingly upon the revenue that beer sales generated.[44]

From 1941, household-use beer distribution as well as that of other types of alcoholic beverages became administered through a so-called ticket system (*kippu sei*). A fixed number of tickets that could be exchanged for the purchase of beer were distributed to each household, but a passbook system was later introduced. From about 1943, it became a further prerequisite that empty beer bottles and caps had to be returned in exchange for new beer. In the Tokyo region, as well as throughout the commercial-use network of restaurants and bars, there were separate allotments of special rations made available for formal ceremonies or soldiers leaving for the front, and some allotments were later provided for workers in the munitions industries.[45]

In 1944, Saipan and Guam fell to the United States, and the mainland came under severe attacks from American B-29s. Due to the bombing, offices, factories, schoolchildren, and adult civilians were evacuated from Japanese cities. In March 1944, the remains of Dai Nippon's Materials, Distribution, and East Asia departments were moved from the firm's head office in Kyōbashi, Tokyo to its plant at Meguro, Tokyo. In 1945, the intensity of the bombing increased, and in the middle of the night on 9 March, the firm's Azumabashi plant was destroyed in an attack that leveled all of Tokyo's lower town, or *shitamachi*. Again, in an attack on Yamanote, Tokyo on 24 and 25 May, about 6,600 tsubo (5.4 acres) of Dai Nippon's plant at Meguro was destroyed, and all of the malt in the silos was burned. In a major early dawn raid on the city of Nagoya on 19 March, the company's Nagoya plant was destroyed, most of the wooden buildings were burned down, and beyond the plant grounds, the workers' dormitories and houses were burned and/or damaged. The same plant was bombed again in another raid on 25 March, and again in large raids on 14 and 17 May. Likewise, on 28 July, Dai Nippon's Kawaguchi plant was damaged in a bombing raid. The destruction continued until the end of the war, causing serious damage and killing many of the company's workers and their families. Most of Kirin's manufacturing facilities and many of its workers suffered a similar fate.[46]

Despite such dire circumstances and government directives, Japan's brewers were able by 1944 to engineer a complete national production, distribution, and taxation network, and they formed the Japan Beer Brewers Association (*Nihon bakushu shuzō kumiai*). Although this system, underpinned by the 1943 Alcoholic Beverage Industry Group Control Law (*Shudan hō*), was designed to regulate wartime beer sales for household, commercial, and special event use, it succeeded simultaneously in laying the groundwork for Japan's entire postwar alcohol production, distribution, and taxation regime. The law also extended to sales, and it bound up all retailers of alcoholic beverages into an integrated Retail Sales Association (*Kōri shubai kumiai*).[47] While beer production was ultimately halted in favor of fuel alcohol production in the spring of 1945, its member firms, which were limited by that time to just Dai Nippon and Kirin, would emerge better prepared to deal with the privations of the postwar era and the challenges to come. As the Allied Occupation unfolded, Japan's beer producers capitalized on their wartime experience as they began brewing fixed quantities of generic "beer," and managing nationwide distribution programs aimed at servicing thirsty US service personnel and collecting their empties for reuse.

Despite the brewing industry's many organizational, technical, production, and management systems that were initiated or improved as a result of the war, Japan's major brewers Kirin, Sapporo, and Asahi do not treat the era at all online. Sapporo and Asahi were created in 1949 out of Dai Nippon Beer, following GHQ's policy of industrial deconcentration. Today, Sapporo maintains a series of beautiful museums in Japan, especially in Sapporo City, and these facilities do acknowledge the war era to a limited extent. The displays there are informed by the company's Japanese-language *shashi* histories, all of which treat the prewar and wartime eras in great detail, and acknowledge explicitly that the technical and systemic advances made during the war formed the basis for the firm's postwar operational growth. These discussions are treated in a logical and straightforward fashion, for they involve a dozen years' worth of production increases and systemic, legal, and operational challenges. Such circumstances and responses could not possibly fail to inform the company's postwar recovery and subsequent expansion. Stark then, is the firm's omission of any mention of the war or its challenges in its online histories.[48] The same is true of Asahi's online histories, which trace the firm's descent from the Osaka Beer Brewing Company (founded in 1889), but skip directly from 1935 to 1949.[49] For Kirin's part, its corporate web sites feature only the most rudimentary history pages in either English or Japanese – a sharp contrast to the many editions of handsome and comprehensive *shashi* that Kirin has published in Japanese.[50] Researchers interested in learning of Kirin's wartime activities who cannot read Japanese are limited to facile and totally undocumented Wikipedia entries that read as follows:

> With the start of World War II, the government imposed strict controls over the entire brewing industry. Sales of Kirin beer dropped drastically. Despite a reduction in operations, Kirin established the foundation for its future research and development efforts. In January 1943 the company created the laboratory at the Yokohama brewery and the research department at the Amagasaki brewery.[51]

The above passage, which was visible in October 2008, has since been deleted. By July 2009, the entire Wikipedia page had been truncated and the "company history" section removed altogether.[52] Similarly, the following synopsis about Dai Nippon Beer (later renamed Sapporo) featured in a purported business and investment web site called *Funding Universe*, includes the following erroneous passage:

> During the 1920s and 1930s Japanese militarists, implementing their plan to make Japan the dominant economic power in Asia, began to centralize the brewing industry. By 1943, the merger of all Japanese breweries was virtually complete: Dai Nippon and Kirin were the only two brewing companies left in Japan. In fact, the militarists were powerful enough to force the Sapporo

division of Dai Nippon to establish joint ventures in the occupied territories of Korea and Manchuria.[53]

This passage is incorrect for two reasons. First, no "Japanese militarists" had control over the brewing industry at any point – it was a privately owned and managed industry that, like all other Japanese industries, was subject to government regulation by the Ministry of Finance and the Ministry of Commerce and Industry. Second, and more importantly, these two companies initiated their moves into Korea in the early 1930s independent of government orders, and long before the passage of the National General Mobilization Law of 1938. They were not "forced" to branch out, nor did they establish "joint ventures" – they established wholly owned subsidiary companies. The internet is littered with erroneous claims such as these, and the firms involved, having surrendered editorial control to misinformed web authors, have thus abandoned their corporate integrity through continued inaction.

This industry's failure to treat the war era, even as a cautionary tale, is unfortunate, especially when so many of its facilities were bombed and its employees and their families killed. The time, I argue, for overlooking Japanese war losses, especially of civilians, is long past, and historians can and often do treat the consequences of war for both Japan and the rest of Asia-Pacific in parallel and not mutually exclusive terms. Kirin and Sapporo, I contend, are in an ideal position to instruct future generations of war's consequences. As Japan aims to expand its business and investment opportunities throughout the Asia-Pacific region, individual corporate efforts to underscore the futility and the hardships of war would be vastly more beneficial to Japan's image abroad than continued neglect or obfuscation of involvement in the government's prescribed wartime production regime.

The optical industry

The leading participants in Japan's modern optical industry are Canon, Minolta, and, chiefly, Nippon Kōgaku (Japan Optical Engineering), or Nikon. The following section deals principally with the dominant firm, Nippon Kōgaku, which was both the leading supplier of optical munitions to Japan's military, and the supplier of optical glass to all other optical firms during the war era. Like most Japanese company web sites, Nippon Kōgaku's corporate history features a simple listing of its major accomplishments, inventions, and factory expansions. Immediately apparent, however, is the glaring absence of discussion in English of the war years, or even of the extensive involvement of the Imperial Japanese Navy (IJN) in the firm's growth.[54] Nippon Kōgaku was founded in 1917 through the consolidation of three smaller firms, but the Great Kantō Earthquake that devastated the Kantō region on 1 September 1923 left the young firm's plant in ruins.[55] Suddenly bereft of its key supplier of optical munitions such as telescopes, bomb sights, and range finders, the IJN leapt into the reconstruction effort and provided extensive developmental funds. IJN support began with the naval limitation conferences in 1922 and 1930, after which Japan's government made determined efforts to promote naval research and development initiatives. Japan's participation in the naval limitation program with the United States and Great Britain thus prompted the IJN to finance the development of new and existing technologies to bolster the fighting capabilities of its existing fleet. Rather than laying new keels for capital vessels, which were limited to a 10:10:7 ratio by tonnage (with Japan's share being 7), the navy secured funds for the expansion of research and development in new fields such as optics, rockets, and so on.[56] For this reason, Nippon Kōgaku's facilities were reconstructed and expanded post haste, and the company brought in foreign technical experts from the German optical firms Leitz and Zeiss to assist with the improvement of its technological and material understanding. Producing optical glass in large melts required an extensive repository of technical skill, and with the aid of their foreign advisors, Nippon Kōgaku amassed the engineering capability necessary both to produce optical weapons for Japan's military, as well as optical glass for other companies producing optical products, including cameras, microscopes, and surveyor's transits, or theodolites. These efforts were underwritten by the contemporary design tenet, "copy, improve, innovate."[57]

Nippon Kōgaku's most impressive achievements were the large, complex range finders and submarine periscopes that it designed and built for the IJN. These range finders, the largest of which were constructed for the superbattleships *Yamato* and *Musashi*, required highly advanced lens and mirror fabrication – key technical demands that would put the company in an excellent postwar position. Perhaps most vital to its postwar foray into camera production, however, was the experience that the firm earned as both a designer of lenses and as a mass-production manufacturer. In the former case, Nippon Kōgaku was called upon by IJN submarine commanders during the Pacific War to produce better periscopes, for the current models did not transmit sufficient light. Too much light was being lost as the image passed through as many as 33 optical components, and submarine commanders were experiencing difficulty spotting targets in the hours of dawn and dusk. In response, Nippon Kōgaku's engineers designed lens coatings to improve the transmission of light, which involved baking lenses with cryolite and other chemical substances at high heat. Not only were these methods successful, they proved to be a key advantage in the company's conversion to postwar consumer product manufacturing. Although Nippon Kōgaku did not itself manufacture cameras for civilian consumers, it did produce Nikkor-brand camera lenses for firms like Kōgaku Seiki and Kwanon (today Canon), and nearly a hundred other optical components makers.

In the 1945 report of the US Naval Technical Mission to Japan, US investigators found that Nippon Kōgaku's lens coatings were superior to those produced by American optical companies, and that Japanese optics were a bright spot in the country's wartime manufacturing record.[58] While other technologies were on par or often inferior to US designs, the mission found that Japan's optics had very desirable qualities. As a result, one of the trophies sought by American sailors stationed in postwar Japan was a pair of Nippon Kōgaku's "Orion" binoculars, which boasted not only superior optics, but also a set of rudimentary eyepiece filters designed to improve night vision by capturing available star and moonlight. Continued manufacture of such products, which were classified as optical munitions, was of course banned by US General Headquarters (GHQ) during the Occupation era. However, when the company applied for permission to resume manufacturing standard civilian binoculars and cameras, GHQ gave its assent, and Nippon Kōgaku thus combined its technical know-how with its experience as a mass-producer of lenses using wartime volunteer labour.

Nippon Kōgaku's experience as a wartime munitions supplier enabled it to overcome the challenges of the postwar era and to retool its operations relatively quickly. Nikon's rapid transition to consumer production in 1945 and 1946 capitalized upon its engineers' wartime technical accomplishments, and despite the destruction of its plants at the end of the war, the firm was soon able to modify its designs to target the civilian photography market. Combined with its knowledge of optical glass and lens manufacturing, prior successes in lens coating enabled Nikon to enter world camera markets. In April 1946, Nikon's engineers applied an optical coating similar to that used in war-era periscopes to the barrels of its *Nikkor* lenses to enhance the transmission of light through the instrument. This enabled the addition of more optical elements, and significantly reduced internal reflections or "flares," which greatly improved the performance of the company's large camera lenses. These advances soon enabled Nikon's lenses to outperform those of German manufacturers Leitz and Zeiss at postwar camera exhibitions. The superior quality of Nikon's lenses was recognized worldwide already by the mid-1950s, and the company points to the "sensation" created by the age of the battlefield "cameraman," whose shots graced the pages of *Life* magazine. At the World Expo in Brussels in 1958, Nikon was awarded the Grand-Prix, Gold, Silver, and Bronze prizes for its lenses and camera designs.[59]

Nikon describes its role as an optical munitions manufacturer as a period of "increased wealth in technical efficiency," and cites its experience in this arena as fundamental to its debut as civilian consumer product manufacturer.[60] Without pressure from Japan's military, it is unlikely that Nippon Kōgaku would have diversified its product line to include cameras for reconnaissance aircraft or similar military use. Whatever their intended application, Nikon's engineers were called upon, often under great duress, to produce state of the art optical weapons and auxiliary equipment, and these investments, fuelled by state funding, enabled the firm to leap into the postwar era and face the challenges of an impoverished market. It is thus inaccurate to suggest that discussion or understanding of Nikon's postwar development is possible without reference to its wartime activities. Importantly, Nikon's *Japanese*-language web site lists those activities in great detail, including the firm's manufacture range finders for the *Yamato*-class warships, as well as infrared vision equipment. Nikon's documentary effort here is much more detailed than it was several years ago, when its Japanese history page was as superficial as its English-language page is at the time of writing.[61] The latter still skips from 1932 to 1945, omitting any reference to the firm's wartime technological accomplishments, presumably to avoid the impression that it profited from the war. Broadly speaking, most Japanese companies that participated as munitions corporations did profit from the war. However, corporate earnings and dividends were tightly controlled and in 1940 the Army Ministry issued the Outline for Calculating Reasonable Profit Margins, which capped the dividend rates of corporations at 12 percent per share.[62] Companies faced increasingly impossible demands from the military even in the closing stages of the war, and as companies like Nippon Kōgaku came under attack by B-29s, its plant directors were ordered to relocate their machinery in caves and forests in order to continue their operations. The war is a charged issue to be sure, but we must remember that by 1945 a large proportion of employees in Japanese factories, and especially in Nippon Kōgaku's lens plants, were women and schoolgirls, not soldiers.

Like Nippon Kōgaku, contemporary optical firms Canon and Minolta provide no details about their wartime operations in their corporate online histories.[63] Both Minolta's Japanese- and English-language online histories are equally superficial, skipping from 1928 to 1956 with but a single entry in between – the issue of a new camera model in 1940. Likewise, in discussing the years 1937–1945, Canon's histories mention only the assumption by Takeshi Mitarai (1901–1984) of the firm's presidency in 1942.[64] There are presently fewer popular online accounts about Nikon in circulation than there are for the companies in the other industries examined above, due perhaps to my own publication several years ago of a comprehensive article on Nippon Kōgaku's corporate development and wartime operations.[65] Other web authors have since quoted, cited, and linked my article in their own stories on Nikon's historical development, and this has, I hope, trimmed the web of potential confusion. Nevertheless, Nikon itself has still not taken ownership of its wartime operations by issuing any corollary history in English, despite the keen interest of its many thousands of product enthusiasts worldwide. Japanese companies are understandably reticent to invoke any memory of the war in their online corporate literature, but if not the companies themselves, what other group or actor may take ownership of such a significant and integral era in Japan's history?

Conclusion

If Japan's leading companies were to begin to address their wartime operational histories online in English, even as they aimed to widen their share of the Asia-Pacific market, it would sow important seeds. Where Japan's elected officials and textbook revision committees have often been criticized for failing to treat the war years in sufficient detail, the collective will of its corporations to discuss the era, especially in the digital realm, would cultivate greater global respect and integrity. However, the companies' continuing reluctance to acknowledge their participation in Japan's prescribed wartime production regime is a setback both corporate and national. We may ask rhetorically, in an era of globalized communication, when exactly will it be seen as historically absurd to omit mention of the years 1937–1945 in even cursory online histories? After 70 years, or 100, or 200? If these major companies survive, and there is every reason to believe that market leaders like Yamaha, Kirin, and Nikon will do so, when might they "safely" discuss in

English their involvement in Japan's war effort? With each passing year, their reluctance to even acknowledge the era, never mind the details, becomes more obvious, and more telling. Indeed, by failing to recognize the war, they call even greater attention to it, which is far more suspect than the inclusion of a brief but accurate chronology on a corporate web site. Naturally, few companies would wish to dwell at any length upon their or Japan's wartime conduct, but documenting the era constitutes an invaluable opportunity to tell a cautionary tale about the consequences of war and the defence of corporate independence. It must be recognized that munitions companies the world over were essential, productive, and profitable even in limited degrees during the period 1937–1945. With shareholders, employees, suppliers, and subcontractors to service, few companies were in a position to be conscientious objectors to war by closing their doors following the passage of wartime mobilization ordinances. Fewer still could refuse to satisfy the demands of their respective militaries, or balk at the suggestion that they begin manufacturing strategic rather than luxury goods, however ridiculous the production targets. Debates over the moral responsibility of wartime manufacturing are important, but we must also note that Japan's participant firms were largely obliterated by US B-29s during the final phases of the Pacific War, and their employees, along with their families, were often killed. These companies have clearly felt a responsibility to document their wartime operations in their Japanese-language *shashi* histories. It is, I contend, essential for all Japanese companies to do the same in English in order both to take back their operational histories and to present them in the proper historical context. In this light, Honda has struck an admirable balance with its English-language online history, and it should be looked to by its industrial and commercial peers as a leader both in product development and historical stewardship.

Notes

1 By "prehistories," I refer to the operational predecessors of firms or divisions that today manufacture a different or wider variety of products, and/or were active during the war era under different names. Honda Giken Kōgyō K.K. (Honda Motor Company, Inc.), "Honda History," http://world.honda.com/history/index.html (JP: Honda Motor Company, Inc.), 7 July 2009.

2 The term "transwar" is used thematically in reference to the period between Japan's invasion of Manchuria on 18 September 1931 and the end of Japan's Occupation by the Allied Powers (1945–52). This was an era of industrial and technological development that progressed continually – a process that did not stop and then begin anew following Japan's surrender to the Allies at the end of the Second World War. The term "wartime," however, is used chronologically to refer to the period from 18 September 1931 to the end of the Second World War on 15 August 1945. The term "postwar" is likewise used chronologically to refer to the period following the Second World War.

3 Michael A. Cusumano, *The Japanese Automobile Industry: Technology and Management at Nissan and Toyota* (Cambridge, MA: Harvard University Press, 1985), p. 14.

4 See especially "The Wartime Economy and Scientific Management, 1937–1945," Chapter 3 of William M. Tsutsui, *Manufacturing Ideology: Scientific Management*

in Twentieth-Century Japan (Princeton, NJ: Princeton University Press, 1998), pp. 90–121; and Michael A. Cusumano, *The Japanese Automobile Industry.*

5   Michael A. Cusumano, "'Scientific Industry': Strategy, Technology, and Entrepreneurship in Prewar Japan," in William D. Wray, ed., *Managing Industrial Enterprise: Cases from Japan's Prewar Experience* (Cambridge, MA: Harvard University Press, 1989), pp. 269–315.

6   Richard J. Samuels, *Rich Nation, Strong Army: National Security and Ideology in Japan's Technological Transformation* (Ithaca, NY: Cornell University Press, 1994).

7   C.G. Grimes, Captain, USN, ed., *U.S. Naval Technical Mission to Japan – History of Mission,* Washington DC: US Government Printing Office, US Naval History Division, 1946.

8   Takemae Eiji, *Inside GHQ: The Allied Occupation of Japan and Its Legacy* (New York: Continuum, 2002), pp. 76–77.

9   For the background on this issue and the motorcycle industry's early development, see Jeffrey W. Alexander, *Japan's Motorcycle Wars: An Industry History* (Vancouver, BC: UBC Press, 2008).

10 Sakiya Tetsuo, *Honda Motor: The Men, the Management, the Machines*, trans. Ikemi Kiyoshi, (New York: Kodansha International USA/Harper and Row, 1982), p. 53.

11 Ikeda Masajirō, ed., *Sōichirō Honda: The Endless Racer*, trans. Kazunori Nozawa (Tokyo: Japan International Cultural Exchange Foundation, 1993), p. 158.

12 Sakiya, *Honda Motor, The Men, the Management, the Machines*, p. 56.

13 Honda giken kōgyō K.K. (Honda Motor Company, Inc.), "Joy of Manufacturing (1936)," http://world.honda.com/history/limitlessdreams/joyofmanufacturing/index.html, 7 July 2009.

14 Ibid.

15 Suzuki jidōsha kōgyō KK, keiei kikakubu, kōhōka (Suzuki Motor Company, Inc., Public Relations Department, Management Planning Section), ed., *Shichijūnenshi hensan: Suzuki jidōsha kōgyō kabushiki keiei kikakubu kōhōka* (*Seventy-Year History: Edited by the Public Relations Department of the Suzuki Motor Company, Inc., Management Planning Section*) (Nagoya: Suzuki jidōsha kōgyō KK, 1990), pp. 11–12.

16 Ibid., p. 12–14.

17 Ibid., p. 15.

18 Ibid., p. 15.

19 Ibid., p. 13.

20 Ibid., p. 17–18.

21 Suzuki Motor Company, "Suzuki no rekishi" (History of Suzuki), http://www.suzuki.co.jp/about/development/index.html, and, "History," http://www.globalsuzuki.com/corp_info/history/index.html, 7 July 2009.

22 Answers.com, "Suzuki Motor Corporation," http://www.answers.com/suzuki%20motor%20company, 7 July 2009.

23 Suzuki, *Shichijūnenshi*, p. 11–12.

24 Yamaha KK (Yamaha Company, Inc.), ed., *The Yamaha Century: Yamaha 100 nenshi (100-Year History of Yamaha)* (Hamamatsu: Yamaha KK, 1987), p. 4.

25 Yamaha, *Yamaha Century*, p. 222.

26 Interview with Hasegawa Takehiko, former president and CEO, Yamaha Motor Company, Inc., *Mōtāsaikuristo* (Motorcyclist), special edition, December 2002 and January 2003, reprinted online at http://www.iom1960.com/kantoku-zadankai/hys-kantoku-zadankai.html, 7 July 2009.

27 Ikeda, *Sōichirō Honda: The Endless Racer*, pp. 28–29.

28 Ibid., p. 11.

29 Ibid., pp. 11–12, 225–26.

30 Yamaha hatsudōki K.K. (Yamaha Motor Company, Inc.), "Enkaku gojūnendai" ("History, 1950s"), http://www.yamaha-motor.co.jp/profile/history/1950/index. html,

and "History, 1955–1959," http://www.yamaha-motor.co.jp/global/about/history/1950/index.html, 7 July 2009.

31 Yamaha Global Gateway, "Senzen no Yamaha kigyō katsudō, 1887–1944" ("Yamaha Prewar Operational Activity, 1887–1944), http://www.yamaha.co.jp/about/history/prewar/index.html, and "Yamaha History," (1887–2003) http://www.global.yamaha.com/about/history.html, 7 July 2009.

32 Wikipedia, "Yamaha Motor Company," http://en.wikipedia.org/wiki/Yamaha_Motor, 26 October 2008.

33 Interview with Hasegawa Takehiko, former president and CEO of Yamaha.

34 Kawasaki jūkōgyō KK, Hikōki jigyō honbu (Kawasaki Heavy Industries, Inc., Aircraft Manufacturing Division), ed., *Gifu kōjō gojūnen no ayumi* (*Fifty-Year History of the Gifu Works*) (Gifu, JP: Kawasaki jūkōgyō KK, 30 November 1987), p. 21.

35 Ibid., p. 41.

36 GHQ of the Supreme Commander of the Allied Powers, "Memorandum AG 360" ESS-E (SCAPIN 301) (18 November 1945), in Nihon Gaimushō, Tokubetsu shiryōka (Foreign Office of Japan, Special Records Section), *Nihon senryō oyobi kanri jūyō bunsho shi (Documents Concerning the Allied Occupation and Control of Japan), Vol. 3: Keizai (Financial, Economic, and Reparations)* (Tokyo: Tōyō keizai shimposha, August 1949), p. 260.

37 Kawasaki, *Gifu kōjō gojūnen no ayumi,* p. 81.

38 Motoyard.com, "Kawasaki Motorcycles," http://www.motoyard.com/Kawasaki-Motorcycle.shtml, 7 July 2009.

39 Kirin Beer K.K., *Kirin biiru K.K. gojū nenshi (Kirin Beer Company, Incorporated: 50-Year History), Kirin Beer K.K.,* 20 March 1957, p. 114.

40 Ibid., p. 115.

41 Ibid., pp. 122–33.

42 Ibid.

43 "Household-use beer distribution system," *Asahi shimbun, 2 June 1940, in Sapporo Beer K.K., Sapporo 120 nenshi (120-year History of Sapporo Beer)* (JP: Sapporo Beer K.K., 1996), p. 300, and Kirin Beer K.K., Kirin biiru K.K. gojū nenshi, pp. 146–47.

44 Kirin Beer K.K., *Kirin biiru K.K. gojū nenshi,* pp. 139–45.

45 Sapporo Beer K.K., *Sapporo 120 nenshi,* p. 301.

46 Ibid., p. 310.

47 Ibid., p. 303.

48 Sapporo Beer K.K., "Sapporo biiru monogatari" ("The Story of Sapporo Beer"), http://www.sapporobeer.jp/english/history/, and "The History of Sapporo Breweries," http://www.sapporobeer.jp/story/index.html, 7 July 2009.

49 Asahi Breweries, Ltd., "Rekishi – Enkaku" ("History – Development"), http://www.asahibeer.co.jp/aboutus/history, and "History of Asahi Breweries," http://www.asahibeer.co.jp/english/companye/history.html, 7 July 2009.

50 "Nenpyo" ("The Kirin History), http://www.kirinholdings.co.jp/company/history/history1.html, and Kirin Holdings Company, Ltd. "Corporate History," http://www.kirinholdings.co.jp/english/company/history/corporatehistory/01.html (and ~02.html), 7 July 2009.

51 Wikipedia, "Kirin Brewery Company," http://en.wikipedia.org/wiki/Kirin_Brewery_Company, 26 October 2008.

52 Ibid., 7 July 2009.

53 Funding Universe, "Sapporo Breweries Limited," http://www.fundinguniverse.com/company-histories/Sapporo-Breweries-Limited-Company-History.html, 7 July 2009.

54 For a more in-depth analysis of Japan's transwar optical industry, see Jeff Alexander "Nikon and the Sponsorship of Japan's Optical Industry by the Imperial Japanese Navy, 1917–1945" in *Japanese Studies*, Winter 2002.

55 These firms were the Iwaki Glass Seisaku-sho, the Fujii Lens Seizō-sho, and the optical division of Tokyo Keiki Seisaku-sho. Nippon kōgaku K.K. (Japan Optical

Engineering Company, Inc.), *Nippon kōgaku kōgyō kabushiki kaisha: gojūnen no ayumi (Fifty Year History of the Nikon Company)* (Tokyo: Nihon Kōgaku, 1967), p. 56.

56 Thomas F. Mayer-Oakes, ed., *Fragile Victory: Prince Saionji and the 1930 London Treaty Issue from the Memoirs of Baron Harada Kumao* (Detroit, MI: Wayne State University Press, 1968), Appendix III C, p. 311.

57 Christopher Howe, *The Origins of Japanese Trade Supremacy: Development and Technology in Asia from 1540 to the Pacific War* (London: Hurst, 1996), p. 284.

58 Captain C.G. Grimes, USN, ed. "Japanese Optics," in *U.S. Naval Technical Mission to Japan – Series X: Miscellaneous Target-Report X-05* (Washington, DC: US Government Printing Office, US Naval History Division, 1945), p. 31.

59 Nippon kōgaku K.K., *Gojūnen no ayumi*, p. 83.

60 Ibid., p. 74.

61 Nikon Corporation, "Kigyō nenpyō" ("Operational Chronology"), http://www.nikon.co.jp/main/jpn/profile/about/history/corporate_history.htm, and "Corporate History," http://www.nikon.com/about/info/history/corporate/index.htm, 7 July 2009.

62 Suzuki, *Shichijūnenshi,* p. 14.

63 Konica Minolta, "History," http://www.konicaminolta.com/about/corporate/history.html, and Konica Minolta, "Enkaku" ("History"), http://konicaminolta.jp/about/corporate/history.html, 7 July 2009.

64 Canon, Inc., "Kiyanon kamera shi, 1937–1945" ("Canon Camera Story, 1937–1945"), http://web.canon.jp/Camera-muse/history/canon_story/f_index_d.html, and "Canon Camera Story, 1937–1945," http://www.canon.com/camera-museum/history/canon_story/f_index_d.html, 7 July 2009.

65 Jeff Alexander, "Nikon and the Sponsorship of Japan's Optical Industry by the Imperial Japanese Navy, 1917–1945," *Gateway Online, 2001*, http://grad.usask.ca/gateway/archive17.html, 7 July 2009. This article was later revised and republished in *Japanese Studies,* Vol. 22, No. 1, May 2002, pp. 19–33.

References

Books and periodicals, English

Alexander, Jeffrey W. *Japan's Motorcycle Wars: An Industry History* (Vancouver, BC: UBC Press, 2008).

—— "Nikon and the Sponsorship of Japan's Optical Industry by the Imperial Japanese Navy, 1917–1945" in *Japanese Studies*, Winter 2002.

Cusumano, Michael A. *The Japanese Automobile Industry: Technology and Management at Nissan and Toyota* (Cambridge, MA: Harvard University Press, 1985).

—— "'Scientific Industry': Strategy, Technology, and Entrepreneurship in Prewar Japan," in William D. Wray, ed., *Managing Industrial Enterprise: Cases from Japan's Prewar Experience* (Cambridge, MA: Harvard University Press, 1989), pp. 269–315.

Grimes, C.G. Captain, USN, ed., *U.S. Naval Technical Mission to Japan – History of Mission*, Washington, DC: US Government Printing Office, US Naval History Division, 1946.

—— "Japanese Optics," in *U.S. Naval Technical Mission to Japan – Series X: Miscellaneous Target-Report X-05* (Washington, DC: US Government Printing Office, US Naval History Division, 1945).

Howe, Christopher. *The Origins of Japanese Trade Supremacy: Development and Technology in Asia from 1540 to the Pacific War* (London: Hurst, 1996).

58   *Jeffrey W. Alexander*

Ikeda, Masajirō, ed., *Sōichirō Honda: The Endless Racer*, trans. Kazunori Nozawa (Tokyo: Japan International Cultural Exchange Foundation, 1993), p. 158.

Mayer-Oakes, Thomas F., ed., *Fragile Victory: Prince Saionji and the 1930 London Treaty Issue from the Memoirs of Baron Harada Kumao* (Detroit, MI: Wayne State University Press, 1968).

Sakiya, Tetsuo. *Honda Motor: The Men, the Management, the Machines*, trans. Ikemi Kiyoshi (New York: Kodansha International USA/Harper and Row, 1982), p. 53.

Samuels, Richard J. *Rich Nation, Strong Army: National Security and Ideology in Japan's Technological Transformation* (Ithaca, NY: Cornell University Press, 1994).

Takemae, Eiji. *Inside GHQ: The Allied Occupation of Japan and Its Legacy* (New York: Continuum, 2002), pp. 76–77.

Tsutsui, William M. *Manufacturing Ideology: Scientific Management in Twentieth-Century Japan* (Princeton, NJ: Princeton University Press, 1998), pp. 90–121.

Books and periodicals, Japanese

Asahi Shimbun newspaper

General Headquarters of the Supreme Commander of the Allied Powers, "Memorandum AG 360" ESS-E (SCAPIN 301) (18 November 1945), in Nihon Gaimushō, Tokubetsu shiryōka (Foreign Office of Japan, Special Records Section), *Nihon senryō oyobi kanri jūyō bunsho shi* (*Documents Concerning the Allied Occupation and Control of Japan*), Vol. 3: *Keizai* (*Financial, Economic, and Reparations*) (Tokyo: Tōyō keizai shimposha [Oriental Economist Newspaper Co], August 1949).

Kawasaki jūkōgyō KK, Hikōki jigyō honbu (Kawasaki Heavy Industries, Inc., Aircraft Manufacturing Division), ed., *Gifu kōjō gojūnen no ayumi* (*Fifty-Year History of the Gifu Works*) (Gifu, JP: Kawasaki jūkōgyō KK, 30 November 1987).

Kirin Beer K.K., *Kirin biiru K.K. gojū nenshi* (*Kirin Beer Company, Incorporated: 50-Year History*) (Kirin Beer K.K., 20 March 1957).

Nippon kōgaku K.K. (Japan Optical Engineering Company, Inc.), *Nippon kōgaku kōgyō kabushiki kaisha: gojūnen no ayumi* (*Fifty Year History of the Nikon Company*) (Tokyo: Nihon Kōgaku, 1967).

Sapporo Beer K.K., *Sapporo 120 nenshi* (*120-year History of Sapporo Beer*) (JP: Sapporo Beer K.K., 1996).

Suzuki jidōsha kōgyō KK, keiei kikakubu, kōhōka (Suzuki Motor Company, Inc., Public Relations Department, Management Planning Section), ed., *Shichijūnenshi hensan: Suzuki jidōsha kōgyō kabushiki keiei kikakubu kōhōka* (*Seventy-Year History: Edited by the Public Relations Department of the Suzuki Motor Company, Inc., Management Planning Section*) (Nagoya: Suzuki jidōsha kōgyō KK, 1990).

Yamaha KK (Yamaha Company, Inc.), ed., *The Yamaha Century: Yamaha 100 nenshi* (100-Year History of Yamaha) (Hamamatsu: Yamaha KK, 1987).

Web sites, English and Japanese

Asahi Breweries Ltd., "Rekishi – Enkaku" ("History – Development"), http://www.asahibeer.co.jp/aboutus/history
—— "History of Asahi Breweries," http://www.asahibeer.co.jp/english/companye/history.html

Canon, Inc., "Kiyanon kamera shi, 1937–1945" ("Canon Camera Story, 1937–1945"), http://web.canon.jp/Camera-muse/history/canon_story/f_index_d.html

—— "Canon Camera Story, 1937–1945," http://www.canon.com/camera-museum/history/canon_story/f_index_d.html

Honda giken kōgyō K.K. (Honda Motor Company, Inc.), "Honda History," http://world.honda.com/history/index.html, (JP: Honda Motor Co., Inc.)

—— "Joy of Manufacturing (1936)," http://world.honda.com/history/limitlessdreams/joyofmanufacturing/index.html

Kirin Beer K.K., "Nenpyo" ("The Kirin History), http://www.kirinholdings.co.jp/company/history/history1.html

—— "Corporate History," http://www.kirinholdings.co.jp/english/company/history/corporatehistory/01.html (and ~02.html)

Konica Minolta, "History," http://www.konicaminolta.com/about/corporate/history.html

—— "Enkaku" ("History"), http://konicaminolta.jp/about/corporate/history.html

Mōtāsaikuristo (Motorcyclist), special edition, December 2002 and January 2003, reprinted online at http://www.iom1960.com/kantoku-zadankai/hys-kantoku-zadankai.html

Nikon Corporation, "Kigyō nenpyō" ("Operational Chronology"), http://www.nikon.co.jp/main/jpn/profile/about/history/corporate_history.htm

—— "Corporate History," http://www.nikon.com/about/info/history/corporate/index.htm

Sapporo Beer K.K., "Sapporo biiru monogatari" ("The Story of Sapporo Beer"), http://www.sapporobeer.jp/english/history/

—— "The History of Sapporo Breweries," http://www.sapporobeer.jp/story/index.html

Suzuki Motor Company, *"Suzuki no rekishi"* (History of Suzuki), http://www.suzuki.co.jp/about/development/index.html

—— "History," http://www.globalsuzuki.com/corp_info/history/index.html

Yamaha hatsudōki K.K. (Yamaha Motor Company, Inc.), "Enkaku gojūnendai" ("History, 1950s"), http://www.yamaha-motor.co.jp/profile/history/1950/index.html

—— "History, 1955–1959," http://www.yamaha-motor.co.jp/global/about/history/1950/index.html

—— "Senzen no Yamaha kigyō katsudō, 1887–1944" ("Yamaha Prewar Operational Activity, 1887–1944), http://www.yamaha.co.jp/about/history/prewar/index.html

—— "Yamaha History" (1887–2003), http://www.global.yamaha.com/about/history.html

3 "Kids these days ..."

Globalization and the shifting discourse of childhood in Japan

Dawn Grimes-MacLellan

What is wrong with kids today?

Around the world, children and youth are increasingly the subject of intense public scrutiny, as crime and violence perpetrated by young people make both national and international headlines and prompt parents, educators and government officials to lament the disintegration of social values. At their most extreme, media reports portray contemporary youth as menacing and fearful, their motives as perplexing as they are impenetrable, a view realized by many Americans as they struggled to come to terms with the senselessness of the Columbine school massacre and how the two average-looking middle class perpetrators evolved into evil personified. These contemporary images of North American youth are in stark contrast to ways in which this period in the lifecourse has long been represented. Romanticized and cherished as a special time of innocence characterized through imagery of goodness, simplicity, naiveté, and self-discovery prior to being corrupted by the worldly temptations of adulthood, childhood in North America draws its traditions from old Norman Rockwell paintings and literary characters such as Tom Sawyer or Huck Finn whose lives in a small Mississippi riverfront town embrace freedom seeking adventure and self-realization. Though mischievous, the Tom and Huck of our memories are generally good-natured, their antics and youthful wonder supporting our collective imagination of childhood as a time of innocence.

Similarly in Japan, contemporary images and discourses of childhood and youth seem to have taken a drastic turn from long-established tradition. Reports of declining academic achievement and increasing incidence of bullying and teenage prostitution, coupled with imagery of youth (both boys and girls) with dyed hair, pierced noses and poor manners, coalesce to suggest for an already angst-ridden population enduring a second decade of restructuring that the future of Japan is in a downward spiral. Fueled by the media, these images contrast the children and youth of today with those of a nostalgic (and largely, imagined) past when children were regarded as treasures and youth obeyed their parents without question, spoke politely to neighbors, and played with innocent exuberance. These days, negative perceptions relating the problems of children and youth are so widely reported in the media that even the most casual observers and infrequent visitors to Japan effortlessly become aware of the "crisis" of childhood permeating throughout Japanese society.

The current ominous foreboding regarding Japan's young people can be traced back more than a decade to the Kōbe schoolboy murders of 1997, when a 14-year-old boy fatally stabbed a 10-year-old girl and strangled an 11-year-old boy, leaving his decapitated head at the entrance of a junior high school in the western part of the city. Since that event, juvenile crime has become a fixture of front page news, and the collective horror initially sparked by what has become known as the "Kōbe incident" is re-visited with each subsequent report. In 2004, for example, when an 11-year-old Nagasaki girl stabbed a classmate to death in a sudden act of rage precipitated by the victim's criticism of her on the internet, shockwaves once again resounded throughout the nation (*Daily Yomiuri* 6/3/04) as the age and sex of the offender pushed the limits once again on perceived boundaries on juvenile crime. It now appeared possible for a child of any age or sex to "snap" for any number of unpredictable reasons. Cases such as these strengthened calls for revisions of Japan's juvenile law (*shōnenhō*), which occurred first in 2000 and then again in 2007, initially lowering the age for criminal punishment from 16 to 14 years and subsequently allowing courts to send minors as young as 12 to juvenile reformatories (*Japan Times* 5/25/07).

In early 2007, as pending revisions to the juvenile law drew increased attention to youth violence, news of yet another horrifying case reverberated throughout the nation. This time, a high school student from Aizuwakamatsu, a city of 100,000 northeast of Tōkyō, walked into a police station carrying the severed head of his mother in a schoolbag (*Japan Times* 5/19/07). As if this most vile repudiation of filial piety were not enough, the public learned through news reports that the student had confessed to the act shortly after spending two hours watching a hip-hop music DVD at an internet café. As this and prior cases suggest, although grisly murders such as these are rare in Japan, they persist in public memory, fueled by a steady stream of media coverage suggesting delinquent behavior is on the rise. Subsequently, they become entwined with widespread apprehension for the future to coalesce into a perception among Japanese adults that the condition of contemporary children and youth is in a state of severe crisis.

The reporting of the 2007 incident also suggests that the contemporary discourse of discontent is as much a statement about Japanese adults as it is about its youth. Wrenching social transformations in recent decades have placed great pressures on the nation, on institutions, families and individuals to re-imagine Japan not only in the present but also for the future, and the 2007 incident channels widespread apprehension about the capacity of contemporary youth, the symbolic future of the nation, to bear the burden required to take care of their elders and achieve future prosperity. In this context, the discourse of youth can be viewed as an expression of national angst in postindustrial Japan at the failed promise of modernity and the prospect of an uncertain future.

The thinly veiled attribution of blame for the problems of Japan's youth through references to hip-hop in coverage of the 2007 incident further complicates Japan's already knotty relationship with the rest of the world and national concerns about the social and cultural side effects of globalization. In the postwar era, Japan has largely embraced the policies of intergovernmental organizations such as the Organization for Economic Co-operation and Development (OECD) and the United Nations Educational, Scientific and Cultural Organization (UNESCO) that have associated education with economic development and industrialization with prosperity, a position that served Japan's export-based economy well until the late 1980s. However, the social impact of ongoing economic restructuring during the extended recessionary period beginning in 1990, the translocation of workers set adrift by the 'hollowing out' of the domestic economy, and an aging population and low birth rate have altered family patterns, employment expectations, and the educational landscape. The discourse of childhood thus channels longstanding cultural and social concerns about globalization, couched in the double-speak of "internationalization", to which is now added additional economic concerns as the longstanding promise of industrialization fades and is replaced by increasing pessimism about the challenges ahead as Japan confronts a new postindustrial era.

While recent social commentary betrays a wavering in the national embrace of education, parents and educators, though desperate to retain a sense of social cohesion and stability, are nonetheless paralyzed to do anything more than join the chorus and lament bygone days. Parents criticize the educational system that they see as failing their children and ultimately society, while teachers argue that a lack of parental support and engagement with today's children is at the root of the problem. Irrespective of where the responsibility may fall, as a prism through which to view public perceptions of a nation's trajectory, the discourse of childhood betrays a profound sense of crisis and anxiety surrounding Japan's future prospects.

Global forces and childhood

As noted above, extreme crimes of violence by young people have taken center stage not only in Japan but in industrialized nations around the world. The school shooting perpetrated by teenagers Harris and Klebold at Columbine High School in Littleton, Colorado (US) in April 1999 symbolized for many the lack of connectedness of today's youth, giving rise to a growing fear of youth due to a sense of imperfect understanding of the causes of their disaffection and little insight as to solutions. A common reaction among conservative social commentators has been to link juvenile crime and violence with laziness, lack of discipline and a decline in traditional values by drawing spurious causal inferences between rising crime statistics and declines in international rankings on tests of scholastic achievement. However, even countries such as Finland, lauded in educational circles for its flexible approach to education and top ranking in recent OECD Program for International Student Assessment (PISA)[1] reports, are not immune, and the November 2007 incident at Jokela High School, where an 18-year-old gunman killed eight of his fellow classmates (BBC News 11/7/07), makes clear the frivolity of pinning the complex issue of juvenile delinquency and disaffected youth on simple statistical relations or a rhetoric of lazy rudderless youth.

Sensationalized media accounts of violence and crime perpetrated by young offenders are but only one of many forces that influence adult perceptions of children and youth and shape childhood experiences. To be sure, the lives of youth and their networks of support are shifting along with their position in the global economy. According to Giddens (2000), social and economic transformations of the postindustrial world have broken down the fundamental building blocks of society and deprived youth of traditional support structures. Family and school, two of the most salient social institutions in the lives of children, now appear ill-equipped to meet the challenges of raising contemporary youth as family restructuring has led to a rise in households with single parents who must prioritize between raising their own children and putting food on their plates. Schools, meanwhile, governed increasingly by OECD principles of global harmonization around free market competition and transparent international standards appear eager to develop graduates possessing the skills necessary to thrive in a 21st-century knowledge economy, but ill-equipped and inappropriately structured to deliver what is required. While traditional networks of support close to home fall into disarray, new global networks are formed as transnational corporations such as Nike cultivate youth as a coveted consumer market, leading kids in India, China and South Korea to respond to this global production of desire by developing worldwide connections around iPods, Nikes and Facebook with their fellow youth in Japan, North America and Europe.

The effect of social change on the evolving experiences of childhood has become a universal phenomena found in all industrialized societies, with children increasingly feeling the effects of global transitions both directly as, for example, targets of marketing messages, and indirectly as witnesses to family change and disruption such as in the case of rocketing divorce rates in China.[2] Increasingly, the notion of childhood as a universal age of innocence, open to imagination and artful expression has all but faded, crossing national boundaries to blossom into a global rhetoric of disaffected youth. Its prevalence in mature industrial societies suggests that the phenomenon is related more to the severe transitions of modernity that penetrate kids' lives than with the nature of children themselves. As Giddens (1991: 22) notes,

> Globalisation means that, in respect of the consequences of at least some disembedding mechanisms, no one can 'opt out' of the transformations brought about by modernity ...

Thus, irrespective of their character, youth are subjected through the process of globalization to a decontextualization or "disembedding" of the particularities of their lives, becoming swept up in an overpowering rhetoric they are powerless to change. Instead, as we have seen, contemporary youth navigating the shifting terrain of 21st-century postmodernity are aligning with and creating new cultures as they disengage from traditional ones. As solidarity takes hold among the formerly exotic and alienation is created by that which formerly comforted, an iPod toting American teenager is as likely to align with a member of his age cohort in Bangalore than his local school teacher spouting nuggets of wisdom from a bygone age.

The changing rhetoric of youth has generated anxiety if not panic among parents, educators, health authorities and government officials worldwide. Changes in child and youth lifestyles has led to physical and mental health concerns and Japan, where the sense of fear is palpable, is struggling along with the rest of the world. Childhood obesity, associated with a reduction in play activity as well as with diet, is of increasing concern in Canada, Japan, the USA and Australia, and is now seen in countries as diverse as Malaysia and Chile. In Britain, more than 50 percent of 3-year-olds have a personal TV in their rooms and those in the 11–15 age group spend on average almost 53 hours per week in front of a TV or computer screen (*Telegraph* 2/7/08) China, India and Thailand are concerned with internet addiction as the production of desire leads to the addiction to its products and China, whose health authorities have placed internet addiction on par with drug addiction and gambling, have opened Internet De-Addiction Centers to address the fallout from burgeoning internet use (Cha, 2007).

While the rhetoric of childhood has changed, it is unclear whether the reality matches this rhetoric and further, whether any changes if they do exist are the product of youth themselves or of inflexible social systems. Herr (2005), who argues for a reconceptualization of so-called "problem students" in American schools, notes that the traditional role of schools has been to guide youth along the path to adulthood by using as teaching moments the inevitable missteps along the way. She describes how in contemporary American schools, this form of guidance has now in large part been replaced by an abundance of inflexible rules that "create criminals" by overly circumscribing behavior and frequently leading to interventions that are now more reminiscent of prison than of an educational institution.

Problematizing the concept of childhood itself

Perhaps the most significant impediment to reconciling contemporary views of children, whether in Japan or other parts of the globe, with those of the past is that childhood of the past has never really been the way in which it is portrayed in the present. Steven Mintz (2009), for example, discusses several myths of American childhood that demonstrate a desire or yearning to view the past through rose-colored glasses. Yet, he (2009: 4) writes:

> There has never been a golden age of childhood when the overwhelming majority of American children were well cared for and their experiences were idyllic. Nor has childhood ever been an age of innocence, at least not for the overwhelming majority of children. Childhood has never been insulated from the pressures and demands of the surrounding society and each generation of children has had to wrestle with the particular social, political, and economic constraints of its own historical period.

Despite the reality, the idealized myths and imagery of childhood past persist, and several scholars have suggested that children and childhood have come to symbolize modern society itself (Aries, 1962; Kessen, 1979; Tanaka, 1997, 2004). The metaphoric impact of childhood, as Tanaka (2004: 133) suggests, is pervasive, having become "a part of our common sense that resides in our memories." We have all experienced childhood, and as such it commands a powerful unifying force. This, coupled with our everyday experiences with children, shapes our perceptions of childhood as natural and constant, despite the fact that we live in a continually changing world. As such, given that children have always existed, "childhood also comes to stand for something timeless, that pure state before learning (of good and bad) occurs" (Tanaka, 2004: 134).

At the same time, Tanaka (1997: 22) suggests that childhood has become symbolic of several aspects of modernity "of a new progressive society, one looking forward to a seemingly better future; of temporariness, that idealized past or originary state that must be guided and transformed; and of immanence, the constant regeneration of that pure originary state." Such views became particularly popular during the Meiji period in particular, as Japanese statesmen sought to introduce and promote Western ideas. In the *Meiroku Zasshi, Journal of Japanese Enlightenment*, for example, Mitsukuri Shuhei wrote: "From infancy until they are six or seven, children's minds are clean and without the slightest blemish while their characters are pure and unadultered as a perfect pearl. Since what then touches the eyes and ears, whether good or bad, makes a deep impression that will not be wiped out until death, this age provides the best opportunity for disciplining their natures and training them in deportment" (Braisted, 1976: 106). It is against such idealized views of children that contemporary children are judged. Thus, as reports of youth violence and commentary on moral decay overwhelm a traditionally positive progressive developmental view of children being able and willing to provide "a seemingly better future," the future seems increasingly bleak when compared to an idealized past.

Japanese childhood in historical perspective

"Little treasures": premodern views of childhood

The standard is indeed high as Japanese children and youth of today must compete with "godlike" counterparts of the past. Though explicit premodern descriptions of childhood are limited, interpretations of children based on rituals, cultural practices and their portrayal in art suggest that children in Japan have long been viewed as gifts from the gods, if not godlike themselves. Tanaka (2004: 59) points out, "Prior to the Meiji period, children were considered godlike and not yet subject to the rules of human society." Further, historical descriptions such as "bestowed by the gods" or "favors from the gods" reflect a cultural conception of children as divine blessings, supported by Buddhist and Shinto legends filled with stories of deities as child prodigies who demonstrate extraordinary characteristics as a very early age (Hendry, 1989: 15–16).

Drawing on the work of Iwamoto (1956), Hara and Minagawa (1996: 13) note that "in various Shinto ceremonies children under 7 years old were traditionally given important roles as mediators between the sacred and profane worlds." The treatment of young children as godlike, or "among the gods" is linked to high mortality rates of the time, as Tanaka (2004: 59) writes: "This understanding of children as godlike and human is tied to the simultaneity of past and present. Death was ever present. Infant mortality was high, and life expectancy throughout the classes was low. A reasonable estimate is that about half of children born reached their fifth year." Further, the death of a child under the age of seven called for treatment that differed from that of older children. Since it was believed that such a young child could return immediately to the other world to be re-born soon after, a young infant might be buried "under the floor of one's house, at road crossings, or at village borders" (Hara and Minagawa, 1996: 14) to keep the soul of the deceased close to home in order to guard remaining family members.

The famous Japanese folklorist, Yanagita Kunio, has been quoted as stating that "children were historically considered gods' mediums and played an important part in local festivals where the gods were supplicated" (Yamamura, 1986: 35). This sacred quality of children, as even gods themselves, is also illustrated prominently in premodern Japanese artwork in which deities are frequently depicted in the form of children. A special exhibition at the Tōkyō National Museum held in 2001 titled "Wonder and Joy, Children in Japanese Art," noted that "from the 12th through the 15th centuries, children were perceived to exist in a liminal state between the sacred and the mundane realms and were considered to be closer than adults to the sacred realm of Buddhist deities and Japanese *kami* (gods)" (Tōkyō National Museum, 2001: 13).

Portrayals of children as divine blessings – indeed, as "gifts from the gods" – also reflect cultural beliefs about child development and lend insight into childrearing practices. During the Edo period (1603–1868), *ukiyo-e* woodblock prints depicted a cultural ideal of a close relationship between mother and child along with a view of children as "little treasures" in local domestic scenes, seasonal festivals and annual events. As noted above, some scholars have suggested that the common expression during this period, "before seven, among the gods," (*nanatsu made wa kami no uchi*) [lit. until the age of seven children are among the gods] reflects the relative instability of life in premodern Japan and encouraged both great care and attention to a child's early years (Shwalb and Chen, 1996: 34). Many life cycle ceremonies associated with the early period of childhood marked developmental milestones and reaffirmed the precious nature of children through ritual celebration. Though many such ceremonies have faded from the contemporary urban landscape in Japan, the annual national celebration on November 15 called the 7-5-3 (*shichi-go-san*) festival continues to mark ages historically considered by Japanese to be important in children's development. As part of this ceremony, parents dress their children in elaborate kimono (sons at ages three and five; daughters at ages three and seven), and take them to a temple or shrine. The transformation that is symbolized through the wearing of kimono signifies the changing child, from an uncertain or liminal position between natural and cultural worlds to that of a human fully embedded in a social world and ready to be guided and trained. Tanaka (2004: 136) writes, "A key age (seven) that signifies a life-course change remains the same, but the child has been transformed from the godlike, or 'among the gods until seven,' to an infant as an empty vessel to be trained as a proper citizen. Today the proverb is used to justify spoiling children who will be disciplined into 'good' citizens when entering school."

Thus, in premodern Japan, children were seen as virtuous at birth, only later in life becoming corrupted by the adult world. This moral sanctity eliminated the need for strict discipline in childrearing, for it was believed that children would naturally come to their own understanding of the world around them and choose an appropriate path (Hara n.d.). Children, it was believed, should therefore be allowed to be active and spontaneous, while the role of adults was to shield children from bad influences, guide them away from danger, and soothe them when upset or crying. Hara (n.d.: 11) writes that "too much scolding and prohibition of children's wants before they 'understand what adults say,' hinders the development of their basic trust in other people," and such views are implicit in expressions such as "the spirit of the three-year-old lasts until age one hundred" (*mitsugo no tamashii hyaku made*). Even today, attention to the development of a positive temperament among young children is part of the conventional wisdom of childrearing, and it is frequently heard in Japan that it is important for mothers to take care of their children at home at least until the age of three in order to nurture this disposition.

"A rich culture of childrearing"[3]*: Tokugawa Japan*

Considerably more is known about perceptions of childhood during the Tokugawa period (1603–1868) due to the high literacy rate even among lower social strata[4] and a proliferation of books on childrearing, including the *Detailed Handbook of Everyday Life and Rituals for Women* (*Onna-Chohhohki-Taisei*) published in 1692 and the six-volume *Guidebook for Childrearing* (*Shohni Hitsuyo Sodate-Gusa*) in 1703, which is thought to have been the first publication of its kind (Hara and Minagawa, 1996: 15). Despite the lingering premodern belief in the godliness of infants and children that persisted to some extent through to the modern era, the Tokugawa period marked a growing interest in the special relationship between mother and child, influenced by Confucian scholars of the time who advocated motherhood as a key feminine virtue.

Descriptions of Tokugawa-era childrearing suggest a close physical relationship between mother and child that nurtured heightened sensitivities of both parties, even before birth. Practices such as *taikyō* or "education in the womb" introduced from China were aimed at cultivating a healthy prenatal environment and, as Japanese of the time believed that "the mother's thoughts, feelings and actions during pregnancy were transmitted to the fetus and continued to influence a child's character, health, and abilities after birth" (Hara and Minagawa, 1996: 15), expectant mothers were instructed to be kind to others and to avoid stressful experiences such as funerals. Conversely, mothers were believed to be sensitive to even the most subtle signals of their offspring.

At this time as well, we see the emergence of various rituals that mark milestones in child development, suggesting that "a rich culture of childrearing" developed during the Tokugawa period (Platt, 2005: 68). The *obiiwai* (sash celebration) ceremony, for example, announced a pregnancy, while ceremonies were also held during a child's third and seventh days of life. Later in the cycle of rituals, the 7-5-3 festival, elaborated on earlier, acknowledged a child's continuing development. While the proliferation of rituals suggests a concern with childhood and childrearing during the Tokugawa period, scholars like Karatani (1993: 124) caution against interpreting these symbolic markers of status change as the actual process of maturation from childhood to adulthood:

> When a child becomes an adult by means of a rite of passage, it is like a changing of masks: depending on the culture, this may involve a change in hairstyle, dress, or name, or it may involve circumcision or the application of make-up or a tattoo. But we should not conclude that a substantive "self" is concealed behind these masks.

Similarly, while the Tokugawa period witnessed a growing interest in childrearing in which parents devoted "sufficient emotional and material resources to the child's upbringing" (Platt, 2005: 68), one cannot assume that the experiences of children and attitudes toward childhood were uniform throughout Tokugawa society. It is reasonable to expect that the experiences of children during the Tokugawa era varied according to the family's location within the highly stratified social system. The Tokugawa period, for example, saw an increased medicalization of childhood, with mothers making regular visits to pediatricians equipped to diagnose illness and prescribe medicine. However, these opportunities were more available to urban women where doctors were more plentiful (Hara and Minagawa, 1996).

The highly varied experience of childhood during Tokugawa Japan according to the child's placement within a highly structured social system extended before birth. During the Tokugawa period, upper-class women married earlier and gave birth to more children than their lower strata counterparts both due to the availability of wet nurses, babysitters and even foster families to help rear the children of wealthy families but more importantly, due to the need to bear sons to carry on the family line in the *ie* system of independent multi-generational families (*ie*) based on patrilineal descent in which all the property, social standing, rights, duties and obligations passes to the eldest children (Platt, 2005). The *ie* system also created dramatic shifts for rural Japan, which had previously been organized around large, complex farming families but which during the Tokugawa period averaged three to four children (Hara and Minagawa, 1996: 15).

Tasaki (in Platt, 2005) states that the imposition of the *ie* system reverberated throughout urban and rural Japanese society, prompting parents to consciously limit the number of offspring to invest sufficient resources toward the raising of each child in an effort to contribute to the long-term health and security of the family. While Platt (2005: 967) argues that these demographic changes – specifically, declining birth rates and high infant mortality rates – together made "each individual child a more precious commodity and a safer investment in the household's future economic health," it is important to understand that each child's "preciousness" and the deemed "sufficiency" of resources required by him or her was highly varied and independently valued according to class, birth order, sex, and geographic location. First-born males were highly prized in the *ie* system, and while infectious diseases such as smallpox and measles contributed to high infant mortality rates, infanticide (*mabiki*, literally "making intervals" as in pulling plants from an overcrowded garden) in rural areas and induced abortions in urban areas were widely practiced during the Tokugawa period (Hara and Minagawa, 1996: 15). With increased access to doctors, induced abortions also became widely practiced in rural areas as a means to limit family size and maintain the long-term intergenerational security of the family.

In Japan since the twelfth century, the first seven years of life were considered the first half of childhood, such that most 15-year-olds in Tokugawa were already filling adult roles, either apprenticing or working for parents or employers. The experiences of Tokugawa children varied according to their social standing. "Higher-rank samurai boys were expected to master the military and literary arts and codes of etiquette, while children of lower samurai helped with parents' side jobs" (Hara and Minagawa, 1996: 16). Agricultural children were expected to help on the farm from age seven until entering the labor force at age fifteen while children of the merchant and artisan classes took care of their younger siblings and helped with household chores. Boys at age ten became apprentices until age 17 when through a *gempuku* ceremony, they began to work for wages (Hara and Minagawa, 1996: 16).

The expansion of schooling during the 17th to 19th centuries in Japan is also linked to the creation of modern concepts of childhood (Platt, 2005). Prior to this period, formal education was limited to samurai who attended public schools in the feudal domains, but the Tokugawa period saw the emergence of *terakoya* (literally, "temple schools") providing specialized single-sex instruction for children of all social strata. Initially attended largely by the children of wealthy merchants, farming families and village headmen (Dore, 1965), over 30,000 schools were established in the later Tokugawa period between 1830 and 1868 in communities across the country and attendance by ordinary children was encouraged, largely by elites in an effort to transmit moral and practical knowledge to the masses out of a sense of panic at what was perceived as widespread moral decay and economic crisis (Platt, 2005: 967). Early in the nineteenth century, the rate of attendance at *terakoya* is thought to have reached as high as 70 percent in Edo, delivering a high-level curriculum of reading, writing and *soroban* (abacus) calculation to all as well as sewing, tea ceremony, flower arranging and other arts and crafts to girls (Monbushō, 1980).

While standard textbooks, teaching manuals, and illustrated books were published for use in *terakoya*, the curriculum was more differentiated than it would become later with the introduction of compulsory education in the Meiji era and continued to be applied flexibly, according to the "character, ability, and life circumstances of each child and family" (Hara and Minagawa, 1996: 17). During the Tokugawa era "[p]lay, work, discipline, and education were woven together in children's lives. In both education and discipline, the overall philosophy was to 'let children learn' rather than to 'teach children'" (Hara and Minagawa, 1996: 17).

Impressionable beings: children in the modern era

The Meiji period (1868–1912) marking the beginning of the modern era of Japan oversaw wide-ranging social, political, and economic transformation. After centuries of almost total self-imposed isolation, Japan's ports were opened up to foreign trade and influence, the Tokugawa shogunate was overthrown and replaced with imperial rule, and the class-based society of feudal Japan was transformed into a representative democracy based on free market capitalist principles (Beasley, 2000). Under the official policy of the Meiji government to search the world for knowledge[5], Japan experienced a period of rapid industrialization, modernization and westernization. The government encouraged transfer of technology both by sending Japanese on study trips to the USA and Europe and through the employment of over 3,000 foreign experts (*o-yatoi gaikokujin*) in such specialist fields as medicine, engineering, science, and foreign language teaching, particularly English, which with the rising prominence of the USA had come to replace French, German and Dutch. Western clothing, dining, and architecture came into vogue. Fiat currency and the infrastructure to support a free market economy were introduced, laying the foundations for Japan's rise as the first industrialized nation in Asia.

The early Meiji period was marked by the eager embrace of science and its application to all areas of life, including childrearing. With modernization came the introduction of mass compulsory education and widespread changes to the daily activities of children. In contrast to the prevailing educational philosophy of the Tokugawa period to "'let children learn' rather than to 'teach children'" (Hara and Minagawa, 1996: 17), the goal of mass education during the Meiji period was to improve and regulate society. By applying scientific principles to the teaching of children, schools would integrate children into institutions of the state, train them in the service of the nation and foster their personal identification with the nation (Platt, 2005: 979).

Along with the changing lives of children during the Meiji period came another shift in the perception of childhood. Considered godly in premodern times and valued according to such criteria as class, birth order, and sex in the highly structured Tokugawa period, the rapid social transformations of the Meiji period engendered a belief in the inherent vulnerability of childhood. Children were seen to be highly impressionable and easily swayed by external influences. This tumultuous period brought with it both recognition of the long-lasting influence of social environment on the lives of children and justification for specialist intervention. During the Meiji period, it was felt that children were born with the potential to do both good or evil, with the outcome determined by childhood experiences. With so much at stake during this crucial stage in the lifecourse, the outcome could not be left to chance or the lay knowledge of parents. As Platt (2005: 975) notes, during the Meiji era it was believed that "childhood is too important to be left to parents, who may not be enlightened enough to appreciate the gravity or complexity of their responsibilities. The proper socialization of children thus requires the intervention of trained experts – in this case, teachers."

The growth of cities in the 1890s brought with it dislocations in family structure and changing social experiences for children as many began to work in factories or other industries. "By the turn of the century, 15 percent of factory labor was provided by elementary school-age children, and those that did not work in factories were often sent out of the home for apprenticeships in smaller commercial and manufacturing shops" (Platt, 2005: 976). Parents, too, were often pulled into this growing economy, moving families into the cities and away from extended family resources, and disrupting childrearing patterns.

The emerging discourse of children during this period combined a concern for the social conditions of modern urban society within which children were being raised and a fear of youth engaged in criminal activity. On the one hand, social reformers and intellectuals eager to share their views of the "social ills" of modern Japan turned to the mass media to raise awareness of the plight of poor children living in new urban slums who were "exposed to such an environment of material deprivation and moral depravity" (Platt, 2005: 977). Concern for these disadvantaged children was mixed with fear toward those children already involved in delinquent or criminal behavior, which social commentators blamed on the influences of slums, broken homes, inattentive parents, lack of schooling and discipline. Public anxiety fueled by rising juvenile delinquency prompted the creation of reformatories to deal with "deviant children as well as the development of a juvenile court system and as such, discourse on children as "social problems" came into public discussion and state policy (Platt, 2005: 978).

While the discourse of "child as problem" became prominent during the later Meiji period, it did not apply to all segments of society, but primarily to members of the former agrarian class, who had felt the effects of severe social dislocations most harshly and who were attracted in great numbers to growing cities to become the working-class who exemplified the problems of urban industrial society. Children of the middle-class, on the contrary, were shaped by the opposite discourse of "child as treasure," and child psychologists, pediatricians, and normal school teachers all urged parents to apply scientific knowledge to childrearing in the areas of hygiene, cooking, nutrition, and psychology in order to protect them (Platt, 2005: 979).

Additionally, these social transformations of the later Meiji period were by no means unique to Japan. With rapid urbanization, industrialization, and westernization, Japanese society came to experience problems similar to those experienced in other industrialized nations, and the concerns voiced by social reformers in Japan about the ills of industrialization were echoed by reformers in

London, Paris, or New York. In this sense, the Meiji period marked the first wave of rapid globalization, with Japan sharing with other nations not only the social and economic effects of industrialization but also the birth of the discourse of "children as problems" that reverberated in urban centers around the globe.

Educational zeal and the "disappearance of childhood"

During the early postwar period (1950s to 1970s), Japan once again underwent rapid social change that transformed people's daily lives. Land reform, ordered by General MacArthur as Supreme Commander of the Allied Powers just after the war ended, brought more equal distribution of assets to members of rural society (Dore, 1959). Subsequently, the rapid pace of industrialization set in motion a decline in the agricultural population as the shift toward manufacturing created jobs in urban areas. This process of urbanization contributed to a proliferation of smaller households, most notably nuclear families, with mean household size shrinking from 4.97 to 3.69 between 1955 and 1970 (Meguro and Morioka, 1983: 207). As the Japanese standard of living rose, rising income levels also led to increased consumption. During this period, there was also increasing social demand for higher levels of education. Between 1950 and 1971, student advancement from lower secondary to upper secondary schools doubled from 42.5 percent to 85 percent, with the number of students proceeding to university or junior college rising sharply as well (Monbushō, 1980). The trend toward increasing educational attainment subsequently fueled the growth of a supplementary educational industry, in particular, the *juku* or cram school boom which grew rapidly in the 1970s. Educational zeal and credentialism brought children's lives under increasingly intense scrutiny, and concurrent with the period of rapid economic growth, the changing environment and experiences of children drew concern from the populace. Despite education being touted both within Japan and abroad as a significant factor in Japan's emergence as an economic superpower, the intense focus on performance and achievement brought with it a groundswell of criticism within Japan, fueling a proliferation of Japanese books on childcare and child growth aimed at tackling concerns about the deterioration of childhood experiences.

Japanese press and social commentators criticized the exchange of childhood innocence for educational competition, foreshadowing the changing discourse, from optimism to pessimism, of Japanese childhood that was to come. As reports of in-school violence (*kōnai bōryoku*) and bullying (*ijime*) were published with increasing frequency in the 1980s, an emerging sense of crisis centered on children and youth began to take shape. Harsh criticism eventually arrived from across the Pacific too as the USA, initially awestruck by Japanese academic achievement in the early days of the economic miracle, now sought to undermine Japanese education, the nation's perceived competitive advantage, by exposing the costs of "examination hell" on Japanese children and youth. Scholars, too, began to examine the impact of educational competition. Drawing upon Postman's (1982) critique of the "disappearance of childhood," Field (1995) argued that overscheduling and demanding responsibilities were threatening the psychological and physical health of Japanese children as well, and in Japan's case, the "disappearance of childhood" occurred in the form of "the endless labor" of education. In her view, the long hours of school, combined with increased after-school learning and less time available for neighborhood playtime, had transformed childhood from a time of carefree play to one of regimentation.

"Children feel the pinch first": contemporary views

As educational competition, symbolized in "exam hell," grew in intensity through the 1980s, criticism both domestic and international swelled and views of Japanese children and youth grew increasingly pessimistic. Then in the early 1990s as economic conditions faltered due to the stock market crash and the collapse of the economic bubble, Japanese society headed into economic stagnation in what has become known as the "lost decade" but from which Japan has yet to fully recover. While the early part of the decade saw increasing reports of juvenile crime, especially cases in which bullying had turned fatal, it was the "Kobe incident" (Kōbe *jiken*) of 1997 mentioned at the beginning of this chapter that marked a loss of innocence that sent the nation into a period of soul-searching that has not been resolved to date. The gruesome nature of the crime, compounded by the tender age of the perpetrator, shattered any remaining images of an idealized childhood in Japan, marking what *AERA* (a popular Japanese weekly magazine) called the "inauguration of the discourse of monstrosity and [the] child" (*AERA* 11/1997). Public perception of the Kōbe killer as evil personified spread like wildfire to subsequently taint the entire spectrum of Japanese youth. As Suwa (1998: 12) states, "[W]e're seeing the emergence of a brand new personality type with which we don't know how to deal."

Though the Kōbe incident created a spiraling sense of crisis unprecedented in the annals of youth crime in Japan, Kawakami (1999) viewed the sense of crisis as long overdue, granting recognition through this sudden shift in public discourse of ongoing gradual social transformations in Japan that might have contributed to the incident. In his best-selling book, *Gakkō Hōkkai* (school collapse), he argued that the crime of *Shonen A*, the pseudonym given to the young offender in the press, had finally forced public attention on the effects both at home and in school of unrelenting social disintegration that had been accumulating over the extended period of economic stagnation.

Chen (1996), like Kawakami concerned with social transformation in Japan, attributes the shifting discourse of children and youth less to changes in the actions and attitudes of young people themselves than to the changing conditions and concerns of adult society. According to Chen, social and economic circumstances drive both perceptions of and actions toward children, the least powerful segment of society. He (1996: 33) writes:

> It is true that the Japanese are said to treat their children with greater care. But current concerns about the rights or plight of Japanese children also show

that despite any special attitudes toward children the society once may have entertained, in modern Japan, when social and economic conditions are poor, *the children feel the pinch first.* [Emphasis added.]

Chen observes that throughout the history of childhood, infanticide, parent-child double suicide, and child abuse have all spiked during periods of social and economic hardship. Goodman (2002: 138), too, notes that "the practice of *oyako shinjū* [parent-child double suicide] has a long history in Japan but high rates have been particularly recorded in times of economic depression." The most recent manifestation of this tendency is a recent upsurge in reported cases of child abuse, as Goodman (2002) notes that in reviewing three prominent national newspapers "it was unusual for more than a few days to pass in the middle of 2001 without a story appearing in the Japanese media about child abuse" (Goodman, 2002: 131).

"Kids these days ..."

During my fieldwork from 2000–2003 at a public junior high school (grades 7–9) in Kōbe, only a mile from the site of the Kōbe incident, I found that despite the shift in discourse about children and youth, many students strongly dis-identified with the view that they were "problems" or "dangerous," explicitly rejecting being positioned as the scapegoat for Japan's problems. Tani-san, a grade 7 girl, for example, addressed the negative perceptions of young people in an article she wrote as part of the personal newspaper (*jibun shimbun*) exercise she completed for summer homework. She wrote:

Kids these days ...
   Kids these days are addicted to video games and lack physical exercise ...
   Kids these days have a lot of stress and easily snap ...
   Kids these days are cold-hearted ...
   I think an increasing number of adults are speaking badly about kids nowadays. However, aren't the things they are saying wrong?
   Even if we like video games, there are also many kids who get out and exercise in sports and club activities. You can't blame video games for kids' lack of physical activity. Those kids probably just like staying at home anyway.
   The increase in stress is most likely due to the growing number of adults focused on educational competition. This might not be bad in and of itself but often there are parents who constrain our ideas, and this might be to blame for our increased stress ...
   In addition, we shouldn't all be lumped together as one. It's not right to say "kids these days ..." on the basis of one or two juvenile offenders. Surely it should be realized that there are lots of kids who behave properly.
   I really wish adults would take a good look at the kids around them and see who we are.

Tani-san is not alone in rejecting the negative discourse that homogenizes her generation as inactive, stressed out, and even dangerous. Other students at my fieldsite have said, in effect, that they are being held responsible for Japan's problems that they themselves have not created. What is notable, however, is that society has become so saturated with negative images and discourse that these have become the "standards" against which not only adults, but children and youth themselves measure their own behavior and ideas. These days, being a good-natured, obedient child in Japan is seen as the exception, rather than the rule.

Concluding thoughts

Given the pervasive social discourse, it is easy to form a negative impression of contemporary children and youth if one does not have the opportunity to interact with them. Moreover, discourses and grand narratives are by their very nature evangelical in the sense that they are highly resistant to the weight of empirical evidence. The Kōbe incident marks a significant shift in the discourse of the child, long viewed as good-natured "treasures," but now seen as "problems," both unpredictable and dangerous. This discourse, however, is symptomatic of more profound and ever-widening cleavages in Japanese society than simply the "crisis of childhood." Rather, these public discourses of childhood reflect the pessimism of postmodern contemporary Japan that has experienced increasingly widespread social and economic disruption during the "lost decade" of the 1990s and has yet to fully regain its footing a decade later.

Though forecasts now regularly appear that Japan has turned the corner, there is a general fear that the current generation of Japanese youth, the "post-Bubble" generation of kids who have grown up entirely during the period of socioeconomic disruption, will not be able to measure up to the task of carrying the nation forward into the future. The shift from optimism to pessimism illuminates a growing national concern about the ability and willingness of youth to successfully navigate contemporary challenges and lead Japan toward a stable and prosperous future. Such views, of course, are socio-historically situated, and Tani-san's narrative contests such a pessimistic view of contemporary childhood and youth.

Just as Japan's education system was seen first to be the driving force behind its economic success in the 1980s and then the cause of its failing since the 1990s despite little change to the system itself, the changing discourse of childhood should be understood not as an objective view of childhood, but rather, as a lens through which to view the country's attempts to grapple with profound social transformations. With childhood "the site of national investments where anxieties about national futures gather" (Arai, 2000: 855) and where "ambiguities and contradictions of modernity are ameliorated into a coherent whole personified through the child" (Tanaka, 2004: 133), discussion of declining morality of children and youth today are expressions of this continuing social and economic malaise, and thus it appears that in public discourse, negative perceptions and attitudes toward children and youth will persist for some time to come.

Notes

1 The PISA survey is an internationally standardized assessment jointly developed by participating countries and administered to 15-year-olds in schools. PISA assesses student performance in mathematics, reading and science literacy. Japan has participated in the PISA survey since its inception. Notably, in 2000, Japanese first year high school students ranked first in mathematical skills and second in scientific literacy, while ranking only eighth in reading comprehension. In 2003, Japan fell to sixth place for math, maintained second for science, and placed 14th in reading. In 2006, Japan's relative ranking dropped again, to tenth in mathematics, sixth in science, and 15th in reading. Japan's dramatic drops in relative rankings in math and science has led to calls for increased attention to these subjects, which is reflected in the new course of study that will become effective in elementary and junior high schools in 2011 and 2012 respectively.

2 China has seen an upsurge in divorce rates in recent years. In 2006, China's Ministry of Civil Affairs reported a 18.2 percent increase in divorces from the previous year. A new law in 2003 simplified divorce filings and allows for a same day divorce with a filing fee of 10 yuan (US$1.36) (*China Daily* 1/24/08).

3 Tasaki, in Platt, 2005: 968.

4 Dore (1965), in *Education in Tokugawa Japan*, estimates that formal education outside the home by the end of the Tokugawa period approximated 40 percent for men and 10 percent for women, remarkable for an agrarian society and considerably higher than that of European countries at the time.

5 The fifth article of the Charter Oath (*Gokajō no Goseimon*) forming the first constitution of modern Japan states that "Knowledge shall be sought throughout the world so as to strengthen the foundation of imperial rule" (De Bary, W., C. Gluck, and A. Tiedemann, eds. (2005: 672) [1958]. *Sources of Japanese Tradition*, Vol. II: 1600 to 2000 (2nd edition). New York: Columbia University Press).

References

AERA special (#45). 1997. *Kodomo ga abunai*. [Dangerous children/Children in danger] Tōkyō: Asahi Shimbunsha. November.

Arai, A. 2000. The "wild child" of 1990s Japan. *The South Atlantic Quarterly* 99(4):841–64.

Aries, P. 1962. *Centuries of childhood: A social history of family life*. R. Baldick, trans. New York: Vintage Books.

BBC News. 2007. Man kills eight at Finnish school. November 7. Electronic document, http://news.bbc.co.uk/2/hi/europe/7082795.stm, accessed December 17, 2008.

Beasley, W. 2000. *The Japanese experience: A short history of Japan*. Berkeley: University of California Press.

Befu, H. 1983. Internationalization of Japan and Nihon *bunkaron*. In *The challenge of Japan's internationalization: Organization and culture*. H. Mannari and H. Befu, eds. Pp. 232–66. Tōkyō: Kodansha.

Braisted, W., trans. 1976. *Meiroku Zasshi: Journal of Japanese Enlightenment*. Cambridge, MA: Harvard University Press.

Cha, A. 2007. In China, stern treatment for young internet 'addicts.' *Washington Post*, February 22. Electronic document, http://www.washingtonpost.com/wp-dyn/content/article/2007/02/21/AR2007022102094.html, accessed December 17, 2008.

Chen, S.-J. 1996. Are Japanese young children among the gods? In *Japanese childrearing: Two generations of scholarship*. D. Shwalb and B. Shwalb, eds. Pp. 31–43. New York: Guilford Press.

China Daily. 2008. More Chinese marry, divorce in 2007. January 24. Electronic document, http://www.chinadaily.com.cn/china/2008-01/24/content_6419204.htm, accessed January 5, 2009.

Daily Telegraph. 2007. Ban children from watching tv, says doctor. February 7. Electronic document, http://www.telegraph.co.uk/news/uknews/1577921/Ban-children-from-watching-TV-says-doctor.html, accessed January 15, 2009.

Daily Yomiuri. 2004. Net posting drove girl to kill. 3 June. Electronic document, http://www.yomiuri.co.jp/newse/20040603wo21.htm, accessed June 3, 2004.

De Bary, W., C. Gluck, and A. Tiedemann, eds. 2005 [1958]. *Sources of Japanese tradition, Vol. II: 1600 to 2000. 2nd edition*. New York: Columbia University Press.

Dore, R. 1959. *Land reform in Japan*. London: Oxford University Press.

Dore, R. 1965. *Education in Tokugawa Japan*. Berkeley: University of California Press.

Dore, R. 1976. *Diploma disease: Education, qualification and development*. Berkeley: University of California Press.

Field, N. 1995. The child as laborer and consumer: The disappearance of childhood in contemporary Japan. In *Children and the politics of culture*. S. Stephens, ed. Pp. 51–78. Princeton, NJ: Princeton University Press.

Fukuzawa, Y. 1899 [1966]. *The autobiography of Yukichi Fukuzawa*. E. Kiyooka, trans. New York: Columbia University Press.

Giddens, A. 1991 *Modernity and self-identity*. Stanford, CA: Stanford University Press.

Giddens, A. 2000 *Runaway world: How globalization is reshaping our lives*. London: Routledge.

Goodman, R. 2002. Child abuse in Japan: "Discovery" and development of policy. In *Family and social policy in Japan*. R. Goodman, ed. Pp. 131–55. New York: Cambridge University Press.

Hara, H. The childhood in Japanese society during the past 100 Years (n.p., n.d.).

Hara, H. and M. Minagawa. 1996. From productive dependents to precious guests: Historical changes in Japanese children. In *Japanese childrearing: Two generations of scholarship*. D. Shwalb and B. Shwalb, eds. Pp. 9–30. New York: Guilford Press.

Hara, H. and H. Wagatsuma. 1974. *Shitsuke* [Japanese ways of childrearing]. Tōkyō: Kobundo.

Helstein, M. 2003. That's who I want to be: The politics and production of desire within Nike advertising to women. *Journal of Sport and Social Issues* 27(3): 276–92.

Hendry, J. 1989. *Becoming Japanese: The world of the preschool child*. Honolulu: University of Hawaii Press.

Herr, K. 2005. Reconsidering Problem Students. In *Classroom Teaching*. J. Kincheloe, ed. Pp. 207–18. New York: Peter Lang.

Iwamoto, T. 1956. *Shintō girei ni okeru yōji no ichi* [The role of children in Shintō rituals.] Tōkyō: Heibonsha.

Japan Times. 2007. Juvenile law revision. May 25. Electronic document, http://search.japantimes.co.jp/cgi-bin/ed20070525a1.html, accessed June 1, 2007.

Japan Times. 2007. Teen tells lawyers he killed mom. May 19. Electronic document, http://search.japantimes.co.jp/cgi-bin/nn20070519a5.html, accessed May 25, 2007.

Karatani, K. 1993. *Origins of modern Japanese literature*. Brett de Bary, ed. Durham, NC: Duke University Press.

Kawakami, R. 1999. *Gakkō hōkai* [School collapse]. Tōkyō: Soshisha.

Kessen, W. 1979. The American child and other cultural inventions. In *American Psychologist* 34: 815–20.

Kojima, H. 1986. Japanese concepts of child development from the mid-17th to mid-19th century. *International Journal of Behavioral Development* 9: 315–29.

Lichtman, R. 1982. *The production of desire: The integration of psychoanalysis into Marxist theory*. New York: The Free Press.

McCormack, G. 1996. *Kokusaika*: impediments in Japan's deep structure. In *Multicultural Japan: Palaeolithic to postmodern*. D. Denoon, G. McCormack, M. Hudson & T. Morris-Suzuki, eds. Pp. 265–86. Cambridge: Cambridge University Press.

McVeigh, B. 2002. Self-orientalization through occidentalism: How 'English' and 'Foreigners' nationalize Japanese students. In *Japanese higher education as myth*. B. McVeigh, ed. Pp. 148–79. Armonk, NY: M. E. Sharpe.

Meguro, Y. and K. Morioka . 1983. The changing role and status of women in Japan. In *The changing position of women in family and society: A cross-national comparison*. E. Lupri, ed. Pp. 207–24. Leiden: E. J. Brill.

Mintz, S. 2009. The changing state of childhood: American childhood as a social and cultural construct. Re-staging Childhood website. Electronic document, http://www.usu.edu/anthro/childhoodconference/pages/reading_material.html accessed November 30, 2009.

Monbushō. 1980. Japan's modern educational system, A history of the first hundred years. Electronic document, http://www.mext.go.jp/b_menu/hakusho/html/hpbz198103/hpbz198103_2_189.html#, accessed January 10, 2009.

Morris-Suzuki, T. 1994. *The technological transformation of Japan: From the seventeenth to the twenty-first century*. New York: Cambridge University Press.

Mouer, R. and Y. Sugimoto. 1983. Internationalization as an ideology in Japanese society. In *The challenge of Japan's internationalization: Organization and culture*. H. Mannari and H. Befu, eds. Pp. 267–97. Tōkyō: Kodansha.

Okano, K. and M. Tsuchiya. 1999. *Education in contemporary Japan, Inequality and diversity*. Cambridge: Cambridge University Press.

Platt, B. 2004. *Burning and building: Schooling and State Formation in Japan, 1750–1890*. Cambridge, MA: Harvard University Asia Center.

Platt, B. 2005. Japanese childhood, modern childhood: The nation-state, the school, and 19th-century globalization. *Journal of Social History* 38(4): 965–85.

Postman, N. 1982. *The disappearance of childhood*. New York: Vintage.

Shwalb, D., and S.-J. Chen. 1996. Sacred or selfish? A survey on Japanese parents' images of children. *Research and Clinical Center for Child Development Annual Report* 18: 33–44.

Shwalb, D. and B. Shwalb, eds. 1996. *Japanese childrearing, Two generations of scholarship*. New York: Guilford Press.

Suwa, T. 1998. Crisis in the schools. *Japan Echo* 25(3): 12–15.

Tanaka, S. 1997. Childhood: Naturalization of development into a Japanese space. In *Cultures of scholarship*. S. Humphreys, ed. Ann Arbor: University of Michigan Press.

Tanaka, S. 2004. *New times in modern Japan*. Princeton, NJ: Princeton University Press.

Tokyo National Museum. 2001. *Wonder and joy: Children in Japanese art*. Tokyo : Tokyo National Museum.

White, M. 1987. *The Japanese educational challenge*. Tokyo: Kodansha.

Yamamura, Y. 1986. The child in Japanese society. In *Child development and education in Japan*. H. Stevenson, H. Azuma, and K. Hakuta, eds. Pp. 28–38. New York: W.H. Freeman and Company.

Yoshioka, H. 1995. Samurai and self-colonization in Japan. In *The decolonization of the imagination: Culture, knowledge and power.* J. Pieterse and B. Parekh, eds. Pp. 99–112. London: Zed Books.

4 Restructuring and returns in Japan 2000–2001

*Dick Beason, Ken Gordon, Vikas Mehrotra
and Akiko Watanabe*

Background on the lost decade

Seven years after the stock market crash of 1989–1990, Prime Minister Hashimoto announced plans for a Japanese style financial market 'Big Bang'[1] in order to stem the growing irrelevancy of Tokyo as a financial center. Indeed, between 1990 and 1995, Tokyo's share of stock market trading volume had fallen from 41% of the world total to just 17%. Initially the PM's plans centered on infrastructure investment, promotion campaigns and financial market deregulation, but it became progressively more evident that the real problem was loss of interest in Japanese companies due to poor performance, opacity and financial crises that had not been adequately addressed. That is, Britain's big bang had succeeded not simply due to improvements in infrastructure, information and deregulation, but also because these changes occurred in the context of a system of transparent accounting rules and improving economic conditions.

At the same time that the 'big bang' was announced in Japan, it was becoming increasingly clear that economic conditions were not improving significantly. Furthermore, between 1993 and 1997 a number of major financial institutions experienced financial difficulty, and the Ministry of Finance essentially admitted that it had been allowing these institutions to avoid reporting losses on real estate investments on the assumption that the real estate market would improve. Gradually, authorities and the institutions themselves began admitting that the outstanding stock of non-performing loans (NPLs) was large, and that many loans not reported as non-performing were likely to become so. The lack of transparency and uncertainty regarding the magnitude of the financial crisis resulted in the 'Japan premium'[2] reaching almost 1% in 1997 (see Peek and Rosengren, 2000).

These circumstances together with investor skepticism about the willingness of corporations to restructure meant the big bang was going nowhere. By 1997 a number of prudential and accounting reforms were initiated that would help promote corporate restructuring (or at least make monitoring of restructuring efforts by shareholders simpler), improve the stability of the banking system through improved prudential policy, and ultimately allow for improvements in corporate performance.

Disposal of NPLs began in earnest for the biggest banks from 1993. Significant changes in bank prudential policy began in 1995 as the Financial Supervisory Agency (FSA) got real teeth. In 1997 the government formally recognized that Japan's bank-centered financial system gave dominance to creditors over shareholders in terms of monitoring, and that the Ministry of Finance's (MOF) implicit guarantees that large institutions would not fail exacerbated the moral hazard inherent in such a system. These implicit guarantees were formally ended in 1997, and major accounting and prudential policy changes were initiated.

Use of public funds to facilitate this process began in 1999, and numerical targets for disposal of NPLs rather than profit targets were established by the government in 2000, along with strict guidelines on classification of problem loans and NPLs. While the use of public funds can correctly be viewed as having created a new moral hazard problem, the accompanying public outcry forced the government to attach important strings to the funds. Specifically, essentially solvent institutions were expected to pay the money back, while weaker institutions had to agree to government brokered mergers and acquisitions, including sales to foreign interests. To date, the injections of public money have indeed been 'one offs,' with most funds repaid and many very large mergers having been accomplished. Public funds injections are no longer available.

In terms of prudential policy, the FSA was established as a regulatory body independent from the tarnished MOF. The key role of the FSA was initially to uncover and report the true magnitude of NPLs, then to work out effective write-down strategies with the institutions. This effectively included the power to order mergers, nationalize banks and declare institutions insolvent. BIS capital adequacy ratios were finally enforced (Japanese authorities had previously argued that cross shareholdings of the banks should be accounted for in a friendly fashion toward such ratios for Japanese banks), and poor accounting and prudential practices were uncovered and corrected. Definitions of NPLs, problem loans and performing loans were made uniform in 1998.

At the same time, it was recognized that more internationally compatible and transparent accounting standards for non-financial corporations were also necessary. This was not simply to bring Japan up to best practice standards, but also to encourage and allow for the monitoring of corporate restructuring. The new standards were announced between 1997 and 2000, with full implementation by 2000. While there remain some differences between the new Japanese and International Accounting standards, the differences are small.

The major changes in the accounting standards relate to rules and reporting with respect to consolidation, fair value definitions and accounting for pension liabilities and expense. With respect to consolidation, the old rules required consolidated reporting only when a parent firm directly or indirectly controlled over 50% of the shares of the affiliated firm. New rules cover ownership and control through directors, former employees, operating decisions, liabilities from the parent firm or 'other means.' The onus is upon firms to show absence of control, rather than vice versa. While it is likely that abuses continue, several highly publicized cases of firms and their accountants flouting the new rules have helped to push firms into line.[3]

Fair value accounting rules have been clarified and strengthened. Fair value accounting of securities and unrealized gains and losses on investments must be included in the income statement, rather than hidden in the balance sheet. Debt must be consistently measured at amortization cost. Equity positions in affiliates or subsidiaries must be reported at historical cost. In a move to prevent firms from using sales and acquisitions of cross shareholdings to manipulate extraordinary items in the income statement, cross shareholdings must now be accounted for at fair market value in terms of shareholder equity in the balance sheet. In order to prevent manipulation of pension funds and reserves firms are required to report pension cost and liability on an accrual basis. Specifically, firms must report contributions on an accrual basis, even if such contributions are not made in a given year. In effect, this prevents firms from inflating income statements by underfunding pensions.

While by no means the only or even the major driver behind restructuring in Japan during the first decade of this century, accounting reform has had important consequences. Fair value accounting provides an incentive to firms to dispose of non-productive or non-core assets with high market value in order to cover loses from write-downs. Together with tighter consolidation requirements, parent firms now have the incentive to sell such assets at market value, rather than sell them to smaller (often non-traded) affiliates and push losses downstream. This has an added benefit to minority shareholders and outsiders in that asset disposals have become more transparent. Disposal of non-productive assets and subsidiaries has allowed parent and affiliated firms alike to focus on core competency rather than shell-game like accounting practices. Firms are now more likely to sever ties with entities that do not positively contribute to consolidated performance.

Taken together, the accounting reforms initially caused the measured performance of parent firms to decline, putting pressure on many of the largest companies to restructure. Specifically, by 2000 the combined impact of the accounting changes was to cause an increase in shareholder equity (especially the accounting of cross shareholdings), leading to a decline in (already pitiful) measures such as return on equity and return on assets (ROA). At the same time, holdings by foreign institutional investors had been steadily rising throughout the 1990s, and these investors, unlike insiders, were particularly concerned with performance measures. Japanese companies that had been accustomed to just giving foreign investors a tour of the factory floor became increasingly concerned with ways to increase performance measures. This has resulted in sales of assets that do not improve ROA, including some unwinding of cross shareholdings.

If one thinks of restructuring in terms of a timeline it becomes evident what kinds of measures are likely to take place in particular order. Disposing of unproductive assets and undertaking measures to reduce shareholder equity are measures that can be undertaken relatively quickly. Increasing margins through cost reducing measures such as shedding unnecessary overhead labor becomes the next step. Finally, exploring efficiency gains in terms of sales and marketing in order to boost sales turnover becomes attractive.

At the same time that prudential policy and accounting standards were upgraded, other 'shareholder friendly' measures were introduced. Share buybacks were allowed since 1996, and steadily increased since then to our sample period. The motives for buybacks in Japan appear to be different than in other countries. Market participants in Japan, and foreign institutional holders in particular, seem to view buybacks by 'good companies' as a signal that the firm is willing to return idle cash balances to shareholders rather than squander them on insiders. Generally, the buybacks coincide with retirement of shares, so that shareholder equity is reduced, causing ROE to rise.

Corporate income taxes were steadily slashed during the period up to 2000, by which time they had fallen from among the highest in the world to equivalent to those paid by firms in California. The decades old ban on holding companies, introduced by General MacArthur, was finally repealed in 1997. While this at first sight might appear benign or negative, it is actually an important ingredient in Japanese restructuring. For the non-financial sector it provides a vehicle for parent firms to hold subsidiaries and affiliates in a more arms-length relationship, adding them or shedding them as the need arises, rather than the messy and difficult-to-sever cross-shareholding mechanism. For financial firms, it allowed for the necessary mechanism to enable mergers, and also for parent firms to enter other business lines without necessarily straying from their core competency.

On the aggregate, some measures of restructuring activity appear meager, and this may account for the reluctance of investors to believe that much has changed. Active takeovers in Japan are still relatively rare, due to the high degree of cross shareholding. A stock-swap scheme was introduced and legalized in 2000 to help facilitate mergers. Despite limited pick-up, M&A deals did expand over the 1990s, with 1999–2000 being particularly active, with about 1275 deals in 1999. On the other hand, according to UBS-Warburg, cross shareholding only partially unwound from about 42% in 1989 to 37% in 1999. For our sample period, therefore, we can only say that incentives to respond to demands of outsiders have increased, but they are far from dominant. The key here seems to be the role of foreign institutions. Foreign ownership in companies listed on Section 1 of the Tokyo Stock Exchange (TSE1) has steadily grown from a meager 5% in 1989, when the bubble collapsed, to about 13% in 1999 just before our sample period, to roughly 25% today.

While foreign investors remain outsiders, their increased representation cannot be underestimated. Japanese households, who have seen their pension funds and insurance investments squandered, increasingly expect global standard performance. This, in turn, has forced fund managers in Japan to follow the lead of foreign institutions and demand measurable performance improvement in terms of return on equity (ROE) and ROA. Between 1985 and 1999, the years of Japan Inc.'s demise, ROE fell from an average 8% for the TSE1 to just 2%. Something had to be done, and the various policy changes we have discussed above came into play.

During the fiscal year prior to our sample period, there were radical changes underfoot in the TSE1 companies. For instance, there were 80 plant closures announced and 37 business units sold while 21 other business units were otherwise transferred. Twenty-eight firms announced debt reduction plans, while 413 announced asset sales. Through joint ventures, mergers and acquisitions, buyouts and absorptions, a total of 534 firms made such announcements. Some 106 firms announced reductions in activities, liquidations and spin-offs. Nearly all of these figures are made against a small or zero base. Obviously, accounting-based incentives and other factors were at work to encourage firms to restructure.

While it is difficult for large firms to layoff or fire workers, except in cases of financial exigency, some progress has been made in that area. The easiest way for large firms to shed labor is to rely more heavily on 'part time' employees, whose hours can be reduced or eliminated easily. 'Part time' in large Japanese firms is often very close to full time, the major distinction simply being classified as such. For all firms, the part-time ratio increased from 15% in 1990 to 18% in 2000. The other major means of reducing employment is to offer early retirement and separation to employees. Early separations increased from 5% of all workers in 1990 to around 11% in 1999.

It is against this background that we have chosen the period spanning fiscal years (FY) 2000 and 2001 for our period of observation. By this time implementation of the aforementioned accounting changes were complete, bringing Japan up to international standards. Most firms had implemented changes in governance from the late 1990s. For example, many firms began to improve the efficiency of their large and unwieldy boards. Firms aggressively began to reduce board positions after 1998, and substitute executive officers in a move to improve efficiency. For the TSE1 during FY1998, for example, total board positions declined by 1376, directorships declined by 2066 and executive officer positions increased by 1806.[4] For most companies the paring of board positions amounted to anywhere from a 20% to 70% reduction. For the most part, the introduction of executive officer positions was altogether new.

In this context, the potential for restructuring announcements to appear as a clear positive signal to shareholders is great. Japanese economic and market performance has been poor for so long that one can argue that bad news is already fully priced in, so that restructuring announcements are less likely to present a mixed signal. That is, Japanese firms that announced restructuring measures during our time frame were already likely to have been somewhat distressed, or at least in need of improvement, and this would not be news to the market. Instead, such announcements should convey the signal that the firm's management was prepared to swallow the bitter pill and turn the firm around. Even if this 'clear signaling' argument is incorrect, Japanese restructuring announcements after 1999 present an excellent research opportunity simply as a result of their frequency. For our randomly selected sample of 300 TSE1-listed companies, we found that 90 firms made a total of 836 restructuring announcements during our sample period. This provides an excellent sample to study both firms that announced restructuring, and those that did not.

Firms that made restructuring announcements from our sample over the FY2001–2002 period had average announcement period abnormal returns of 0.3%, ranging from -23.1% to +20.6%. In general announcement period returns are not statistically significant, either as a group for all firms or for sub-categories announcing specific restructuring programs. While this is somewhat surprising given the generally positive performance improvements following these restructuring announcements, the skeptical response of market participants is consistent with the observations in Kang and Shivdasani (1997), who also fail to detect significant market response to the restructuring announcements made by Japanese firms in the late 1980s.

An important contribution of this paper is to determine whether restructuring announcements against the background of increased transparency, greater incentives for improved performance and a history of poor financial performance and returns indeed enhance firm performance and returns. We have collected data on a comprehensive list of restructuring measures for a randomly selected sample of firms, rather than focusing on one or a few special types. Furthermore, we analyze this data in terms of actual impact on firm performance as well as benefits of such measures to shareholders in terms of equity returns. In terms of the data set, we have focused on a market characterized by a relatively large number of different types of restructuring announcements, where distress is likely to be widely known and priced-in, and which is randomly selected. With this approach we hope to avoid some of the selectivity involved in previous studies.

Institutional agents in the Tokyo market were crucially aware of the need for many firms to restructure during the 1990s and into the next decade. Restructuring announcements were well reported in the financial press, and financial analysts typically dissected such announcements thoroughly. A major concern for investors was the importance of insiders and stakeholders in limiting the scope for restructuring, and we believe this forms the basis for skepticism. In other words, it is more likely that agents were either waiting to see evidence of an impact of announced restructuring measures on firm performance, or were highly doubtful that meaningful actions were being taken in response to the announced measures. This is interesting in that firms had for so long avoided any mention of restructuring that one would have expected more dramatic market response to such announcements.

Sample and restructuring announcement characteristics

We randomly selected 300 TSE1 firms from a current total of 1743 TSE1 firms. We exclude consideration of firms in the financial sector due to the incomparability of performance data for such firms relative to the rest of the sample. There are other reasons for excluding financial sector firms, including the fact that restructuring measures in that sector are often quite different from other sectors, and have often included radical transformations including de-listing of the original entity. Firms from all other industry groupings in the TSE are represented. For our sample period of FY2000–FY2001, some of the selected firms had to be eliminated either because they were newly listed during or after our sample period, or were not traded for significant periods. After such elimination, 289 firms remained from our original sample of 300. Among these firms, 90 made restructuring announcements during the sample period for a total of 836 such announcements.

Restructuring announcements were found by searching for all newspaper articles and announcements for the sample of 300 firms in the *Nihon Keizai Shinbum*, Japan's major business and financial daily. This was accomplished by using the 'C-brain' online search and research service from the same source. We then grouped these into 45 restructuring announcement types within six major categories. We have used all announcements during the period, rather than selecting only certain types of announcements as is typically the case in this literature.

While we included every type of restructuring announcement made by our sample of firms during FY2000–2001, we have categorized them in a fashion that makes comparison with previous studies possible. In particular, we were able to group announcement types into categories that are comparable to those of Kang and Shivdasani (1997), a study that examined restructuring during the bubble period of the late 1980s. While comparison of our results with those of Kang and Shivdasani is interesting, it should be noted that the bubble period is very different from our sample period for a number of important reasons. As noted earlier, accounting standards and transparency were radically different, and economic conditions were much stronger with fewer firms subject to financial fragility. Furthermore, Japan in the late 1980s was at the zenith of its bank-centered financial system, and restructurings were largely undertaken at the behest of creditors, rather than being management driven.[5]

The full list of announcement types and frequencies studied is presented in Table 4.1. We consider six major categories of announcement types: contraction actions, employment changes, expansion actions, internal reorganization actions, changes in internal control and financial restructuring. We further consider breakdowns within each of these categories for a total of 45 detailed restructuring action announcement types. Our list of categories is among the most comprehensive in the literature.

Among the six major types of restructuring announcements, contraction measures, employment changes and internal organization measures can generally be viewed as cost reduction or cost control measures. Internal control and financial restructurings are typically governance related changes, though they may have cost and other performance implications as well. Expansion measures include foreign expansions that may result in production cost reduction, and also includes expansion of marketing networks that may result in increased sales revenue or improved sales turnover. Generally, other studies have found that restructuring announcements yield small positive response in returns, though with limited or no response in firm performance after such announcements (Brickley and Van Drunen, 1990). The exception to this finding seems to be in the case of layoffs in the United States, where Chen *et al.* (2001) find a negative impact of such announcements on returns, presumably due to signaling issues discussed earlier.

Table 4.1 Corporate responses to changing business conditions

1. Contraction actions:	**236**
Asset sales (sales of subsidiary shares/operation units/real estate) – Divestitures	60
Spinoff unit - Divestitures	16
Cut/postpone capital expenditures (infrastructure/equipment investments)	5
Withdraw from line of production/business operation	29
Cut production/production capacity (mostly domestic)	25
Suspend production operations (mostly domestic)	6
Consolidate subsidiaries/production plants/operation units/offices/branches	64
Close domestic production plants/operation units/offices/branches	22
Close overseas production plants/operation units/offices/branches	9
2. Employment changes:	**123**
Domestic layoffs	20
Overseas layoffs	13
Temporary layoffs (mostly domestic)	8
Employee transfer / secondment (to different subsidiaries/plants/operation units)	33
Reduce director/executive salary/bonus	7
Reduce manager salary/bonus	5
Reduce employee salary/bonus	4
Performance-based salary/bonus/pension for managers/employees	8
Recruit for voluntary early retirement / offer early retirement incentives	25
3. Expansion actions:	**250**
Increase domestic production	4
Increase overseas production	47
Expand distribution channels	10
Setup new plants/operation units/distribution channels or start new line of production/business operation	40
Establish subsidiary	13
Increase capital expenditures	30
Joint venture or strategic alliance / business and capital tie-up	70
M&A (merger via increased cross holdings and acquisitions	29
Partial acquisition (acquisition of units/divisions)	7
4. Internal reorganization actions:	**173**
Cut production/operating costs	75
Modernize/improve production techniques/equipments/facilities	8
Lower inventory	8
Shift/change product line	6
Reorganize existing production process/operation units	42
Improve product distribution efficiency	22
Outsource part of production/operation	9
Change pricing policy (increase product price)	3
5. Changes in internal control:	**26**
External directors/supervisors	6
Appointed executives	5
Turnover of CEO (resignation, reduction in number of CEO, new appointment)	6
Improve governance (more frequent management meetings, setup of supervisory board, increase accounting transparency)	9
6. Financial restructurings:	**28**
Reduce/terminate cross holdings	4
Main banks grant write-offs of company loans	3
Bond issue	3
Write off of non-performing assets (loans to subsidiaries)	2
Receive financial support from main banks	1
Report special loss arising from restructuring costs	15

Restructuring announcements and operating performance

Naturally, we would like to test whether the observed list of announcements from our sample of firms has had a positive impact on firm performance and returns. A casual reading of the business press would suggest that market participants in Japan during our sample period were highly skeptical and weary.[6] For most of the first decade following the collapse of the bubble economy in Japan, Japanese firms were very leery of making restructuring announcements. Stakeholder rights rather than shareholder rights were paramount, and managers of large firms were protected from takeover by cross-shareholdings. Restructuring was associated with layoffs and considered 'un-Japanese.' Case law in Japan effectively prevented layoffs in large firms except in the case of financial exigency.[7] Government, for its part, tried to convince the populace and market participants that economic recovery was on its way. Given this history, one can understand that there might have been skepticism on the part of shareholders as to whether restructuring announcements would actually pay off in terms of firm performance. We can model the tests of these hypotheses a number of ways. We are concerned with the potential impact of restructuring announcements on firm performance and returns, so we must define two basic 'models' of such impacts and define our performance measures.

Our first measure of performance is ROA, defined as operating income scaled by book assets. ROA captures two key component ratios of performance, sales turnover and margin, as shown in the decomposition below (where EBIT refers to Earnings Before Interest and Taxes, or operating income):

$$\text{ROA} = \frac{\text{EBIT}}{\text{Sales}} \times \frac{\text{Sales}}{\text{Assets}} \tag{1}$$

ROA is not influenced by extraordinary items and financing charges, and represents asset efficiency and profitability. Since we are concerned with how restructuring affects performance, we focus on the change in ROA over a one (as well as two) year horizon after the restructuring announcement (compared with ROA a year before the announcement).

Specifically, we estimate the following equation where the R terms represent the six restructuring announcement categories, and the I terms correspond to two-digit industry codes. The C terms represent control variables such as foreign ownership. On the basis of this mapping, we hypothesize the following baseline model for our statistical analysis.

$$\Delta ROA_i = \alpha + \sum_{r=1}^{6} \gamma_r R_r + \sum_{k=1}^{7} \eta_k I_k + \lambda_c C_c + \mu_i \tag{2}$$

where the C terms represent the six restructuring announcement categories, and the I terms are ticker categories that correspond to two-digit industry codes.

In (2), ΔROA is measured as the one or two year change in ROA. The one (two) year change is the change in ROA from one (two) year before the announcement until one year after. The announcements will be considered on

Table 4.2 Industry adjusted mean and median one period change in return on assets (ROA)

Restructuring action	Mean	Median
Contraction	0.0096	0.0036
	(0.001)	(0.001)
Employment changes	0.0123	0.0036
	(0.0004)	(0.001)
Expansion	−0.0031	−0.0014
	(0.29)	(0.33)
Internal reorganization	0.0095	0.0036
	(0.0003)	(0.0006)
Changes to internal control	−0.0021	0.0000
	(0.73)	(0.62)
Financial restructuring	0.0225	0.0205
	(0.0008)	(0.0001)
All	0.0042	0.0011
	(0.012)	(0.005)

Source: Author

Note: ROA is calculated as Earnings Before Interest and Taxes divided by Total Assets. Change in ROA is calculated as the difference between ROA at the end of the first fiscal year following the restructuring announcement and the ROA at the end of the fiscal year preceding the announcement. Industry adjusted ROA is calculated as ROA for the firm less the median ROA for all firms belonging to the same two-digit industry code matched by fiscal year. A total of 836 restructuring plans, classified into six broad categories, were announced by 90 firms from a randomly selected sample of 300 firms over the 2000–2001 period. P-values are provided in parentheses.

the basis of the individual announcement types and a single variable capturing all announcements. Industry dummies are the seven non-financial four-digit ticker codes in the TSE1. The model for performance is essentially an event-type analysis on whether the defined performance variable for the announcing firms responds to an announcement of restructuring in period 0. The null hypothesis for equation (2) is that the coefficients on announcements are individually equal to zero (we can remain agnostic with respect to the sum of coefficients).

Of course, it may take the firm many periods to respond positively or negatively to an announced restructuring measure. We have found that the results are robust to lag structure, and we have reported the one-year change measure. The results in terms of restructuring announcements and performance are quite ubiquitous; firms in Japan for the period under analysis seem to deliver on restructuring announcements. We can see this in stylized fashion in Table 4.2, where announcement types and changes in industry adjusted ROA are presented. Contractions, employment changes, internal reorganizations and financial restructuring type announcements are positively related with improvements in ROA. Category 'ALL' here is a simple dummy variable representing whether firms made any of the six categories of announcements. The significance of this variable for industry adjusted mean and median ROA is not as large, since it includes the impact of expansion and internal

Table 4.3 Pair-wise correlations for restructuring announcements

	C1	C2	C3	C4	C5	C6
C1	1.0	.233 (.0001)	−.117 (.0039)	.23 (.0001)	−.046 (.254)	.101 (.013)
C2	.233 (.0001)	1.0	−.15 (.0002)	.163 (.0001)	−.031 (.4429)	.217 (.0001)
C3	−.117 (.0039)	−.151 (.0002)	1.0	.114 (.005)	−.08 (.049)	−.119 (.0033)
C4	.23 (.0001)	.163 (.0001)	.114 (.005)	1.0	−.015 (.71)	−.02 (.621)
C5	−.046 (.254)	−.031 (.443)	−.08 (.049)	−.015 (.71)	1.0	−.041 (.315)
C6	.101 (.013)	.217 (.0001)	−.119 (.0033)	−.02 (.621)	−.041 (.315)	1.0

Source: Author

Note: Pair-wise correlation coefficients for restructuring announcements made by a random sample of 300 firms listed on the Tokyo Stock Exchange over the 2000–2001 period. A total of 836 announcements of various types were made by 90 firms from the sample of 300 firms over this period. The restructuring announcements are classified into six types. C1 refers to Contraction type events. C2 refers to employment changes. C3 refers to expansion actions. C4 refers to internal reorganizations. C5 refers to internal control changes. C6 refers to financial restructurings. P-values are provided in parentheses.

control type restructuring announcements as well. Apparently expansion activities and internal control changes during this period were not positively correlated with higher industry adjusted returns.

With 90 firms out of the random sample of 300 firms making over 800 restructuring announcements, it is obvious that firms are announcing and undertaking multiple restructuring actions. In Table 4.3 we present the correlation coefficients between the six major announcement types. Perhaps not surprisingly, categories which are individually positively correlated with improvements in ROA tend to be positively and significantly correlated with each other. Categories which appear to be uncorrelated with improvements in ROA (categories Expansion and Internal Control Changes) tend to be negatively correlated or uncorrelated to all other restructuring announcements with the exception of expansions, which are positively correlated to internal reorganizations. Overall, announcements of the type that are found to be positively correlated with performance improvements are correlated with each other. Managers seem to try several types of actions in an effort to improve firm performance.

In Table 4.4 we present our findings with respect to a specification of model (2). We model changes in ROA as a function of the six categories of announcement type, the seven industry/ticker categories, and percent of foreign ownership. Foreign ownership is included under the assumption that firms with greater foreign ownership are more likely to introduce performance-enhancing measures.

Table 4.4 Restructuring announcements and changes in ROA: OLS regression estimates

Dependent variable	One period change in ROA	Two period change in ROA
Constant	−0.009 (0.13)	0.0093 (0.15)
C1	0.006 (0.16)	−0.0013 (0.85)
C2	0.009 (0.07)	0.014 (0.03)
C3	0.0007 (0.87)	−0.0013 (0.81)
C4	0.015 (0.002)	0.015 (0.01)
C5	−0.002 (0.73)	−0.013 (0.32)
C6	0.002 (0.79)	−0.002 (0.78)
% Foreign	0.037 (0.07)	0.0022 (0.95)
Industry dummies	YES	YES
Adj. R-sq	0.172	0.144
F-stat	3.070	2.680

Source: Author

Note: Regression of change (one and two period) in ROA on restructuring announcements, industry dummy variables and foreign ownership. One (two) period ROA changes are measured as the ROA at the end of the first (second) fiscal year following the restructuring less the ROA from one fiscal year prior to the restructuring announcement. C1 refers to Contraction type events. C2 refers to employment changes. C3 refers to expansion actions. C4 refers to internal reorganizations. C5 refers to internal control changes. C6 refers to financial restructurings. P-values are provided in parentheses.

We have estimated (2) using both one and two period changes in ROA for robustness, although we only discuss and tabulate the one-period change in ROA to conserve space. As in the univariate correlations, employment reductions and cost reducing internal organizational changes contribute to improvement in both one and two-period changes in ROA. Category 1 contraction-type actions and category 6 financial restructuring do not have a statistically significant impact on changes in ROA in the multivariate analysis. A possible explanation for this comes from the results in Table 4.3: there is a significant degree of correlation between these two announcement types. This collinearity will bias against finding a statistically significant impact of announcements on improvements in ROA. Our attempts to deal with this issue do not conflict with the results of Table 4.3, except to enhance the impact of category 2 announcements, employment changes.

Restructuring announcements and returns

As discussed at the outset of this paper, we are also interested in the question of whether restructuring announcements by firms have a significant impact on returns. The question is of interest in terms of international comparisons, but there are important market specific reasons for examining the issue in the Japanese context. Generally speaking, restructuring announcements have small, short-term positive impact on returns in the context of the U.S. market. There are exceptions, and some announcements tend to give mixed signals, such as layoff announcements (see Chen *et al.*, 2001). The general finding of small positive impact on returns gives rise to the question of whether firms might consider making restructuring announcements that are pure window dressing, simply for the sake of boosting short-term returns.

This question is particularly interesting in the Japanese context, and is an issue often raised by market participants. That is, given the lengthy period of poor economic performance, and poor performance by most firms in Japan specifically, might firms in that context consider making restructuring announcements in order to help boost returns, having observed the U.S. experience? While the Japanese context is not so simple, in that restructuring announcements were initially avoided by firms for a very long period after the market and economic collapse began in late 1989, it is certainly plausible that managers in Japan might be tempted to follow such a course. There is no question that many market participants viewed and continue to view restructuring announcements in that market with great skepticism. While one seldom hears suggestions that the firms are engaging in crude price manipulation, the general criticism is that the announced actions simply represent 'too little too late,' and can be expected to be of limited impact.

In this chapter, we have already addressed the issue of substance: for our sample and period of analysis, restructuring announcements as a whole do boost firm performance. Furthermore, specific types of restructuring announcements, especially those related to cost control, do positively affect firm performance as measured by improvements in ROA in a statistically significant fashion. For our purposes here, therefore, the only question which remains is whether in fact our skeptical market participants are willing to pay for such announcements. Specifically, do restructuring announcements in Japan for the period of analysis boost returns in a statistically significant fashion?

In Table 4.5 we consider the relation between the six major restructuring categories, as well as the overall announcement dummy variable, and three returns measures. In this table, the interval $[-1, +2]$ indicates returns measured from one day prior to an announcement to two days after the announcement, and so forth. The results are generally not significant, with only expansion activity announcements (category 3) showing even modest positive impact at the usual levels of significance across all time periods. On the basis of these univariate results, it does not appear that the market is generally prepared to reward firms for making restructuring announcements. Indeed, if anything, market participants are

Table 4.5 Restructuring announcements and stock returns

Event type	Day [-1,2]	Day [-1,1]	Day [-1,0]
Contractions	−0.0089	−0.0045	0.002
	(0.4)	(0.56)	(0.71)
Employment changes	−0.046	−0.027	−0.011
	(0.08)	(0.2)	(0.48)
Expansions	0.019	0.017	0.015
	(0.08)	(0.05)	(0.09)
Internal reorganizations	−0.008	−0.007	0.004
	(0.68)	(0.67)	(0.68)
Internal control changes	0.019	0.012	0.01
	(0.47)	(0.45)	(0.49)
Financial restructurings	0.0067	0.01	0.008
	(0.59)	(0.24)	(0.36)
All	−0.0067	−0.0019	0.003
	(0.49)	(0.81)	(0.59)

Source: Author

Note: Announcement dates are based on reports in the Nihon Keizai Shinbum. A total of 836 restructuring plans were announced by 90 firms from a randomly selected sample of 300 firms over the 2000–2001 period. All returns are adjusted for market using the TOPIX Index. P-values are provided in parentheses.

more prepared to reward growth related announcements than typical restructuring announcements.

We must consider a fully controlled model for returns and restructuring announcements before we can formally conclude that the market is unwilling to pay for restructuring announcements. Our basic model here assumes a mapping between restructuring announcements and returns. The logic is just the extension of the relationship between restructuring announcements and performance outlined in equations (1) and (2). If restructuring enhances performance, then we hypothesize that restructuring announcements should enhance returns. The model to be tested is presented in equation (3), with the null hypothesis that the coefficients on restructuring announcements should be statistically insignificant.

$$RET_i = \alpha + \beta.MKT_i + \sum_{r=1}^{6} \gamma_r R_r + \sum_{k=1}^{7} \eta_k I_k + \lambda_c C_c + e_i \tag{3}$$

Results of estimating (3), using both market-adjusted returns (based on the TOPIX Index) and raw returns with the TOPIX Index return as an explanatory variable, are presented in Table 4.6. None of the announcement categories appear

Table 4.6 Restructuring announcements and returns: OLS regression estimates

Dependent variable	Market-adjusted return	Raw return
Constant	−0.016	−0.016
	(0.51)	(0.53)
TOPIX Return		0.87
		(0.05)
%Foreign	0.05	0.048
	(0.44)	(0.47)
Contraction-type events	0.016	0.016
	(0.24)	(0.25)
Employment changes	−0.018	−0.019
	(0.23)	(0.22)
Expansion events	0.022	0.022
	(0.15)	(0.15)
Internal reorganizations	0.0004	0.004
	(0.77)	(0.77)
Internal control changes	0.008	0.007
	(0.73)	(0.76)
Financial restructurings	0.017	0.019
	(0.52)	(0.49)
Industry fixed effects	YES	YES
Adj. R-sq	−0.034	0.019
F-stat	0.81	1.11

Source: Author

Note: Market-adjusted as well as raw returns are measured over three days centered on the restructuring announcement date. Market-adjusted returns are calculated by subtracting the return on the TOPIX Index. %Foreign refers to equity ownership by foreign institutions. Industry fixed effects are based on two-digit industry classifications. P-values are presented in parentheses.

to enhance returns. Despite the previous evidence presented, that restructuring announcements do indeed appear to enhance performance, we cannot generally reject the null hypothesis that such announcements do not positively impact returns. While we present only the two-day announcement return regressions in Table 4.6, the results were robust with respect to other returns windows. The relation between expansion measures and returns disappears in the multivariate analysis, suggesting a spurious correlation. Unlike their counterparts elsewhere, market participants in the Japanese market are not typically willing to ante up for restructuring announcements, despite evidence that such activities positively affect firm performance. Despite meaningful reforms in terms of accounting practices and transparency, market participants in the immediate post-reform and post-tech bubble period appear to be skeptical about restructuring announcements by Japanese firms.

Conclusions

In this chapter we considered restructuring announcements in the Japanese business press for 300 randomly selected firms from the first section of the Tokyo Stock Exchange. We found that 90 firms from that sample made over 800 restructuring announcements. We grouped these announcements into six major categories, namely contraction events, employment changes, expansion actions, internal reorganizations, internal control changes and financial restructurings. We first considered the issue of whether firms that made such announcements had improvements in performance as measured by ROA. We found that restructuring plans involving cutting back production or employment, internal reorganization (often with similar motives), and financial restructurings were associated with positive and significant improvements in ROA. This finding was robust to lag structure.

We also considered the relationship between restructuring announcements and returns. We found no evidence for a positive relationship between announcements of restructuring activities and returns. This finding was in stark contrast to the results found for restructuring and performance. Despite significant improvements in governance and accounting regulations after 2000, it appears that market participants remain skeptical of firm-level efforts to generate meaningful reforms.

Notes

1 The term is borrowed from a similar regulatory change in London in 1980.
2 The term 'Japan Premium' as used in the business press typically referred to the premium on offshore interbank overnight borrowing by Japanese banks of a certain risk class relative to foreign banks of a similar risk class.
3 Most notably here is the suspension of activities of Price Waterhouse Cooper in 2006 after nearly 40 years of operation in Japan.
4 Toyo keizai data, 1999.
5 For example, after the first oil shock in the mid-1970s, Mazda's main bank (Sumitomo Bank) carried out a full-scale restructuring of the firm, including replacement of top management. In the mid-1990s, after the main bank system began to crumble and the large Japanese banks found themselves in trouble, other shareholding groups began to flex their muscle. In the Mazda case, Ford Motor Co. became the de-facto monitor of the company and initiated radical restructuring. More generally, see Aoki, Patrick and Sheard (1994).
6 See, for e.g., 'Corporate Japan's Stealth Makeover,' *Businessweek*, September 29, 2003; and 'Barbarians at the gate, vultures overhead,' *Asia Times Online*, September 23, 2003.
7 Contrary to popular belief, layoffs and dismissals are not illegal in Japan, but a long history of case law, together with specificity of human capital, has made them costly. Generally speaking, firms with more than 10 employees are expected to avoid layoffs through reduction of hours for non-tenured employees (Beason, 1992). This has been reaffirmed in several court rulings, including the Shuhoku Bus Case (1968), the Toyo Sanso Co. Case (1979) and the SAS case (1995).

References

Aoki, Masahiki, Hugh Patrick and Paul Sheard, 1994. The Japanese Main Bank System: An Introductory Overview. In Masahiki Aoki and Hugh Patrick, eds., *The Japanese Main Bank System*. Oxford: Oxford University Press, pp. 1–50.

Asia Times Online, 2003. Barbarians at the Gate, Vultures Overhead. September 23, 2003.

Beason, Richard, 1992. Intertemporal Substitution and Labor Supply in Japan. *Journal of Human Resources*, 27, 511–533.

Blackwell, D.W., Marr, M.W., Spivey, M.F., 1990. Plant-closing Decisions and the Market Value of the Firm. *Journal of Financial Economics*, 26, 277–288.

Brickley, J.A., Van Drunen, L.D., 1990. Internal Corporate Rrestructuring: An Empirical Analysis. *Journal of Accounting and Economics*, 12, 251–280.

Businessweek, 2003. Corporate Japan's Stealth Makeover. September 29, 2003.

Chen, Peter, Vikas Mehrotra, Ranjini Sivakumar, and Wayne W. Yu, 2001. Layoffs, Shareholders' Wealth, and Corporate Performance. *Journal of Empirical Finance*, 8, 171–199.

John, K., Ofek, E., 1995. Asset Sales and Increase in Focus. *Journal of Financial Economics,* 37, 105–126.

Kang, Jun Koo and Anil Shivdasani, 1997. Corporate Restructuring During Performance Declines in Japan. *Journal of Financial Economics*, 46, 29–65.

Kang, Jun Koo and Anil Shivdasani, 1995. Firm Performance, Corporate Governance, and Top Executive Turnover in Japan. *Journal of Financial Economics*, 38, 29–58.

McConnell, J.J., Muscarella, C.J., 1985. Corporate Capital Expenditure Decisions and the Market Value of the Firm. *Journal of Financial Economics*, 14, 399–422.

Nihon Keizai Shinbum, various, Searched through C-Brain online database.

Peek, Joe, and Eric S. Rosengren, 2000. Determinants of the Japan Premium: Actions Speak Louder than Words. *Journal of International Economics*, 53, 283–-305.

Warburg Dillon Read (Now UBS), 2000. New Japan Part I. January 4, 2000.

5 An overview of corporate governance reform in post-bubble Japan

Institutional change and selective adaptation

Masao Nakamura

Corporate governance practices and institutions in transition

For convenience, we regard Japan's corporate governance reform in the 1990s and early 2000s as a transition from Japan's traditional bank-based corporate governance system (Institution I) to a new US-type corporate governance system (Institution II).

Notable issues that must be dealt with in the transition

In achieving this transition, a number of important issues must be dealt with by the government and also the affected organizations, including business corporations. These issues include the clarification of the meaning of a corporation as related to its owners' (shareholders') individual rights. Another issue is the treatment (protection) of minority shareholder rights, relative to the rights of majority shareholders. It is well known that, in Japan's bank-based corporate governance system that was in place at most Japanese corporations until the early 1990s, the company management had to pay attention only to the company's majority shareholders (i.e., banks and other financial institutions, the other industrial firm shareholders who form keiretsu) but could safely ignore the company's individual and minority shareholders.

We regard the US practice of caring for minority shareholder rights as reflecting Western liberal norms. We also regard US practice of protecting individual shareholder rights (protection of the rights of owners of private property) as reflecting Western liberal norms.

Consistency with these US practices is an important principle for corporate management to follow based on shareholder value maximization. (Shareholder value maximization is not consistent with the Japanese traditional corporate operating criterion based on stakeholder value maximization. As discussed below, the stakeholders of a firm include not only the shareholders but also the employees, creditors, suppliers and often major customers of the firm.)

Pursuing shareholder value maximization leads in general to the requirement that the market for corporate control must exist and must function well. For example, mergers and acquisitions (M&As), both friendly and hostile M&As, must be freely allowed to take place so that firm management can focus on shareholder value maximization. Without such a well-functioning market for corporate control, firms may end up having to keep inefficient production units, which contribute negatively to firm value. Such inefficient production units may become productive units if they become subsidiaries of another firm. Such transactions of M&As apply not only to firms' production units but also the whole firms themselves in liberalized M&A markets. Under such a scenario the shareholder value maximization principle continues to hold since unprofitable firms will cease to exist.

In what we will refer to as Japan's Institution I, few of these practices associated with liberalized M&A markets and the shareholder value maximization principle were present until the 1990s. How Japan moves from Institution I to Institution II while incorporating (at least partially) these and other US practices, many of which reflect Western liberal norms, is of interest, and will be discussed below.[1,2]

Our approach

In order to focus on selective adaptation, we primarily consider Japan-specific factors as surrogates for Japanese norms. In empirical studies some of these factors are proxied by some other observable factors while others are treated as unobservables. Since these factors often explain a significant fraction of variation in the dependent variable of interest, it is worthwhile investigating the role they play in an institutional change situation like the one Japan has been going through with its corporate governance system. In the selective adaptation framework that we use here for explaining Japan's transition in corporate governance practices and institutions, it is postulated that the interactions between local (Japanese) norms and the Western liberal norms underlying the laws, institutions and practices associated with the Anglo-American corporate governance system will determine the manner by which Japan will select to implement (or enforce) the parts of the Anglo-American corporate governance practices. It is also the case that certain phenomena that are associated with certain Japan-specific factors (norms) are often not explainable using economic theory.[3]

Norms underlying the Japanese business behavior

Many studies in the literature have investigated various aspects of the normative nature of Japanese life. Even though there is no single unique and agreed on set of norms and values underlying all aspects of Japanese life, many researchers seem to agree that the following norms distinguish cultural characteristics of Japan from those of the United States.[4,5] These norms span overlapping areas of Japanese business behavior and hence are not exclusive.

Often cited Japanese norms identified in Japanese business behavior

1 *Group behavior:* Reischauer (1988: 128) notes the "Japanese tendency to emphasize the group at the expense of the individual." Reishauer (1988: 133, 685) also notes that "associations of business enterprises, from groups of petty retailers by street or ward to nationwide associations of great banks or steel producers, are more wide spread and more important a feature in Japan than in America." As we discuss later, this is consistent with the important role many types of corporate groups (referred to as keiretsu below) continue to play in the Japanese business system.

2 *Consensus:* Consensus is the goal ... To operate their group system successfully, the Japanese have found it advisable to avoid open confrontations (Reischauer, 1988: 136).

3 *Long-term relationships:* Until the early 1990s, long-term employment was the norm for most regular workers in Japan.[6] This is still the case but, after the massive restructuring that took place at almost all Japanese corporations from the 1990s through the early 2000s, the size of the workforce of regular employees who enjoy long-term employment has shrunken in most companies.[7] Despite this, many public opinion polls continue to suggest that most of the Japanese public prefer long-term employment security.[8] These preferences are reflected in many company decisions.

4 *Vertical keiretsu relationships among corporations:* Japan's large manufacturers (e.g., Toyota) and their parts suppliers in auto, electronics and other assembly-based manufacturing industries are typically organized in vertical production keiretsu groups (e.g., Toyota group), where the core assembler owns small pieces (e.g., 20–30%) of their key (first-tier) suppliers which in turn own small pieces of the second-tier suppliers, etc. Many Japanese firms believe that this form of industrial organization is more efficient than alternative forms such as fully vertically integrated firms owning both assembler and parts supply operations, or assembler firms buying from completely independent parts suppliers.[9] Vertical keiretsu group firms have managed to "sustain hybrid relationships – close, dependent, long-term alliances, absent majority ownership, or contingent contracts – because (partly for cultural reasons) of a generally low taste for opportunism: strong norms favoring trust, obligation, and reciprocity in relationships, backed up by such reputation-enforcing formal mechanisms as supplier associations" (Ahmadjian and Lincoln, 2001: 685; Sako, 1996). In Japan's assembly-based production setups, keiretsu relationships provide organic bonding among member firms and have important implications for their business relationships. The social and economic infrastructure in which Japanese supply networks are embedded makes abrupt termination of stable partnerships difficult. Ties between assemblers and their key suppliers have, in many cases, been in place for 30 years or more (Japan Fair Trade Commission, 1993). For example, Ahmadjian and Lincoln (2001) note "Lifetime" employment and low levels (by Japanese norms) of job rotation within purchasing departments enable

purchasing managers to develop strong personal bonds with their suppliers' representatives.

5 *Importance of group-oriented values:* Many authors have noted that Japanese businesses emphasize group-oriented values in their decision-making. For example, Bartlett and Ghoshal (1998: 50) state: "In contrast to European family capitalism and American managerial capitalism, the Japanese cultural heritage has fostered a form of management Chandler called 'group capitalism.' As many observers have noted, the homogeneity of Japanese society, its isolationism during the Tokugawa period, and the influence of Eastern religions and philosophies have reinforced strong Japanese cultural norms that emphasize group behavior and value interpersonal harmony. Such values carry over into the country's commercial organizations and have helped shape distinctive management styles and organizational practices. ... At a corporate level, the group-oriented values were reflected in the zaibatsu and other enterprise groups, which paternalistically watched over their affiliated companies. Within the organization, such values were evident in the widespread norm of lifetime employment commitments – by both employer and employee – and such managerial practices as nemawashi or ringi, which institutionalized information sharing and joint decision making." Lincoln *et al.* (1986: 343) also conclude that, in general, there is wide agreement that Japanese decision making is group and consensus-oriented and involves low delegation of formal authority to positions held by individuals.

6 *Trust and networks:* Lincoln (2006: 219) describes Japanese customer-supplier relationships as follows: "At a micro-level, 'the trust, reciprocity, and stability typical of customer-supplier dyads in Japanese industrial goods markets' have facilitated keiretsu firms to enjoy cooperation, synergy, and knowledge-sharing in product and process development. At a more macro-level, webs of cross-shareholdings, director transfers, and preferential trade and lending flows have functioned both as information systems and as governance structures to disseminate while conserving and protecting knowledge assets" (Lincoln and Gerlach, 2004; Williamson, 1996). By the same token, the breaks and "holes" in the network (Burt, 1992) – e.g., between direct competitors or rival groups – have at times presented formidable barriers to Japanese firms' collaboration and learning.[10]

7 *Male/female behavior.* Reischauer (1988: 175, 183–184) notes: "The laws now give women full legal equality. But Japan is still definitely a 'man's world,' with women confined to a secondary position. Many Westerners wonder indignantly why Japanese women do not agitate more aggressively against their unequal status. (Japanese men are blatantly male chauvinists and women seem shamefully exploited and suppressed.) Despite the great gains made by women in recent decades, social limitations on them and discrimination in employment remain severe." This aspect of Japanese culture is probably why exceptionally few Japanese women are found in high-level managerial and other professional positions compared to countries in the West. Despite the massive transfer of US managerial methods to Japan

since the end of World War II, equal employment opportunity laws of the type implemented in the US have not been fully transplanted nor enforced in Japan. Despite Japan's general acceptance of Western liberal norms, female employment conditions are generally marginal in comparison with the conditions males enjoy. Japan's decision not to accept to enforce US-style equal employment laws fully seems consistent with the notion that Japan behaved according to selective adaptation in this regard.

Comparing Japan's corporate governance practices before and after the corporate governance reform: Japan's selective adaptation

In this section, we apply a selective adaptation framework to analyzing Japan's reactions toward US-style corporate governance practices. For most practical purposes, it is reasonable to think that all legal and institutional settings required by Japanese corporations for adopting US-type corporate governance practices have been laid out by Japanese government reform measures. Nevertheless, how fully proposed US practices get implemented and enforced in the end by Japanese corporations depends on the selective adaptation behavior of Japan's businesses, government, courts and public, among other actors.

a) State variables for describing Japan's corporate governance

We focus on several major issues in corporate governance here. They are: legal protection of shareholders' rights, particularly those of minority shareholders; issues associated with large shareholders (i.e., concentrated ownership); and the agency cost (to all shareholders) that arises because firms' managers do not implement policies to maximize shareholder value.

We use the following state variables to measure the change in the functioning of the aspects of corporate governance mechanisms that are related to the issues given above before and after the reform. These state variables are not necessarily mutually independent or exclusive in that if some factors affect one state variable, it is possible that the same factors also affect some other state variables.[11] Nevertheless we view these state variables as one way to capture essential aspects of Japan's corporate governance mechanisms.[12]

- (s1) Degree to which shareholder value maximization is achieved
- (s2) Degree to which outside independent directors are involved in boards of directors' decisions
- (s3) Degree of competition in the market for corporate control (i.e., activities associated with M&As)
- (s4) Degree of transparency and information disclosure in accounting, financial and other reporting to investors
- (s5) Degree of the protection of minority shareholders

(s1) Describes the degree to which the management is faithful to shareholders' objective to maximize firms' share value. Prior to the reform, Japanese firm management was able to pursue their own objectives which were significantly at variance with shareholder value maximization. Agency costs of this sort were a significant source of economic inefficiency.

(s2) Measures the degree to which the board of directors functions as a governance body. If the board is controlled by insiders, which was the case before the reform, it might be difficult to reduce the agency costs of the sort given by (s1).

(s3) Measures how active the market for corporate control is. While Japanese banks played some role as a substitute for the market for corporate control before the reform, they were not able to replicate the benefits of a more competitive market for corporate control.[13] Inability to replace a firm's bad management team with a more competent one in a timely manner has been a major source of agency cost, of the sort given by (s1), and a source of significant economic inefficiency. We are interested in how the reform impacted the degree of competition in the market for corporate control.

(s4) Measures the fair and transparent availability of firm information that is relevant to all investors concerned. Information disclosure and transparency is the basic prerequisite for efficient functioning of the stock market, allowing investors to evaluate the shares they own. Efficient stock markets also give managers information about the cost of capital which is required for their investment decisions. Efficient stock markets are also essential for developing an active market for corporate control. Japanese bank-based corporate governance mechanisms were insider-oriented and often lacked transparency in various respects.

(s5) Describes the degree to which the individual rights of investors, and particularly those of minority investors, are protected. It is well known that under the old bank-based corporate governance system, up to 70% of most listed firms in Japan were owned by financial and other corporate shareholders who were sympathetic to the incumbent management. Hence firm management generally paid little attention to individual and other minority shareholders' rights.

b) Japanese business norms and instruments that affect the degree of acceptance of new institutional settings and practices in corporate governance

Japanese business norms

We discussed above some of the norms and related issues that characterize Japanese behavior in Japan's business, and society in general.[14] Some of these norms are particularly important for shaping Japan's acceptance of new US-style practices of corporate governance. We list below some of the business norms in concrete terms.

(N1) Corporate groups. Group-oriented behavior reflecting economic efficiency effects may underlie Japanese keiretsu behavior, especially including vertical production keiretsu. Economic efficiency gains have not been verified for horizontal keiretsu, but horizontal keiretsu groupings have proven to be highly potent poison pills and have functioned as such since the early 1950s.

(N2) Consensus. Consensus as the goal, and avoidance of open confrontations. This kind of value system might encourage out-of-court settlements and impede transparency and full acceptance of new laws by individual business firms and shareholders.

(N3) Group-oriented value maximization as the objective for corporate decision making. Until the end of the 1980s up to 70% of most Japanese listed corporations' outstanding shares were held by banks and other financial institutions, as well as other industrial firms. This allowed company managers to ignore the rights of individual shareholders while pursuing other objectives. For example, some authors suggest that Japanese corporations have pursued firms' stakeholders value maximization (e.g., Aoki, 1988; Araki, 2005; Jacoby, 2005)[15] and value-added maximization.[16] These sorts of objective functions, for example, put much weight on the welfare of firms' employees as well as the welfare of suppliers, customers and creditors.

One of the cornerstones of Japan's corporate governance reform is formal acknowledgement by the Japanese government of shareholder value maximization as corporations' primary objective in their decision-making.[17] Japan's new company law and other related laws focus on this point. Legal terms for the protection of shareholders' rights have been clearly set out, as in the US.

Instruments that facilitate adoption of new institutional settings and practices

If firms and investors see the immediate or potential benefits of new laws, those laws may be implemented promptly with full force. The reasons for such full acceptance are in most cases economic and are in some cases humanitarian. There may be little reason for businesses to reject new rules if they perceive those rules are obviously better suited for modern economic activity compared to the old rules, other things being equal. Such an element of perception and legitimacy may be needed for having new rules to be accepted by economic agents.[18]

Another reason that may facilitate acceptance of new laws is when new rules complement the existing old rules in some ways. In this case too the utility of implementing the new rules is obvious. If such legitimacy or complementarity in the new laws are not obviously present and yet the new laws are adopted by the government, investors and businesses alike may not seriously implement the new rules and may instead look for loopholes.

In circumstances where new laws and institutions proposing new corporate governance practices have elements of legitimacy and/or complementarity as discussed above, these new practices will likely be accepted. Their acceptance will further be facilitated if the practitioners concerned and the general public perceive that the new laws are consistent with their personal belief.

We expect that those new corporate governance practices, implied by new reform laws, are more likely to be adopted seriously if Japanese practitioners have a favorable perception about the legitimacy and complementarity of the new laws implemented. (We regard these laws as being more consistent with the Japanese norms.) Otherwise, the new laws implemented may not be fully practiced. In the following we call perception, legitimacy and complementarity the instruments for selective adaptation. In the following discussion, we argue that adoption of new practices is likely if at least some, if not all, of the instruments that favor acceptance of the new practices can be found a priori.

c) State variables before and after the reform

In applying a selective adaptation framework to Japan's corporate governance reform below, we consider how Japanese business norms (N1)–(N3) interact with Western liberal norms which drive to enhance each of the state variables (s1)–(s5). However, in our selective adaptation analysis we use the three instruments (perception, legitimacy, complementarity) instead of the liberal norms directly in calculating the relevant interactions. We proceed as follows. For each state variable and the associated US corporate governance practices which are thought to enhance the value of the state variable, we consider interactions between the instruments and the relevant Japanese norms. If the overall effects of the interactions are positive, we conclude that Japan (and the underlying Japanese norms, in particular) accepts the relevant US practices by selective adaptation and hence the state variable will increase its value as a result of the reform.[19] Table 5.1 shows our framework of analysis for shareholder value maximization (s1).[20]

Shareholder value maximization (s1)

Because of the general perception among Japan's policy makers and the public in the 1990s that Japan's outdated bank-based corporate governance system was one of the main causes for the near collapse of the Japanese economy, it did not appear difficult for the notion of shareholder value maximization to be accepted by both businesses and policy makers. There was general agreement that Japan's bank-based corporate governance system was too insider-oriented and that the US-style market-based system, with the clear management objective of shareholder value maximization, needed to be implemented. In order to achieve this objective, many laws were revised. Japan's new company law, in particular, was set up to provide a new framework within which Japanese corporations can organize their business activities and corporate structures so they are consistent with their respective profit maximization. To secure investor confidence, Japan's new Financial Instruments and Exchange Law of June 2006 was enacted. This law updates and consolidates all existing exchange laws, including the Securities and Exchange law. It introduces the notion of flexibility in its mandate on regulating financial instruments.

Table 5.1. A framework for selective adaptation analysis: Japanese and Western business norms' interactive influence on Japanese corporate governance state variable: s1(shareholder value maximization)

Japanese business norms	*Instruments of selective adaptation for Western liberal business norms*		
	(1) Perception	*(2)* Legitimacy	*(3)* Complementarity
(N1) Corporate groups (keiretsu)	– (possible conflict between keiretsu and individual firms)	– (possible conflict between keiretsu and individual firms)[a]	+ (each supplier's shareholder value maximization reduces moral hazard and agency costs among vertical keiretsu firms)
(N2) Consensus as the goal, and avoidance of open confrontations	– (possible conflict between shareholders and other stakeholders)	– (possible conflict between shareholders and other stakeholders)	?
(N3) Stakeholder value, value added and other group-oriented value maximization as the objective for corporate decision making	– (possible conflict between shareholders and other stakeholders)	– (possible conflict between shareholders and other stakeholders)	+ (paying serious attention to traditionally ignored shareholders' rights to some degree may even improve corporate governance)

Notes: Each cell represents possible impacts on the state variable in question (s1 in the present case) of the interaction between each of the Western business norms instruments and each of the Japanese business norms if is promoted. (–), (+) and (?) mean, respectively negative, positive and ambiguous impacts on adoption of the state variable in question. For example, Japanese perception of shareholder value maximization in the context of (N1) corporate group is likely negative because of possible conflict between keiretsu and individual firms. For the same reason legitimacy to promote (s1) shareholder value maximization will be negative. On the other hand, shareholder value maximization at each keiretsu member firm may improve that firm's governance by reducing moral hazard and agency costs and hence the complementary role of shareholder value maximization may have a positive impact on strengthening the corporate group (N1). Overall, negative interactions between the Western and Japanese business norms are likely to dominate. Hence our selective adaptation analysis implies that shareholder value maximization is less likely to be adopted by Japanese firms.

a For example, crossholding and other types of intra-group shareholding are not compatible with each firm's shareholder value maximization.

Source: Author

Interestingly enough, Japan's initial acceptance of the notion of shareholder value maximization did not necessarily lead to straightforward acceptance of various business mechanisms or business strategies that are associated with the US-style shareholder value maximization.

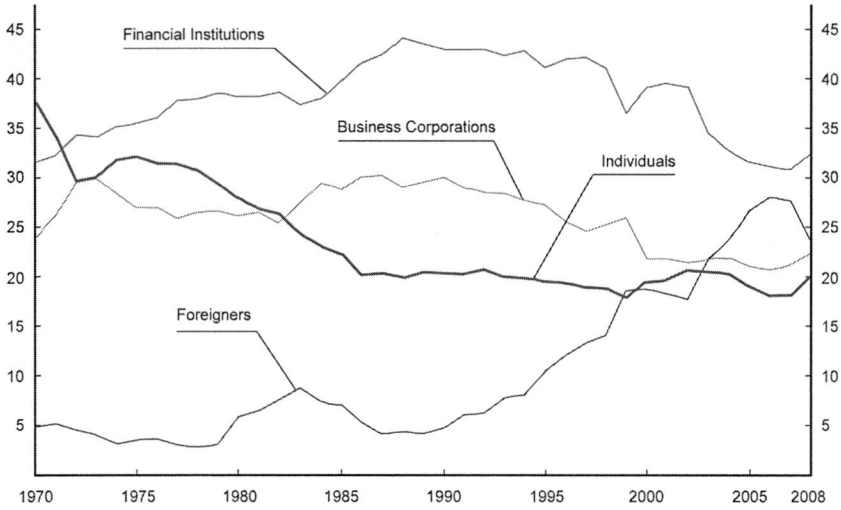

Figure 5.1 The ownership structure of listed firms in Japan, 1950–2008

Source: Tokyo Stock Exchange, *2008 Survey of Japanese Listed Firms*, Tokyo Stock Exchange, Tokyo, 2010

Notable changes regarding shareholder value maximization (s1) have taken place in the interactions between corporations and their individual and institutional shareholders. General decline in bank shareholding has been replaced by a substantial increase in shareholding by individuals and investment funds (see Figure 5.1). These new shareholders clearly view shareholder value maximization as an important objective to be pursued by the firm management.

Nevertheless, our selective adaptation framework provides predictions which are consistent with recent developments in Japanese corporate governance. As is shown in Table 5.1, the standard Japanese business norms provide little support in terms of the perception and legitimacy of shareholder value maximization (s1). For example, Japanese business leaders and company employees who value stakeholder welfare (e.g., norms N2 and N3) do not necessarily share positive perceptions nor appreciation for shareholder value maximization. Keiretsu and other firms with multiple equity connections (N1) are not necessarily in a position to promote shareholder value maximization for any one firm within a corporate group. Japan's new laws acknowledge shareholders' ownership of their firms. However, if the majority of outstanding shares of a corporation are owned by friendly keiretsu firms as is seen from Figure 5.1, the new laws telling corporations to follow shareholder value maximization does not provide legitimacy and the general perception is that it may not necessarily be useful for individual shareholders either.[21,22]

Initial reactions[23]

Many domestic and foreign individual shareholders as well as investment fund managers began taking advantage of the new opportunities, where they could question the managers and directors of the firms whose shares they held.

Many legal suits were brought against corporate managers and directors. The thrust of these legal suits is to question the validity of managers' and directors' actions in the light of shareholder value maximization and their mandated responsibility.

During the court proceedings for these shareholders' legal suits, the Japanese courts initially showed their acceptance of the notion that shareholder value maximization must serve as the essential guidance for managers and directors. Proposed poison pills at many firms were rejected by their shareholders in their general shareholders' meetings in June 2006, the first year when Japan's new company law became operational.

These legal suits convinced many managers and board directors that they might face potential legal cases against them from their companies' shareholders if their business decisions result in major losses to their companies and hence damage their market value. It is for these reasons that Japanese managers began taking time to listen to their investment fund shareholders who have active suggestions to make regarding corporate activities.

Reactions in later stages

After the initial transient period, it became clear to many Japanese managers that Japanese corporations could not accept the US-style shareholder-driven corporate management. Stakeholder value maximization theory was often used as a tool to rebut attempts by investment firms, both foreign and domestic. Firm management began to devise new poison pills to fight off hostile takeovers. This move was helped by Japan's shareholding patterns, in which large fractions of Japanese corporations' outstanding shares are still owned by keiretsu firms and other related corporations. Poison pills based on keiretsu relationships and cross shareholding began to emerge. (These are potent tools as poison pills, the effectiveness of which was proven during most of the post-World War II period (e.g., Morck and Nakamura, 1999).

Outside independent directors' involvement in the board's decisions (s2)

Under Japan's new company law, corporations now have options to choose between the traditional Japanese style corporate board system and a US-style executive committee system. Outside directors play different roles depending on which system a company chooses to adopt.[24] Using our selective adaptation framework similar to one shown in Table 5.1 for (s1), we can show that directors who are strictly outsiders to firms' operations are less likely to be acceptable to the firms as members of their boards. That is, the perception of (s2) is negative. Such outsiders are not likely to generate enough confidence in the company managers. Outside

Table 5.2. Percentage of outside directors at Japanese corporations

% outside directors	0	1–20	21–40	41–60	61–80	81–100
% corporations	56.2	31.4	9.1	2.5	0.0	0.8

Source: Yoshikawa (2003)

Table 5.3. Comparison of firm performance by the type of corporate governance (outside directors), Tokyo Stock Exchange, first section firms

	June 28, 2002	*June 30, 2005*	*Growth in sales revenue, 2002–2004*	*Growth in ordinary profit, 2002–2004*
New committee system (31 firms)	166.948 bn ¥	162.256 bn ¥ (-2.8%)	7.1%	36.9%
Traditional system with auditors	2689.191 bn ¥	3431.376 bn ¥ (+27.6%)	9.2%	51.7%

Source: Nikkei, August 16, 2005.

directors are not likely to generate enough confidence because few insiders think outside directors can understand all complex relationship-based business issues that are often important for firms' operations and decision-making. This does not provide legitimacy to (s2).

We also note that many of the outside directors that firms appoint come from their related firms.[25] On this basis, selective adaptation theory predicts that keiretsu firms whose inter-firm business relationships are particularly complex are less likely to choose to have the US-style outside director-based boards.

Consistent with our observation, Table 5.2 shows that Japanese firms generally use relatively few outside directors regardless of their origins.

A number of Japanese firms have implemented the new US-style committee system as part of their corporate governance system.[26] A recent survey of Japanese listed firms show that, statistically, those firms that had adopted the US-style committee system lag their peers who continued to use the traditional Japanese system in terms of firm performance (Table 5.3).

Competition in the market for corporate control (s3)

There is no question that Japan's M&A activities became much more active after the reform.[27] One of the fundamental issues raised about the Japanese business system was that, under the bank-based corporate governance system, it was difficult to cut inefficient parts of the company in order to grow more promising areas of business. An active market for corporate control allows firms to exchange component parts in order to form mutually more efficient corporations. With this process, more share value is generated.

We see that Japanese business norms (e.g., stakeholder value maximization) are consistent with friendly mergers but are not consistent with hostile takeovers on the basis of the public perception and legitimacy. Thus using our selective adaptation framework we can show that Japan's acceptance of a competitive market for corporate control will be more prevalent for friendly takeovers and mergers. On the other hand, hostile takeovers are less likely to be acceptable to Japanese businesses and society in general, even though hostile takeovers can play a positive complementary role in improving failing firms' quality of management.

Even if this prediction turns out to be the case, we should not underestimate the potential gains in economic efficiency from this new state for Japan's M&A markets. Until the 1980s, there were virtually no large-scale friendly mergers, let alone hostile mergers. The few large-scale mergers that took place generally were value-losing events. One main reason for such failures was the difficulty for different Japanese firms of integrating two highly firm-specific management systems, particularly with respect to personnel management systems. Japan's new company law allows more prompt reorganization of merged business units.

Another function of an active M&A market in the US is that the threat of a hostile takeover would often be effective for improving the quality of firm management, and, if needed, such a takeover could allow the incumbent management to be replaced by more competent management, which may improve economic efficiency, thereby creating more value in the process. While Japan's bank-based corporate governance system worked satisfactorily until the 1980s as a substitute for the market for corporate control,[28] it was not able to cope with the massive problems in the 1990s. This was particularly so because the lack of proper governance of the banks themselves led almost all Japanese banks to suffer from massive bad loan problems and most of them, facing banktrupcy, had to be bailed out by the Japanese government.

Based on selective adaptation we predict that Japan's reform will not bring many hostile mergers, and, as a result, there may be less efficiency gain than might otherwise be associated with such mergers or the threats of them.

We conclude that selective adaptation theory implies Japan's M&A markets after the reform, unlike those found in the US, will not be well balanced, in that most active transactions will still be friendly M&As. Relatively few possibilities for hostile takeovers are expected.

This is consistent with what we have observed so far for post-reform M&As: most domestic M&A activities are between affiliated firms and they are friendly mergers by definition.[29]

Transparency and information disclosure in accounting, financial and other reporting to investors and to the public (s4)

Transparency and information disclosure is essential for protection of all investors. It is particularly important for minority shareholders who may not have legal access to company books and other sources of information. Japan's corporate governance reform resulted in significantly increased requirements for transparency and information disclosure for corporate activities and protection of investors. The primary laws that are relevant here are the new company law, the new financial instruments and exchange law and the revised certified public accountants' law. In addition, Tokyo and other Stock Exchanges impose their own disclosure rules on the listed firms.

Japan's new company law now requires corporations to use consolidated financial statements as their primary means of reporting. It also requires corporations to report the value of financial securities and unrealized losses and profits annually.[30] Since Japanese firms conduct large numbers of transactions with their affiliated keiretsu firms of all kinds, individual (typically minority) shareholders would have difficulty figuring out corporations' overall soundness unless their consolidated statements are available. Japanese firms also own large amounts of securities, often including stocks of affiliated companies, to maintain their keiretsu relationships. New rules require corporations to report their financial positions for these securities annually. In the past many firms used their affiliated firms to manipulate their financial positions. For example, parent firms always post significant amounts of profits while their unlisted subsidiaries post losses. Under the new rules on disclosure and reporting, these questionable reporting practices are expected to decline. This is a positive implication for public investors.

However, we point out that, given Japanese corporations' persistent reliance on transactions with their related firms, these new laws are not likely to eliminate fraudulent accounting practices involving affiliated firms. Third-party monitoring of these interfirm transactions between affiliated firms is difficult at best and firms are likely to continue conducting questionable or illegal transactions in these areas.[31]

Another implication of consolidated financial statement-based reporting is that detailed stand-alone financial statements for each of the business unit companies under a holding company are no longer required. Since public investors invest in listed holding companies, not in their individual business units, such stand-alone financial reporting for each business unit might not appear essential. Yet, these business units are often the objects of M&As, and in those cases, potential acquirers and their shareholders, as well as the shareholders of the potential target firms, could become concerned about the accuracy with which specific segment information related to the unit being transacted is being disclosed. Disclosure requirements in this regard would be essential for transparent transactions of M&As.[32] (s4) receives modest support in terms of the positive public perception, legitimacy and complementarity.[33]

We expect that the new financial instruments and exchange law and revised CPA law will significantly improve corporations' reporting transparency and protection of both investors and creditors.

Protection of minority shareholders (s5)

Selective adaptation implies that Japan may choose corporate governance practices which are not as effective as in the US system for protecting minority shareholders. Japanese business norms do not generally support viewing minority shareholders' rights as an overwhelmingly important matter compared to the majority shareholders' rights. This suggests relatively little public support exists for positive perception and legitimacy. Although Japan's new laws will allow minority shareholders a new voice in the general shareholders' meetings and hence recognize their complementarity role, the rights of majority shareholders might still prevail in many cases.

In particular, if a firm's majority shareholders consist of keiretsu and other corporate and institutional investors who are friendly to the firm management, minority shareholders' objections raised in the general shareholders' meeting may not go anywhere.

A number of recent events are consistent with this implication of selective adaptation behavior. We discuss these below.

Stable shareholding as a poison pill

Facing potential hostile takeover threats, many Japanese firms have resumed their efforts to establish their base of stable shareholders which deteriorated considerably since the burst of Japan's financial bubble in 1990. These stable shareholders typically consist of affiliated (or keiretsu) firms, banks and other financial institutions, and other corporations some of which may also engage in cross shareholding. They are friendly in the sense that they do not sell off their shares in opportunistic manners. While some of this type of shareholding may enhance efficiency for the firms involved, most lack any compelling foundations in terms of shareholder gains. The primary purpose of many recent incidents of stable shareholding appears to be to guard the incumbent management against hostile takeovers. Stable shareholding proved to be highly effective as a poison pill. If up to 70% of a firm's outstanding shares are owned in pieces by many friendly corporate shareholders, no outsiders can succeed in their hostile takeover bids. As expected, most of the hostile takeover or unsolicited TOB attempts failed in Japan.[34]

Example: Steel Partners versus Bull-Dog Sauce

A couple of years ago poison pills were virtually unheard of in Japan. But a recent survey reports that, as of May 15, 2007, 14% of Japanese firms listed in the first sections of Tokyo, Osaka and Nagoya stock exchanges, and 8% of all listed firms (316 listed firms), have already implemented or are planning to implement anti-takeover defense schemes.[35] This is despite the argument by Warren Lichtenstein, chairman and chief executive of the Steel Partners (and many other investors from the US) that "companies with poison pills in the US typically have demonstrated poorer returns on invested capital, resulting in many of them being redeemed."[36]

Since the early 2000s, Steel Partners has been aggressively buying shares for takeover purposes of Japanese companies such as Bull-Dog Sauce (a maker of condiments), Yushiro Chemical Industry (machinery lubricants maker), Myojo

Foods (noodle maker) and brewer Sapporo Holdings. However, Steel Partners so far failed in all its offers to takeover the target companies. Steel failed either because of the target company's anti-takeover measures or friendly tenders by other companies.

Bull-Dog's defense began with its shareholders' approval of the company-proposed measures on June 24, 2007, to fend off Steel Partners' US$260 million takeover bid, including a warrants issue on terms that would dilute Steel Partners' stake. Steel Partners asked the Tokyo District Court for an injunction, but the court rejected Steel's request on June 28, 2007, arguing that the defensive plan is legal and dismissed a request for an injunction by Steel Partners. Steel Partners appealed to the Tokyo High Court.

The Tokyo High Court rejected Steel's appeal on July 9, 2007. Steel Partner's final appeal to Japan's Supreme Court also failed on August 7, 2007. Bull-Dog became the first Japanese company to have successfully avoided a hostile takeover using a poison pill. Bull-Dog's poison pill, which is one of the most popular ones being adopted by many Japanese companies, allows the company management to issue stock warrants to general shareholders so that the potential acquirer's stake will be diluted.

It is by no means obvious that Steel Partners' offer would have disadvantaged most of Bull-Dog's general individual shareholders. Nevertheless, Bull-Dog's management was successful in convincing them that Steel Partners, as company owner, would jeopardize Bull-Dog's ongoing business operations. More than 80% of shareholders voted for the management.[37]

The main argument used successfully by the management was that Steel Partners, being ignorant of Bull-Dog's business, will focus on maximizing the returns to shareholders at the expense of other stakeholders such as employees, customers, suppliers, banks and the like.[38,39] This argument by the Bull-Dog management is consistent with the stakeholder value maximization discussed above.[40] The potential problem with this is that it can be used to support incompetent management.

It is expected that, if Steel Partners decided to terminate its TOB and accepted the management warrants issue plan, Steel Partners would make about 5 million yen (about US$4.2 million). On the other hand, after paying all the costs related to their anti-takeover activities, Bull-Dog's financial conditions are expected to deteriorate significantly, registering significant amounts of losses throughout the 2007 fiscal year.[41]

Whether Japanese court ruling on the Bull-Dog case will make it harder for investment funds as well as other potentially hostile acquirers to gain acceptance in Japan remains to be seen. This is particularly so given our analysis above that hostile takeovers might not be part of Japan's selective adaptation behavior. But it might be that, by passing hostile takeover opportunities, Japanese shareholders may also be passing significant economic gains.[42]

We should note also that, despite the real difficulties Japanese minority shareholders face, there have been some successful revolts in general shareholders' meetings, where important management proposals on corporate governance were rejected. Such proposals can be rejected if more than one-third of the firm's shareholders oppose.[43]

Concluding remarks

We have applied a selective adaptation framework to analyzing Japan's corporate governance reform which started in the 1990s. The reform was undertaken with a conviction that Japan's discredited post-World War II bank-based corporate government system must be replaced by a US-style corporate governance system. The US corporate governance system was chosen as Japan's model because of the robust economic performance of the US economy. Japan's reform has introduced new laws which emphasize: shareholders' rights and shareholder value maximization, minority shareholders' rights; competition in the market for corporate control; and transparency and information disclosure. With strong public support, the Japanese parliament promptly passed these new laws which reflect Western liberal norms.

We have shown that, despite the US-style corporate governance laws and institutions that have come into effect for Japanese businesses, Japanese businesses' actual implementation of corporate governance practices so far were quite selective and uneven.

Our predictions based on application of our selective adaptation framework are mostly consistent with the observed levels of implementation of various aspects of US corporate governance practices (i.e. state variables (s1)–(s5)). Our analysis shows how (Western liberal norm-based) US-style corporate governance practices interact with Japanese business norms, and shows why some practices are more likely to be adopted than others.

We tentatively conclude that Japan's corporate governance reform will achieve increased competitive activities in the market for friendly M&As and see also significantly improved practices in disclosure and transparency, since Japanese public see positive perception and legitimacy in US corporate governance practices in these areas. On the other hand, corporate governance practices reflecting shareholder value maximization, outside directors and hostile M&As will receive less support because of the lack of the positive perception and legitimacy that these practices generate, even though these US practices may contribute positively in complementary ways under certain circumstances in Japan.

Notes

1   We should note that Western liberal norms and the business practices associated with them (e.g., individual rights, competition, transparency) are well accepted in Japan. In formulating specific business policies, however, these liberal norms are not uniformly and consistently applied. Selective adaptation explains this behavior as a consequence of Japanese compromise behavior, incorporating both Japanese and Western liberal norms.

2   Different authors give different predictions. Some predict that Japan will accept US-style corporate governance practices. For example, Hoshi and Kashyap (2001) note that Japan's corporate governance system in the twenty-first century will become like the system found in the US.

3   For example, Gilson and Milhaupt (2004) found that, as of March 2003 no firm which was a member of a bank-centred horizontal keiretsu group, had adopted the executive committee system of governance. Explaining this in economic terms is difficult.

4   These items on the list are not exclusive nor exhaustive. In the following, we define cultural norms and the associated values broadly and consider norms in a business as well as non-business context together.

5   Most of the discussions that follow hold in a comparative context for other countries in the West. We focus on Japan–US comparisons below because our interest is comparisons between Japan and the US regarding corporate governance practices.

6   But, as noted above, regular workers in Japan tend to be (prime-age) male workers (e.g., Nakamura, 1993).

7   Many Japanese corporations now use sent-in workers as well as regular workers side by side at their worksites. Sent-in workers are formally employees of manpower companies and generally enjoy little employment security.

8   Kiyokawa and Yamane (2004) report that 65% of managers and 71% of workers in Japan believe lifetime employment is desirable for employees.

9   The assembler firm's minority ownership position versus its suppliers means that the assembler firm can remain relatively small and allows suppliers to manage themselves independently, thus eliminating the types of agency costs many large vertically integrated firms typically suffer.

10 Compared to the Japanese keiretsu-based network model, the Silicon Valley network model of innovation and entrepreneurship involves less durable interfirm ties than are typical in Japan and more informal encounters of individuals "doing lunch" and otherwise transacting business in a bounded geographic space (Saxenian, 1994).

11 For example, the factors that increase state variables such as (s1) below will also benefit all shareholders, including minority shareholders (s5). We define protection of minority shareholders as a separate state variable, (s5) because increased (s1) may benefit large shareholders more than minority shareholders. This is because large shareholders have power over the firm management and hence can influence it to their advantage, unlike minority shareholders.

12 Highly developed economies, compared to developing economies, tend to have high levels of achievements in these state variables (e.g., Shleifer and Vishny, 1997; Porta *et al.* (1999).

13 Morck and Nakamura (1999).

14 Since societal norms and business norms are often intermingled and are not generally separable, we discuss them together below.

15 Aoki (1988: 154) describes the Japanese firm as a coalition of the two constituent bodies (shareholders and quasi-permanent employees) which share the uncertain returns from the firm's production activities. This model differs from the neoclassical model of the firm in which the shareholders are the owner and an exclusive residual claimant. Recent surveys show that Japanese executives think that shareholders are only slightly more important than employees. Executives are still in favour of distributing incremental profits equally among shareholders employees, internal reserves and investment (Araki, 2005: 51). Jacoby (2005) argues that these views are shared by the general population.

16 Tsurumi and Tsurumi (1991) present empirical evidence that value added maximization was followed as the corporate norm by Japanese semiconductor firms during the 1970s and 1980s.

17 Note that, unlike stakeholder value or value added maximization, shareholder value maximization is concerned with firms' residual values net of all expenses including workers' wages.

18 Potter (2003, 2004) proposed using perception, legitimacy and complementarity as instruments in explaining how selective adaptation proceeds in a foreign culture.

19 Note that in our calculation of the above interactions, the Western norms underlying particular US corporate governance practices that drive each of the state variables are not explicitly enumerated. We use the three instruments instead in these calculations. Use of the instruments this way allows us to make inferences about Japan's selective adaptation behavior in a practical manner. Use of the instruments this way would also make it possible to statistically test our hypotheses on selective adaptation when appropriately designed data (e.g., survey data) on corporate governance became available.

20 See Nakamura (2008, 2009) for selective adaptation analysis with respect to s2–s5.

21 Our conclusion is consistent with Roe (2001) who suggests that shareholder value maximization is, empirically, less likely to be accepted in countries where product market competition is weak (e.g., European markets) than in countries where product market competition is strong (e.g., the US).

22 Limited empirical evidence consistent with this prediction is also available. For example, a recent event study by Beason et al. (forthcoming) show that, for a randomly chosen sample of 90 firms listed in the first section of the Tokyo stock exchange in 2000–2001, little statistically significant positive relationships exist between the 836 restructuring announcements by the firms and their subsequent stock returns. Even though these restructuring activities were undertaken to enhance the firms' share value, the market was apparently not convinced.

23 See Nakamura (2006) for a brief survey on this.

24 In the new system majority members of each of the three executive committees must be from outside.

25 Most outside directors on Japanese company boards are not really independent directors. Many are sent in by their banks, affiliated companies, etc. (e.g., parent firm, subsidiary firm, keiretsu firms, etc.).

26 Firms adopting this system have some flexibility in designing how these three committees (appointment, compensation and auditing committees) relate to the board of directors. For example, Sony adopted the US-style system but Canon and Matsushita Electric Industries did not.

27 E.g., Arikawa and Miyajima (2007). However, the volume of M&As involving Japanese firms is still small by international comparison. The amounts (in billion dollars) of M&As reported for different countries for the first six months of 2007 are as follows: US (1,372.7); UK (632.3); Spain (217.6); Italy (208.5); Canada (185.4); France (159.9); Germany (155.1); Australia (110.4); and Japan (81.3).

28 E.g., Morck and Nakamura (1999).

29 In 2005, there were 3,734 reported transactions of M&As in Japan; 2,725 (73%) of these were between group (affiliated) firms, while the remaining 1,009 (27%) involved non-group firms. Furthermore the fraction of in-group M&As has been increasing since the early 1990s (Development Bank of Japan, 2007).

30 Prior to the reform, financial statements on stand-alone firms were the only required form of reporting. Firms did not report unrealized gains or losses of the securities they owned until they were sold in the market.

31 An example is the recent scandals in illegal accounting (e.g., creating of non-existing sale between related firms) by Fujitsu's and NEC's related firms (Nikkei, July 3, 2007).

32 A recent example of this involved Mitsubishi Motor's selling itself to Daimler Chrysler, while hiding the company's record on recallable manufacturing defects, etc. In the

end, Daimler Chrysler sold back all the shares of MMC to MMC and also received compensation for the lack of disclosure of manufacturing defects of the MMC.

33 Nevertheless we expect that the level of disclosure and transparency in Japan will continue to be less than that in the West for activities involving intra-keiretsu group transactions. One factor that contributes to transparency is revision of Japan's certified public accountants law, which has gone through a number of revisions since the 1990s. All revisions were intended to strengthen CPAs' monitoring capacity and improve quality of accounting auditing of Japanese listed and unlisted corporations. A number of scandals triggered these revisions. The most recent revision of 2007 requires accountants to audit and report fraudulent book keeping by firms with more stringency. It will also be accompanied by strengthen the penalty terms for accountants who violate the rules. The 2007 revision is expected to become operational in early 2008.

34 These include Oji Paper's attempt to absorb Hokuetsu Paper, Rakuten's attempt to takeover Tokyo Broadcasting System and Livedoor's attempt to takeover Nippon Broadcasting System.

35 Yomiuri Shinbun, Tokyo, May 17, 2007.

36 Empirical support for this statement, however, is somewhat mixed. See, e.g., Bebchuk and Cohen (2005), Gompers *et al.* (2003), Hermalin and Weisbach (2003).

37 Business press reports that the Tokyo District Court decided that: "Ultimately, (Steel Partners) has the view of disposing of its target company assets and must be seen as solely concerned with pursuing its own profit. As such it is appropriate to label (Steel Partners) … as an abusive buyer." (A. Tudor, Reuter, July 9, 2007.) The Japanese Supreme Court also argued that Steel Partner's takeover would not be consistent with Bull-Dog's survival as an ongoing concern. Their argument dose not seem to fully support the shareholder value maximization principle.

38 Before appealing to Japan's Supreme Court, Lichtenstein commented: "We feel we have no choice but to appeal to the Supreme Court of Japan as Bull-Dog Sauce's actions breach the principles of shareholder equality. We also categorically dispute the High Court's characterization of Steel Partners as an 'abusive bidder.' Our track record as an investor since 2002 clearly shows that Steel Partners is a long-term shareholder whose interests are aligned with those of the Company." The Japanese Supreme Court did not agree.

39 This argument, often used by the incumbent management in Japanese firms, can be effective if it has shareholder support. It is, however, not the case that Japanese courts always side with the incumbent management.

40 This seems also being interpreted in Japan to be consistent with maintaining the target firm as an ongoing concern.

41 Their expected loss for the first six months of the 2007 fiscal year is over US$10 million. They also expect to register losses for the entire fiscal 2007 year.

42 Whether this has negative economic efficiency implications is another serious question.

43 In its general shareholders' meeting held in February, 2007, Tokyo Steel's management proposal to make Tokyo Steel become one of Osaka Steel's subsidiaries was rejected because about 42% of shareholders opposed the proposal. The minority shareholders argued that the management proposal would seriously disadvantage the company shareholders. It was thought that many of the shareholders who voted against the management are individual shareholders owning a less than 1% of Tokyo Steel shares. We note that this opposition to the management was originally organized by the Singapore-based Strawberry Asset Management which used the internet extensively to achieve this. Without such major efforts by a skillful investment fund, the Tokyo Steel management would have won.

Works cited

Ahmadjian, C.L., and Lincoln, J.R., "Keiretsu, Governance, and Learning: Case Studies in Change from the Japanese Automobile Industry," *Organization Science* 12, 2001, 683–701.

Aoki, M., *Information, Incentives, and Bargaining in the Japanese Economy*, New York: Cambridge University Press, 1988.

Aoki, M., "Monitoring Characteristics of the Main bank System: An Analytical and Developmental View," in M. Aoki and H. Pratrick (Eds.), *The Japanese Main Bank System: Its Relevancy for Developing and Transforming Economies*, Oxford: Oxford University Press, 1994.

Araki, T., "Corporate Governance Reforms, Labor Law Developments, and the Future of Japan's Practice-dependent Stakeholder Model," *Japan Labor Review* 2, 2005, 26–57.

Arikawa, Y., and Miyajima, H., *Understanding the M&A boom in Japan: What drives Japanese M&A?* RIETI discussion paper series, Research Institute of Economy, Trade and Industry, Tokyo, 2007.

Bartlett, C.A. and Ghoshal, S., *Managing Across Borders: The Transnational Solution*, 2nd edn. Boston, MA: Harvard Business School, 1998.

Beason, D., Gordon, K., Mehrotra, V., and Watanabe, A., "Restructuring and Returns in Japan 2000–2001," this volume, 79–95, 2011.

Bebchuk, L.A., and Cohen, A., "The Costs of Entrenched Boards," *Journal of Financial Economics* 78, 2005, 409–433.

Burt, R., *Structural Holes: The Social Structure of Competition.* Cambridge, MA: Harvard University Press, 1992.

Development Bank of Japan, *Do M&A Improve Corporate Financial Performance in Japan?*, Development Bank of Japan, Tokyo, 2007.

Gilson, R. J., and Malhaupt, C., "Choice as Regulatory Reform: The Case of Japanese corporate Governance," Columbia Law and Economics Working Paper No. 251, 2004.

Gompers, P., Ishii, J., and Metrick, A., "Corporate Governance and Equity Prices," *Quarterly Journal of Economics* 118, 2003, 107–155.

Hermalin, B., and Weisbach, M., "Board of Directors as an Endogenously Determined Institution: A Survey of the Economic Literature," *Economic Policy Review*, April, 2003, 7–26.

Hoshi, T., Kashap, A., *Corporate Financing and Governance in Japan: The Road to the Future*, Cambridge, MA and London: MIT Press. 2001.

Jacoby, S.M., "Business and Society in Japan and the United States," *British Journal of Industrial Relations* 43, 2005, 617–634.

Japan Fair Trade Commission, *A Survey of Transactions of Auto Parts (Jidosha Buhin Torihiki ni Kansuru Jittai Chosa)*, (in Japanese), Tokyo, 1993.

Kiyokawa, Y., and Yamane, H., "Japanese Views on Labor (nihonjin no rodokan)," (in Japanese), *Ohara Shakai Mondai Kenkyujo Journal* 542, 2004, 14–33.

Lincoln, J.R., "Interfirm Networks and the Management of Technology and Innovation in Japan," in D.H. Whittaker and R.E. Cole (Eds.), *Perspectives on Technology Management (MOT) in Japan*, Oxford: Oxford University Press, 2006.

Lincoln, J.R., and Gerlach, M.L., *Japan's Network Economy: Structure, Persistence, and Change*, New York: Cambridge University Press, 2004.

Lincoln, J.R., Hanada, M., and McBride, K., "Organizational Structures in Japanese and U.S. Manufacturing," *Administrative Science Quarterly* 31, 1986, 338–364.

Morck, R., and Nakamura, M., "Banks and Corporate Control in Japan," *Journal of Finance* 54, 1999, 319–339.

Morck, R., Nakamura, and A. Shivdasani, M., "Banks, Ownership Structure, and Firm Value in Japan," *Journal of Business* 73, 2000, 539–569.

Nakamura, M., "Japanese Industrial Relations in an International Business Environment," *North American Journal of Economics and Finance* 4, 1993, 225–251.

Nakamura, M. (Ed.), *The Japanese Business and Economic System: History and Prospects for the 21st Century*, New York: Palgrave Macmillan, 2001.

Nakamura, M., "Mixed Ownership of Industrial Firms in Japan: Debt Financing, Banks and Vertical Keiretsu Groups," *Economic Systems* 26, 2002, 231–247.

Nakamura, M., "Japanese Corporate Governance Practices in the Post-bubble Era: Implications of Institutional and Legal Reforms in the 1990s and early 2000s," *International Journal of Disclosure and Governance* 3, 2006, 233–261.

Nakamura, M., "Selective adaptation of Anglo-American Corporate Governance Practices in Japan," in M. Nakamura (Ed.), *Changing Corporate Governance Practices in China and Japan: Adaptations of Anglo-American Practices*, London and New York: Palgrave Macmillan, 2008, 235–278.

Nakamura, M., Japanese Corporate Governance Reform, Globalization and Selective Adaptation, working paper, Sauder School of Business, University of British Columbia, May 2009.

Porta, R.L., Lopez-de-Silanes, F., and Shleifer, A., "Corporate Ownership Around the World," *Journal of Finance* 54, 1999, 471–517.

Potter, P.B., "Globalization and Economic Regulation in China: Selective Adaptation of Globalized Norms and Practices," *Washington University Global Studies Law Review* 2, 2003, 119–150.

Potter, P.B., "Legal Reform in China: Institutions, Culture, and Selective Adaptation," *Law and Social Inquiry* 28, 2004, 465–495.

Reischauer, E.O., *The Japanese Today: Change and Opportunity*, Cambridge, MA: Harvard University Press, 1988.

Roe, M.J., "The Shareholder Wealth Maximization Norm and Industrial Organization," *University of Pennsylvania Law Review* 149, 2001, 2063–2081.

Sako, M., "Suppliers' Associations in the Japanese Automobile Industry: Collective Action for Technology Diffusion," *Cambridge Journal of Economics* 20, 1996, 651–671.

Saxenian, A., *Regional Networks: Industrial Adaptation in Silicon Valley and Route 128*, 1994, Cambridge, MA: Harvard University Press.

Sheard, P., "Interlocking Shareholdings and Corporate Governance," in M. Aoki and R. Dore (Eds.), *The Japanese Firm: Sources of Competitive Strength*, Oxford: Clarendon Press, 1994, 310–349.

Shleifer, A., and Vishny, R.W., "A Survey of Corporate Governance," *Journal of Finance* 52, 1997, 737–783.

Tokyo Stock Exchange, 2005 Survey of Japanese Listed Firms, Tokyo Stock Exchange, Tokyo, 2006.

Tsurumi, Y., and Tsurumi, H., "Value Added Maximization Behavior of Firms and the Japanese Semiconductor Industry," *Managerial and Decision Economics* 12, 1991, 123–134.

Williamson, O., *The Mechanisms of Governance*, New York: Oxford University Press, 1996.

Yoshikawa, Y., *Corporate Governance for Improving Firm Value (kigyo kachi kojo notameno corporate governance)*, (in Japanese), Toyo Keizai, Tokyo, 2003.

6 Competing in the new global economy

Exploring the roots of Japanese scientific and technological innovation

Ken Coates and Carin Holroyd

Before the economic crisis of 2008–2009 hit, most governments around the world agreed that scientific and technological innovation held the key to 21st-century economic success. Even in the midst of the greatest downturn in a generation, countries and companies retained their belief that the new economy, based on the commercialization of science and technology, would outstrip traditional manufacturing in international importance. In an economic environment driven by the marriage of commerce, science and cutting edge technological innovations, Japan has been among the most successful of the Western nations. The number of patents, typically a benchmark for innovation, has jumped dramatically.[1] So, too, has the level of government investment in training, research and commercialization of science. Japan devotes more of its GDP to research and development than all but a couple of countries, and has focused on science and technology as the cornerstone of its attempt to remain highly competitive in the new global economy.

Globalization, and the current economic crisis, has raised the bar on international competitiveness. The emergence of new high technology economies in China, Taiwan and India presents major challenges to the leading Western nations, particularly the United States of America. The nature of technological innovation has altered fundamentally the economic balance and the central equations of national competitiveness. Countries like Israel, Finland and Singapore are using scientific and technological initiatives to transform their economies. Others – most notably Malaysia – have invested heavily in science and technology in hopes of leaping forward to the cutting edge of the new economy. This chapter reviews Japanese policies for the promotion of scientific and technological innovation and assesses some of the sectors in which Japan is at the scientific forefront. Japan's policies show its determination to prepare itself for the challenges of the globally competitive 21st century. Its scientific work and collaborations demonstrate how the research taking place in Japan influences and is influenced by other countries.

Leading industrial nations have long been at the forefront of technological innovation, aided through the second half of the 20th century by substantial university systems engaged in basic research, spin-offs from military developments, and significant corporate investments in research and development. This, combined with innovative approaches to product design and marketing, enabled the United States, Japan, Germany, Italy and the United Kingdom to maintain and expand their industrial bases. End-of-century developments, however, brought unexpected and dramatic changes. The emergence of the internet collapsed commercial distances, supported new services and products, and generated dramatic economic expansion, including the short-lived dotcom euphoria that engulfed the United States and other nations. While the internet attracted the greatest share of public attention, other scientific and technological developments promised equal if not greater change. Biotechnology, robotics, nanotechnology, pharmaceuticals, ubiquitous computing, advanced health care equipment and genetic engineering associated with plants, animals and human beings are among the new and expanding fields that have leapt from the scientific laboratory to the marketplace. It is in this economic and technological environment that Japan is endeavouring to maintain its competitive stature.

The foundations of Japan's 21st-century innovation economy

Japan has invested heavily in scientific and technological innovation. Even in the midst of the post-bubble recession, when most Western observers assumed that Japan would be hard-pressed to calibrate its economy in order to compete effectively on the international stage, the Japanese government devoted billions of yen to the construction of scientific facilities, urged greater academic–business collaborations, and pushed the business community to expand their research and development capabilities. Japan's science and technology efforts have been impressive and the country is surprisingly effective at converting scientific and technological advances into commercial products and services.

The Japanese innovation strategy, no less than efforts in other countries, has experienced uneven results. Policies to link regional economic development to scientific and technological investments have been less than successful. One of the largest initiatives in the country, Kansai Science City, has fallen far short of achieving its lofty ambitions.[2] A rapid restructuring of the national university system injected a commitment to commercialization into the hitherto aloof elite Japanese research universities but it will take time to achieve real results. In Japan, as elsewhere, expensive dollar investments in basic science generate a great deal of scientific data, but conversion of research results into marketable products and services can often take decades. On a broader scale, products and services designed and tested in the Japanese market are not assured of international success, a lesson that the country's leading mobile internet provider, DoCoMo, learned at considerable expense.

The current push for scientific and technological innovation bears all the hallmarks of contemporary globalization. The internationalization of scholarship means that scientists and technologists the world over are aware of the state of research and discovery in other nations. It also means that Japanese researchers are working alongside international scholars in such fields as nanotechnology, biotechnology, quantum and ubiquitous computing, tele-health, alternative energy sources, and robotics. While basic science is fundamentally important to national and global progress, it is the intersection between research and commercialization that holds the key to economic success. It is here, even more than in the well-funded laboratories and national research institutes, that Japan holds particular advantage, with a nation-wide commitment to bringing academics, government researchers and corporate developers together to produce viable and valuable products and services.

If there are key lessons to be gleaned from the Japanese experience, they lie primarily at the intersection of science, technology and commercialization. Japan does more science, with better equipment and more scientists, than most leading nations, at a scale several times larger than comparative populations would suggest. Japanese firms also do a considerable amount of research and development, demonstrating consistent commitment to advanced scientific and technological innovation. Japan draws heavily on funding and expertise from a broad spectrum of companies and supports work at the intersection of science and commerce, long a hallmark of the Japanese economy. Japanese scientists and technologists have well-established patterns of speaking to and working with designers, marketers and business people, and the government of Japan is encouraging even greater effort in this area.

A look at Japan's financial commitments, innovation strategy and commercial developments over the past decade is particularly interesting. How much money a country can afford, or cannot afford not to, invest in research and development generates considerable debate. Table 6.1 shows that most industrialized countries have been increasing their investments in research and development. Japan, however, stands out in the percentage of its gross domestic product (GDP)

Table 6.1 Spending on research and development

	1995	*2000*	*2002*	*2006*
Total R&D (% of GDP)				
EU-25/27	1.72	1.80	1.83	1.76
Japan	2.69	2.99	3.12	3.39
USA	2.51	2.72	2.67	2.62
OECD	2.09	2.24	2.26	2.26
Business R&D (% of GDP)				
EU-25/27	1.06	1.15	1.17	0.95
Japan	1.89	2.12	2.32	2.60
USA	1.80	2.04	1.87	1.70
OECD	1.40	1.56	1.54	1.35

Source: OECD Countries Spend More on Research and Development, Face New Challenge. 23 December 2004 (http://www.oecd.org/document/2/0,2340,en_2649_201185_34100162_1_1_1_1,00. html; OECD in Figures 2008 – Science and Technology>Research and development (I), 2006.

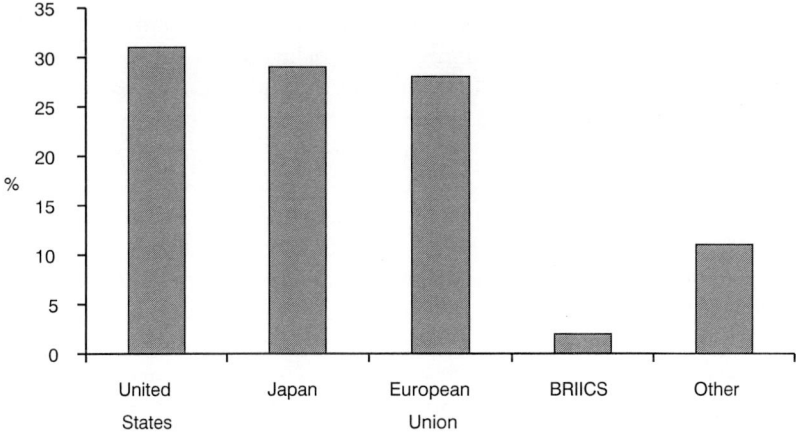

Figure 6.1 Share of countries in triadic patent families 2005

BRIICS refers to Brazil, China, India, Indonesia, the Russian Federation and South Africa.
Source: OECD, Patent Database, June 2008.

committed to this field. While in 2006, for example, the European Union (EU) average investment stood at 1.8% and the Organisation for Economic Co-operation and Development (OECD) average was 2.3%, Japan invested 3.4% of its extremely large GDP in research and development. Importantly, Japan also has an extremely high rate of business investment in research and development: 2.6% of GDP as against an OECD average of 1.4%.

This Japanese investment is paying off. Figure 6.1 shows the percentage share of total triadic patent families held by various countries. (Triadic patent families are described by the OECD as a set of patents that are registered at the European Patent Office, the Japan Patent Office and the United States Patent and Trademark Office. Using triadic patent family data focuses on patents of higher value, as patentees only register in all three countries if they deem it worthwhile, and allows for greater international comparability.) Japan was responsible for over 29% of worldwide patents in 2005 (the USA was responsible for 31% and the European Union 28.4).[3] When the percentage of triadic patent families are normalized using GDP and population, Japan ranks second worldwide after Finland (by GDP) and third after Finland and Switzerland (by population).

Japan is one of a handful of countries at the leading edge of research in many of the scientific fields that promise to revolutionize life in the twenty-first century. With the enactment of the Science and Technology Basic Law in 1995, Japan declared it would become an "S&T nation."[4] The advent of the Basic Law began a period of broad and deep reforms designed to modernize and revitalize the management and research structure of universities and to encourage greater government-industry-university collaboration. Historically, industry had been almost exclusively responsible for research and development in Japan. Universities graduated generalists who developed their specialized skills and knowledge while working for Japanese companies, and the universities themselves were managed by the Ministry of Education – with little commitment to commercialization. Informal connections permitted a limited flow of ideas across the academia–industry divide, but relations were far from close or symbiotic.

The arms-length relationships between university researchers and the private sector changed slowly over time. The first changes to the system were precipitated first by the oil crises of the 1970s and then by the 1990s collapse of the bubble economy. One of the resulting realizations that came out of the oil crisis was that government and industry had to work together to develop alternative sources of energy. This led to the creation of NEDO (the New Energy and Industrial Technology Development Organization), a large public R&D organization encouraging cooperation across the academy, industry and government.[5] The economic stagnation of the 1990s also spurred both government and industry to look at ways to re-energize the economy. A focus on science and technology and the encouragement of collaboration was determined to be one of the solutions. In January 2001, the Council for Science and Technology Policy (CSTP) was established within the Cabinet Office. Chaired by the Prime Minister, it includes 14 members, including six cabinet members heading ministries closely related to Science and Technology and seven executive members drawn from industry and academia.[6]

The First Science and Technology Basic Plan (FY1996–2000) increased government expenditures on research and development and focussed on the creation of a new research and development system.[7] Total government expenditures exceeded ¥17 trillion, competitive research funds were dramatically increased including support for 10,000 PhD students and post-doctoral fellows, and the promotion of industry–academia–government collaboration began in earnest. In 2001, the Second S&T Basic Plan (FY2001–2005) was launched with significant involvement from CSTP. Its key policy objective was to promote and prioritize basic research on national/social subjects. The amount of competitive research funding was doubled and again collaboration was enhanced. Some ¥21.1 trillion was invested in this Second Plan. Japan announced its aim of having 30 Nobel Laureates within the next 50 years. The First and Second Basic Plans were designed to solidify the foundation of science and technology in Japan. Public opinion polls, surveys of researchers (with a particular focus on female and younger scientists) and international comparisons of R&D funding and academic results (e.g. national share of S&T articles) were all undertaken to determine what Japan needed to do to be an advanced science and technology-oriented nation.

The Third S&T Basic Plan, launched in March 2006, called for annual government R&D spending of C$30 billion annually for five years.[8] This plan aims first to return to society, by enhancing the quality of life of its citizens and by commercializing the discoveries that have already been made, the last decade's investment in research and development.[9] The Third Basic Plan focuses on commercialization of technologies and public education of the potential of many of these discoveries to revolutionize life as it is currently known. Its major policy goals are stated as achieving a quantum leap in research and development, making breakthroughs in advanced science and technology and in sustainable development, developing a reputation as "innovator Japan", and creating a healthy aging society and a society with assured security. Within its overall strategy, the government identified four priority fields: life sciences (including biotechnology), information technology, environmental research and nanotechnology/material science. Several secondary priorities, including energy, *monozukuri* (manufacturing) technology, scientific and technological infrastructure and frontier science (outer space and oceans) were also identified. Japan's Basic Plan also continued the emphasis on promoting research among young scientists and female researchers, attracting more foreign researchers, spurring senior scholars and developers to further action and encouraging and strengthening industry–academia–government collaboration. The government placed very strong emphasis on patents and patent management, the funding of research through competitive grants, and maintaining a national system of evaluation. Japan placed a great deal of importance on the formation of research clusters, paying close attention to the seminal work, *The Competitive Advantage of Nations* (1990) by Harvard business professor Michael Porter, and seeking to combine research and innovation with old-style regional economic development.

A cornerstone of the Japanese science and technology effort was a major reorganization of the Japanese university system, completed over the objections of many faculty and administrators, which began in 1998. One of the primary goals was to encourage greater university–industry collaboration and thus broaden the impact of academic research. The ambition – to make the prestigious and highly accomplished national Japanese universities more responsive, more independent, and less like a branch of the national government – was striking. Even more noteworthy was the fact that the government largely succeeded in its goal, moving with dramatic speed in a sector long known for sober second thought and slow change. Laws such as the Law to Promote the Transfer of University Technologies allowed academic researchers to engage in commercial activities, as consultants, researchers, managers and even owners, thus breaking the long-standing formal division between the academy and the commercial sector. The results supported the government's initiative. In 1999, there were 28 university start-up companies in Japan. Five years later, under the new legislation, there were over 1,100. More than 300 had started operations in 2004 alone. University technology licensing offices expanded from 16 in 2000 to 39 in 2005.[10] And the biggest and most impressive accomplishment lay in the area of patents. In 2005, the number of patents awarded in Japan surpassed those granted in the United States, providing Japan with global leadership in an area that had long been something of a national embarrassment.

The Japanese government also placed a high priority on science and technology clustering, believing that combining industry, government and academic research in a single location would produce economies of scale and much greater collaboration. In 2001, METI started an initiative to create industrial clusters, hoping to revitalize regional economies in the process. A list of 19 projects was later pared down to 17, with the clusters involving 250 universities and close to 6100 companies. The Shikoku Techno Bridge has 300 companies and 5 universities collaborating in the health, welfare and environmental fields. The Tokai Project to Create Manufacturing Industry attracted 770 companies and 30 universities.[11]

MEXT (the Ministry of Education, Culture, Sports, Science and Technology) launched an Intelligent Clusters Project in 2002, creating 12 clusters designed to enhance connections between academic knowledge and industrial development. Outside of the formal plan, existing academia–industry–government clusters expanded, including Tsukuba Science City near Tokyo and Kansai Science City near Osaka and Kobe. In the clustering enterprise as in other areas, the government used direct investment, its influence over universities, and its commitment to science and technology advances to cajole, encourage and compel widespread engagement. Although the cluster initiative only recently started, it is not yet clear that this effort will generate the expected results. The imperatives of scientific innovation rest uneasily with the political and social requirements of regional economic development, particularly the effort to revitalize medium and smaller centres.

While the Japanese government is building and largely paying for the scientific, academic and administrative infrastructure to support the country's push toward science and technology pre-eminence, research, development and commercialization is also occurring in research laboratories and corporations across the nation. Japan's scientific leadership is evident in both areas identified as governmental priorities, like nanotechnology, and in other sectors in which Japan has been doing interesting and cutting-edge work for years including robotics, ubiquitous computing and the mobile internet.

The establishment of aggressive policy and subsidies and even the allocation of sizable sums of money to support scientific and technological innovation are no assurance of commercial success. A summary of some of the developments in each of these areas demonstrates the range, creative intensity, and impact of the Japanese innovation effort. The following is meant to be suggestive, rather than comprehensive, and to provide an overview of the commercialization of Japanese scientific and technological advances. Science no longer happens in national isolation. Japanese scientists work with scientists from other nations and each country's work influences the other. In many of the sectors in which Japan is playing a leading role its work has been influenced by and is influencing what occurs in other parts of the globe. Furthermore, commercialization efforts emerge in an intensely competitive international environment; indeed, governments around the world are supporting, encouraging and subsidizing innovation activities in all of the key areas of opportunity.

Mobile internet

In late June 2007, the Apple iPhone was launched to much fanfare. Enthusiasts touted its combination of mobile phone and personal digital assistant (PDA). What few mentioned outside of Asia was that almost everything the iPhone could do, the Japanese had been able to do on their mobile phones for years. Indeed, a unique convergence of policy, science, and commerce launched Japan into the mobile internet industry very early on, resulting in several national firms emerging as global leaders in both technological innovation and commerce success.

For several years in the 1990s, the internet had provided the best example of how Japanese regulation and policy stifled scientific and commercial creativity.[12] While Western nations revelled in the dot.com boom, Japan had moved very slowly to expand internet access, charging users among the highest fees in the industrialized world and offering comparatively poor service. That changed with the introduction of the mobile internet. In 1999, the mobile phone-based internet was introduced by a company called NTT DoCoMo (which means "anywhere"). The firm came to market with a portable telephone with a small screen with about 11 lines that allowed users to send e-mail and access a few internet sites. The system was named i-mode, with the "i" standing for information. Users only had to push a button to change the mode from phone to e-mail. Within just over a year, DoCoMo had five million users and three rival companies had entered the market. In one of the fastest technological uptakes in the lightning-fast internet revolution, by June 2006 there were 80 million subscribers to Japanese mobile internet services. Importantly, the service was unique to Japan. Most of the websites are available only in Japanese and hence have no significant audience outside the country.

Mobile internet users soon had access to a wide range of commercial services, ranging from train schedules, restaurant menus, hotel and dinner reservation systems, taxi cabs, GPS services, and numerous information sources, including news, sport scores, weather and traffic reports. Much of the information is targeted at specific age groups and a considerable amount of content is free. Japanese consumers showed themselves ready to pay for internet services and content, capitalizing on a micro payment system facilitated by the mobile internet. Companies recognized that there were literally millions of potential consumers using their mobile phones to access the internet and raced to bring their services to market. DoCoMo users now have access to about 12,000 official i-mode sites (which DoCoMo monitors to ensure that they are interesting, appropriate and easy to use) and 100,000 unregulated internet sites. Among the unregulated sites are both many abridged versions of regular websites and others that have been specially designed for the mobile environment. Not all the content is serious. In fact, as one writer summed it up, "Much of that content is about sex, sports, sex, astrology, sex, animation and sex." Nonetheless, along with sex, sports, astrology and animation are the practical sites listing transportation routes and schedules, restaurant and concert information, sports scores, stock prices, short games and music clips. There also many unique sites – a Starbucks locator service; a site "that brokers deals between drivers and cargo companies; Photonet that lets subscribers deposit their personal photos which can then be accessed by prospective dates; Warikan-kun "where after-work groups of imbibing colleagues can easily calculate how much everybody has to pay – including a discount for people who came later – and a proportionately higher charge for the boss," and many others.

About three-quarters of i-modes official sites are free. These make money by selling products or services through their web sites. Tsutaya, a big video and CD rental chain, earned more than ¥100 million a month in 2000. (Tsutaya sometimes sends redeemable electronic coupons to its i-mode users. During these video rental promotions, revenue from rental fees jumps by 60%.) According to the President of DoCoMo, the fee-charging sites usually charge ¥100–300 to subscribe. Most need about 10,000 subscribers to remain in business. Others, with over two million subscribers each paying about ¥200 a month, have total monthly sales of about C$4 million.

The Japanese mobile internet system is succeeding because it is simple to use, portable and offers an easy payment system, making it very attractive to consumers. Equally, the combination of ordering over the internet, an exceptionally efficient home delivery system and the use of convenience stores and depots at train stations as parcel pick up sites has made e-shopping very convenient. At the same time, both content providers and the parent company are able to make money. Content providers earn revenue through subscription fees and/or through the products or services they sell through their web-sites. DoCoMo makes money by charging a 9% commission to the content providers and monthly fees and data downloading costs to users. A typical i-mode user spends about ¥400 (C$3.95) a month on content subscriptions and ¥2,000 on downloading content. As of 2005, the mobile internet e-commerce market was estimated to be US$6.3 billion.

The mobile internet in Japan succeeded because it is so well suited to Japanese life. Many Japanese spend a good portion of their day away from home – it is not uncommon for people to travel two hours each way to work on a daily basis – and many activities require long waits in line. The mobile internet phone allows access to the internet at any time from anywhere. I-mode users, therefore, have very different usage patterns from people who go online from personal computers. The average time spent online for a Japanese personal computer internet user is 30 minutes per session, while the typical i-mode subscriber goes online for about 2 minutes. Much of what made the mobile internet popular in Japan did not translate into other markets. NTT DoCoMo and other Japanese mobile internet companies partnered with overseas firms to develop markets in other countries but had mixed success. South Korea has had the largest uptake of the mobile internet with more than half of South Koreans indicating that they access the internet over their mobile phones.

Japanese innovation centred on the i-mode did not stop with the initial application. In January 2001, DoCoMo launched its Java technology which makes possible many more complicated functions like networked games, real-time stock prices, chat software, business support programmes and, possibly most importantly, software enabling secure mobile commerce transactions. Competitors, including KDDI, J-Phone and J-Sky, entered the marketplace, adding new services and, equally importantly, competitive prices. By 2002, companies were launching 3G systems which added music and video capabilities. Then digital camera-equipped cell phones capable of taking, sending and receiving photographs came along. Music, video and photo sharing over the mobile phone came next along with the option of developing an integrated personal portal site. Even more importantly, mobile phones are now being used as "wallets" with the phone having the capability to store rail passes, tickets, money and even to act as a door key. Fingerprint security devices ensure that the phones cannot be used by anyone but the owner. At home, the phone can be hooked up through broadband access to the television, radio and personal computer.

In 2009, one of the areas of interest for NTT DoCoMo is the development of phones that can be operated without having to be held in a hand. Some mobile internet analysts believe that cell phones in their current form will not survive and in fact, the term "handset" will soon become a quaint term referring to a past age! By 2020, wireless phones will become accessories, stylish devices worn on the body. One prototype is shaped like a pair of headphones and is controlled by using the eyes. The interface detects the movements of the eyes, translating the position and line of sight into commands operating the phone. A second prototype is worn like a ring and sounds are heard by placing this "ring" finger in the ear. Another glimpse of the future gives mobile phones the ability to show what lies beyond obstructing buildings by using GPS and a variety of sensors to gather data on the surrounding area so that users can learn about what lies beyond where the device is pointed.[13]

At the height of global euphoria about the mobile internet, DoCoMo launched an aggressive international expansion. Partnerships with companies in America, Europe, Asia and other regions laid the foundation for a permanent international expansion. The plans fell afoul of the dot.com market adjustment, and DoCoMo was forced to pull back dramatically. DoCoMo's 3G phones were not an immediate success in other markets, competition forced prices to unsustainable levels, and the commercial mobile internet in other countries failed to match the reach and impact of the nation-specific Japanese mobile system. Within Japan, however, the mobile internet became the cornerstone of a rapidly expanding e-commerce and mobile phone-activated consumer market. Along with South Korea and ascendant markets in Taiwan, Hong Kong and Singapore, Japan remains among the most effective and innovation mobile internet environments in the world, albeit with a commercial model that has proven difficult to export.

Nanotechnology

Nanotechnology, the manipulation of matter on a molecular and atomic scale to build tiny machines, has enormous potential for fields as diverse as electronics, biotechnology and medicine. The backbone of nanotechnology is carbon-walled nanotubes, invented in 1991 by NEC's Sumio Iijima. Nanotubes are cylindrical objects made of tiny carbon atoms. They are much stronger than steel, resilient and lightweight with good thermal conductivity. The tiny machines they are used to build can be injected into bodies to repair organs and fight disease, put into space or underwater to mine resources or used as energy sources for phones, watches and computers. So great is the potential of nanotechnology, proponents say, it could bring about the Second Industrial Revolution. Nanotechnology researchers aim to be capable of developing everything from fingertip-sized supercomputers to non-degradable plastics that allow the development of a biochip that can be embedded in the human body, to lighter and stronger new materials that can be used to make featherweight bullet proof vests and super tough lightweight coatings for aircraft. As in other high technology sectors, nanotech is intensely competitive internationally, with countries around the world subsidizing major research and development initiatives in this fast-moving sector.[14]

The Japanese government believes the successful development of nanotechnology to be important to the nation's economic future. Estimating that the impact of nanotechnology on the domestic economy will be about C\$310 billion by 2010, the government has been investing close to C\$1 billion annually since 2001 in R&D in nanotech materials. It has set up four nanotech centres of excellence, four nanotech intelligent clusters and four nanotech centres for common use. Concentrating resources in large research centres appears to be particularly important for nanotechnology research as it is such an interdisciplinary and expensive area of research. It is not only the Japanese government involved in the research. Ten major Japanese companies (including NEC, Hitachi, Sony and Fujitsu) have nanotechnology research centres. One of the challenges of the industry is that carbon nanotubes are expensive to produce. Companies that produce them, like Mitsui's wholly owned subsidiary, Carbon Nanotech Research Institute, Inc., which has the largest production facility in the world, are focussed on bringing down the cost. Generally, the best way to do this is to produce nanotubes in large quantities and take advantage of economies of scale. Mitsui has decided not to wait for the market to develop: it is giving nanotubes free to manufacturers in Japan to encourage them to find unique ways to use the material.

Japan is not the only country interested in nanotechnology. The USA, Canada, Europe, South Korea, China and Taiwan among others are also investing in nanotech research. (The US government has estimated the global nanomarket to be US\$1 trillion by 2050.) There are many aspects of nanotechnology research – nanomaterials, nanobiology, environment and energy, nanoprocessing technology, IT and electronics. While the US is leading in some areas like nanobiology, Japan appears to be focusing on the IT/electronics and nanomaterials fields. Its real strength, however, is in commercialization, driving products to market faster. "The EU and US are superb at creating ideas, but they are not as good as Japan at materializing those invented technologies," according to Shuji Tsuroka of Mitusi's Carbon Nanotech Research Institute, Inc.[15]

Photovoltaic homes

The development of photovoltaic panels, which convert sunlight to electricity, provides one of the useful illustrations of the Japanese approach to innovation and commercialization of science and technology. Japan's long-standing interest in energy conversation and alternate energy sources accelerated in the late 20th century. The signing of the Kyoto Protocol highlighted Japan's commitment to energy conservation while also drawing attention to the country's shortcomings in this area. The initiative accelerated with the creation of the Advanced PV Generation programme in 2001, part of an ambitious plan to expand the use of a variety of renewable resources within the country. A national goal for the production of electricity through photovoltaic means was a 20-fold growth, from 4.8 GW by 2010 to 100 GW by 2030. Support was provided for scientific and technological research in this field, but more was needed to overcome consumer resistance to the new and expensive technologies.[16] In this area, the Japanese government again believed that they could see promising commercial opportunities.

In the case of photovoltaic research – an area where the Japanese commitment to science-based innovation meshed with the political priority of reducing dependence on imported oil – the national government made major efforts to convince home owners to commit the US$20,000 needed to install a proper system. A generous series of national and local subsidies, which started at 50% of the costs in 1994 and expired in 2006, provided incentives to homeowners willing to use photovoltaic electricity. By the early 2000s, Japan was recognized as an international leader in the field of domestic photovoltaic systems, having convinced thousands of consumers and, importantly, many of the leading residential construction companies in the country to use the system. Japanese firms soon led the photovoltaic industry. Sharp accounted for almost one-quarter of the world's production; the next three largest Japanese firms – Kyocera, Sanyo and Mitsubishi Electric – produced another 24%. Tokuyama dominated the supply of silicon needed for the panels, with 20% of the total. Until 2006, and the end of the home use subsidies, Japanese firms controlled almost half the world market. They had taken the leadership from the Americans in 1998 and were producing four times the number of photovoltaic modules as the US in 2004. However, German companies led by Q-Cells made quick and dramatic inroads into the photovoltaics market after 2006. The German government put millions of euros into the research and subsidization of solar cells. The result was that 18% of the world's solar production came to be concentrated in Germany and in 2007 Q-Cells came to be the industry leader. In November 2008, in an attempt to regain its top position, Sharp announced an alliance with Enel Spa, Italy's largest utility and Europe's number two power company, to set up a plan to produce thin-film solar cells in Italy.[17]

This sector provides insights into Japanese stimulation of scientific research and commercialization. The initial support for research in the field was matched by an aggressive campaign of subsidies and promotion for residential installations. This, in turn, allowed the private sector to develop both the economies of scale and the manufacturing expertise necessary for commercial viability. Over a relatively short period, photovoltaic energy generation moved from the laboratory to the marketplace. In the process, Japan emerged as the global leader in photovoltaic exports, establishing market domination that other countries will have difficulty matching. The combination of government signaling, research support, consumer subsidies and commercial responsiveness helped Japan create a classic 21st-century industry, with prospects for continued expansion. When the homeowner subsidies ended, Japan has had difficulty holding on its early competitive opportunities in the area, discovering that German investment and encouragement of solar panel research shouldered Japanese products aside in several crucial markets.

Robotics

Over the past two decades, Japanese companies and research institutes have been investing heavily in advanced robotic technology. Industrial robots have long been popular in a range of industries. Japan still accounts for about 45% of the worldwide stock of operational industrial robots. METI has begun promoting the next generation of robots – those that can be used in daily life as security guards, cleaners, receptionists or child minders. NEDO, a METI-affiliated institution, hoped that commercialization of these kinds of robots would begin by 2010. The Japan Robot Association predicts that the Japanese market for these next generation robots will reach US$14 billion by 2010 and more than US$37 billion by 2025.[18] NEDO used the 2005 Aichi World Exposition to showcase a number of these robots in action. There were cleaner robots, security robots and wheelchair robots to move people with disabilities.

Mitsubishi Heavy Industry's robot Wakamaru can hold simple conversations, patrol a house, take pictures (the cameras are in his eyebrows) and alert the home's owner via e-mail if it finds a problem. It went on sale in September 2005 for about C$15,000. Secom Robot X is a security robot designed to patrol schools and factories. Equipped with a flame sensor, fire extinguisher and a camera, Secom looks like a small vehicle and can move at up to 10 kph. PaPeRo (Partner Personal Robot) is NEC Corp.'s childcare robot that can remain in the home and interact with members of the family. PaPeRo walks, dances, connects to the internet autonomously and interacts with users so that it develops its own personality. It can distinguish ten different users by face and voice and recognize about 650 words. NEC is continuing to work on PaPeRo's communication skills and even hopes to give it a sense of humour.

The development of humanoid robots designed to look like people and fit into the human environment is an important area of robotic research. Humanoid robots can be used to operate machinery, act as tour guides, carry things or assist the ill or physically disabled. They may perform tasks that are dangerous for humans like cleaning up toxic spills or going into mineshafts or tunnels. Honda's Asimo, a spaceman-like robot unveiled in November 2000, is probably the most famous humanoid robot. Asimo can walk up stairs (its advanced "i-walk" technology is the culmination of 14 years of research and many lumbering prototypes),[19] can run at 10 kph, switch lights on and off, open and close doors, respond to simple voice commands and recognize faces. Asimo currently serves as a tour guide and greeter at a number of high-tech companies in Japan.

Inspired by the Kobe earthquake, many Japanese researchers began work on the development of rescue robots. These snake-like machines are designed to manoeuvre through small cracks in rubble with cameras and microphones to find people human rescuers cannot access. One rescue robot, IRS Soryu (Blue Dragon) is 1.2 metres long, remotely controlled and can bend at its two joints or even roll on its side to pass through small openings. Kohga, another rescue robot, looks like "a three-foot long string of big metal sausages, each with a small, tank-like tread".[20] Kohga may become contorted going through the rubble but it should always be able to untangle and pull itself along. The National Institute of Advanced Industrial Science and Technology (AIST) and the Tokyo Institute of Technology have developed a transformer or self-reconfigurable modular robot. This robot has the ability to adapt to its environment by changing shape in response to its surroundings. A collection of small, linked robotic modules, it operates without any outside support. A camera can be attached to the head. This kind of robot could be used in rescue operations, planetary exploration or in any situation where it is not known in advance what environment may be encountered.[21]

Pet robots are probably the most well known of the Japanese robots. While they are developed as toys they utilize many new robotic technologies including sensory perception, verbal interaction, emotional expression and tele-manipulation. All of these will also have an impact on the development of future humanoid and helper robots. Sony's AIBO (short for Artificial Intelligence Robot) is probably the most well known. The third-generation AIBO was launched in September 2005 and comes with improved communications functions, takes photos with a built-in camera and allows the photos to be transmitted to the owner's personal computer through a wireless LAN. AIBO can be put on "house-sitting" mode and transformed into a guard dog that detects noises and voices and records them, takes photos and transmits the data to a mobile phone.[22]

Paro, although a pet robot, was developed as a substitute for real animals. Programmed to behave as if it were alive, Paro has "tactile, vision, audio, posture sensors (and) seven actuators beneath its soft white artificial anti-biotic fur." Designed for use in hospitals and elderly care facilities as a kind of robot therapy, Paro encourage patients to talk and brings them comfort and peace of mind, thereby also reducing problem behaviour. Workers report seeing very elderly people who had not shown much response for years, smile, talk and interact with Paro as if it were alive. Paro was entered in the *Guinness Book of World Records* in 2002 as "the world's most soothing robot".[23]

Japan is definitely the market leader in robotics with about 28% of the world market. It is followed by the United States and Germany. South Korea, however, is probably most like Japan in how it sees robots in its future. The South Korean Ministry of Commerce, Industry and Energy expects global robotics to turn into a US$150 billion industry by 2016. South Korea sees robots being used to help with the country's aging population and pictures a robot in every home in the next decade and a half. South Korea is even experimenting with warrior robots – a robotized chassis with a machine gun – and guardian robots for patrolling its border with North Korea.[24] Japan brings a unique set of attributes to the robotic sector, including government support, major industry investments, and a high level of social and consumer acceptance of machine-based services. Indeed, the comfort level that many Japanese consumers have with scientific and technological innovation have helped the country retain its place as the world's leading developers, consumers and innovators in the robotics field.

Ubiquitous computing

The next phase of digital technology – ubiquitous computing or the idea of one person accessing many computers – is another area of substantial Japanese commitment. Ubiquitous computing involves embedding electronic tags or ucodes in virtually everything through the use of bar codes, radio frequency identification (RFID) chips, smart cards and electronic tags. Coded chips can be attached as electronic tags to all sorts of products and services as has already been done for industrial equipment, fax machines and digital cameras.

To access the information contained in all these embedded tags, people carry ubiquitous communicators, PDA-like devices that read the ucode tags and retrieve the relevant data. The information is then stored in a huge database that allows for the incorporation of context – information on how a particular piece of data is of importance to the individual accessing it. Potential applications are numerous and include hospital safety (before a drug is administered a nurse or doctor checks the ucode on the medicine bottle with the individual patient), supply chain management (allows for the traceability of consumer goods), communications (tags are embedded in pavements and street signs to provide information to tourists about local landmarks and to the sight impaired about obstacles or directions) and food safety (codes are attached to food packages containing information on how the food was produced and distributed and indicates if a package has been tampered with). One of the variations on ucodes is active tags that continually monitor a product. These can be used, for example, for placement in food shipments to monitor the temperature and other conditions throughout its journey.

A leading version of the use of ucodes is the T-Engine, founded by Ken Sakamura. This system is "arguably the most advanced ubiquitous computing platform in the world", according to Jan Krikke of *Pervasive Computing* magazine.[25] The T-Engine Forum is an initiative initially set up by five Japanese chipmakers and 17 other Japanese technology firms. It now has 500 members – nearly all of Japan's blue-chip and large global companies. The T-Engine has government associations in Singapore, China, South Korea, Taiwan, Vietnam and Thailand and 60 academic partners, mostly from Asia. The T-Engine Forum works on a standardized system to ensure compatibility, overcoming earlier problems where weak standardization, designed to allow developers to modify the operating system to suit their own requirements, brought in subtle differences which meant that systems were not compatible. Ubiquitous computing is being tested in Kobe and in the Ginza area of Tokyo. When entire cities are tagged, robots equipped with ucode readers can be tasked with making deliveries of food or medicine. Japanese firms are very optimistic about the medium-term commercial potential of this new and pervasive technology.

Ubiquitous computing has yet to catch on with consumers in the same way as have other scientific and technological developments. Indeed, the sector remains substantially laboratory-based, with some promising commercial tests underway, largely in pre-consumer applications. Japan has established a significant international leadership role in this important field, and has been working very hard with other Asian nations to establish industry standards that could well protect Japanese innovations in the near to medium term. Most importantly, ubiquitous computing demonstrates the constant commitment to innovation and scientific expansion within the Japanese system, as the country's officials, business leaders, scientists, inventors and consumers look eagerly for the next commercializable opportunity.

Conclusion

Since the bursting of the Japanese "bubble", Western commentators have consistently underestimated the level of innovation and creativity in Japan. To a degree that few observers have credited, the Japanese government made a formidable commitment to basic science and technology research, rapidly expanding its level of support and priority for this internationally competitive field. Japanese firms have remained engaged in the scientific enterprise, partnering with each other, with a transformed and re-energized academic community, and with government agencies in pursuit of new basic science discoveries and commercially exploitable opportunities. The commitment to fields like robotics, the mobile internet, nanotechnology, biotechnology, health and photovoltaic panels has been matched by a willingness to experiment with administrative measures such as reorganizing the national university system, investing in major science-based urban clusters, and encouraging a culture of government–business–academia collaboration.

Japan's innovation strategy is not necessarily the best in the world. Finland comes out on top on many of the key indicators. Japan benefits, of course, from the size of its economy and the breadth and depth of its investments in science, technology and innovation.

Perhaps the key lesson from Japan is the importance of cooperation in the national interest. Collaboration – between firms in related sectors and between government, universities and colleges and the private sector – likely holds the key to national success in innovation. Japan has competing economic interests and divided political loyalties, but a strong national government with the resources to invest in major innovation projects has managed to preserve the country's role as a global leader in innovation. Governments and businesses would do well to pay close attention to developments in Japan and to the Japanese model for scientific and technological innovation; unfortunately, there has long been much more interest in describing Japan's "Lost Decade" of the post-bubble economy than in looking at the major investments made in the country during this allegedly dormant period. While the Japanese model cannot be transferred directly to other countries, the Japanese experience illustrates one national approach to ensuring competitiveness and prosperity in the 21st century. In the midst of the 2008–2009 downturn, with traditional manufacturing in retreat and with concerns about environmental sustainability and fiscal stability constraining revival efforts, Japan's commitment to scientific and technological innovation might well provide yet another strategy for adapting to rapidly changing economic conditions. Both the science and the markets for new products and services are truly global in nature, as is the competition for the ideas, the personnel and the opportunities. The 21st century, it seems, is destined to belong to the countries that best combine research, innovation, and commercialization. As the government, business and academic collaborations of the past decade reveal, Japan is determined to be one of those countries.

Acknowledgements

This chapter is based, in part, on K. Coates and C. Holroyd, *Innovation Nation: Science and Technology in 21st Century Japan* (London: Palgrave Macmillan, 2007).

Notes

1 For details on Japan's performance in patents, see the statistical material provided by the Japan Patent Office (http://www.jpo.go.jp/index_e/public_information.html).
2 The uneven development of Kansai Science City is described in Holroyd and Coates, *Innovation Nation: Science and Technology in 21st Century Japan* (London: Palgrave Macmillan, 2007).
3 OECD Science, *Technology and Industry Scoreboard, 2007.*
4 For a copy of the Science and Technology Basic Law, see http://www.mext.go.jp/english/kagaku/scienc04.htm.
5 The organization's history, including the conditions of its establishment, is described at http://www.nedo.go.jp/english/introducing/what.html.
6 Cabinet Office Government of Japan, "Council for Science and Technology Policy" (http://www8.cao.go.jp/cstp/english/about/administration.html).
7 The First Science and Technology Basic Law (http://www.mext.go.jp/english/kagaku/scienc04.htm).
8 The details of the plan can be found at http://www8.cao.go.jp/cstp/english/basic/3rd-Basic-Plan-rev.pdf.
9 Science and Technology Basic Plan, Government of Japan, 28 March 2006, http://www8.cao.go.jp/cstp/english/basic/3rd-BasicPlan_06-10.pdf.
10 John Walsh, Yasunori Baba, Akira Goto and Yoshihito Yasaki, "Promoting University-Industry Linkages in Japan: Faculty Responses to a Changing Policy Environment", *Prometheus,* 26 (2008).
11 For details on the plan, see http:///www.rieti.go.jp/users/cluster-seminar/pdf/028-1_e.pdf See also Katryn Irbata-Arens, *Innovation and Entrepreneurship in Japan*, Cambridge: Cambridge University Press, 2005.
12 This section is drawn from *Japan and the Internet Revolution* by Carin Holroyd and Ken Coates and also in "Entering the Internet Race: The Early Years of the Internet and Internet Commerce in Japan", *Journal of Internet Banking and Commerce,* Spring 2005, 10(1).
13 "Cellular Firms Eye Hands-free Future", *Nikkei Weekly,* December 15, 2008, 15.
14 This section is drawn from Holroyd and Coates, *Innovation Nation.*
15 Kurt Hanson, "Mitsui Mines for Nanotech Gold", J@pan Inc. July 2003.

16 Paul Parker, "Residential Solar Photovoltaic Market Stimulation: Japanese and Australian lessons for Canada. *Renewable and Sustainable Energy Reviews* 12(7) 1944–1958.

17 "Sharp Ups Ante in Solar-cell Competition", *Nikkei Weekly*, 8 December 2008.

18 "Robots Dance and Play at Japan exhibition", *MSNBC*, June 9, 2005.

19 "Business: Dr. Doi's Useless Inventions", *The Economist,* 23 December – 5 January 2001, Vol. 357, Issue 8202, 102.

20 "A Slithering Lifesaver", *Newsweek,* 20 October 2003, E2.

21 Shogo Matsuda, "Transformer 'bots get Modular to Shift Site-specific", *Nikkei Weekly*, 15 May 2006. Visit to AIST Science Square Tsukuba, June 2006.

22 Details about the AIBO and its house-sitting capabilities can be found at http://support.sony-europe.com/aibo/downloads/en/Quick_EN.pdf.

23 See the report reports on Paro available at http://www.parorobots.com/whitepapers.asp.

24 Andrew Salmon, "I, Robot – Is This the Face of the Future?", *South China Morning Post,* 6 May 2007.

25 Jon Krikkem "T-Engine: Japan's Ubiquitous Computing Architecture is Ready for Prime Time", *Pervasive Computing* (May–June 2005), http://csdl2.computer.org/comp/mags/pc/2005/02.b2004.pdf.

7 Soft power and the globalization of Japanese popular culture

William M. Tsutsui

The rise of Japanese pop culture has been one of the undeniable global phenomena of the late twentieth and early twenty-first centuries. This rapid ascent and global diffusion has been remarkable in its speed and breadth. Japanese anime (animation) and manga (comic books/graphic novels) have become youth favorites internationally; Japanese video games and television series claim devoted followings around the world; *sudoku* number puzzles have replaced crosswords in popularity and pushed up pencil demand globally; Japanese fashion defines chic in Asia as well as Europe. As Timothy Craig has put it,

> In short, Japanese pop culture is ubiquitous, hot, and increasingly influential. Once routinely derided as a one-dimensional power, a heavyweight in the production and export of the "hard" of automobiles, electronics, and other manufactured goods but a nobody in terms of the "soft" of cultural products and influence, Japan now contributes not just to our material lives, but to our everyday cultural lives as well.[1]

Move over Toyota, Honda, and Hitachi, these days Japan means Hello Kitty, Super Mario, and Miyazaki Hayao.

Over most of the past century and a half, the impact of Japanese culture on Western life has generally been figured in terms of highbrow art forms. In the late nineteenth century, Japan's colorful *ukiyo-e* prints famously inspired the French Impressionists; in the early twentieth century, literary forms like *tanka* and *haiku* influenced American modernist poets and Japanese aesthetics inspired architects like Frank Lloyd Wright; after World War II, urban art-house cinemas screened the cerebral works of Kurosawa, Mizoguchi, and Ozu. Western scholars, having focused for so long on Japan's sway over American and European elite culture, have been caught a little off-guard by the global ascent of Japanese pop since World War II. Although academic studies are now available in English on topics from Japanese hip-hop to television game shows to Pokémon, Western scholars have yet to explore fully the factors that explain Japanese popular culture's current worldwide appeal, let alone the forces in postwar Japanese society that unleashed the imaginative energies of manga and anime, *tokusatsu* (special effects) films and *kawaii* (cute) character goods. Understanding the historical roots and contemporary manifestations of what Douglas McGray has famously referred to as Japan's "Gross National Cool" is a project still far from complete.[2]

The current catch phrase applied to issues such as these is "soft power." The Harvard political scientist Joseph Nye coined the term, which has now migrated from academic and policymaking circles to general use, in the second half of the 1980s. Soft power, Nye wrote, is "the ability to get what you want through attraction rather than coercion or payments. ... When you can get others ... to want what you want, you do not have to spend as much on sticks and carrots to move them in your direction."[3] Hard power consists primarily of the military and economic capabilities that a country possesses and can deploy on the international stage, while soft power arises from a country's culture, values, and ideas, what CNN has called "the art of influencing people to like you."[4] In his 2004 book *Soft Power: The Means to Success in World Politics*, Nye argues that hard power and soft power together are responsible for the rise and decline of states. In the American case, he observes, a powerful military and economic might can be used as coercive forces against other countries, but the people of the world are also influenced by the attractive power of America's culture and values, including Hollywood movies, popular music, and the vision of an "American lifestyle" founded on freedom, democracy, and prosperity. Thus, as Nye suggests, "[S]oft power is more than just persuasion or the ability to move people by argument. ... It is also the ability to attract, and attraction often leads to acquiescence."[5] At least in theory, then, states should be able to use the soft power of cultural appeal, just like the hard power of tanks and development loans, to further their national agendas globally.

With this in mind, three central questions – all of which scholars have been actively wrestling with of late – emerge when considering Japan today and the dramatic international ascent of Japanese pop culture over the past several decades. First, how did Japan come to show such creativity in its entertainment products? What, in other words, is the source of the imaginative explosion behind Japan's postwar pop culture boom? Second, why has the rest of the world been so attracted by things like anime, manga, Hello Kitty, video games, monster movies, and Japanese fashion and food? What, in short, explains the appeal of Japanese products on a global scale? And third and finally, given the phenomenal international rise of Cool Japan, what is the meaning, not to mention the potential utility, of the resulting soft power? That is to say, how might Japan be able to capitalize on the mass popularity which its pop culture creations now enjoy around the world?

Atomic inspirations

First of all, then, how can we determine the origins of the remarkable creativity that has driven contemporary Japanese popular culture?

Historically, it is possible to identify a wide range of potential genealogies for the distinctive visual and narrative characteristics of Japanese pop, from the highly graphic woodblock prints of the Edo period to colorful and kinetic popular entertainment forms like *kabuki* theater and *bunraku* puppetry. Most scholars, while acknowledging the importance of such long historical legacies, tend to locate the imaginative spark for forms like anime and video games in Japan's less distant past. The current mainstream interpretation of the roots of Japan's pop creativity is that offered most assertively, articulately, and repeatedly by Murakami Takashi, the celebrated and influential "*otaku* chic" or "geek chic" artist.[6] According to Murakami, who has put forth his views in a series of high profile exhibitions and catalogues, most notably an extravaganza called "Little Boy: The Arts of Japan's Exploding Subculture" held at Japan Society in New York City in 2005, the origin point of Japan's extraordinary pop ingenuity was the atomic bombings of Hiroshima and Nagasaki. In Murakami's analysis, the Japanese people have never fully come to terms with defeat in World War II, occupation by the United States of America, and a pattern of postwar subservience to America that has left Japan perpetually infantilized (hence the ubiquity of "cute" in Japanese youth culture) and somehow deformed (hence the prevalence of monsters in the Japanese imagination). Since the frank discussion of the war's legacies and the asymmetric relationship with the United States have been all but taboo in polite society in Japan, Murakami argues that it has fallen to popular culture to explore the unresolved tensions of the postwar period. Thus, in popular cinema, manga, anime, video games, and avant-garde art, we see a compulsive reiteration of apocalypse, nuclear mutation, grotesque metamorphosis, technological escapism, masculine insecurity, social vulnerability, and other themes and imageries through which postwar Japanese struggle to find some sort of closure for war, surrender, and ongoing dependence on America. Combine this almost existential quest described by Murakami with the market realities of postwar Japan (specifically, a large and increasingly wealthy population, with a significant "baby boom" generation of young postwar consumers eager for mass entertainment), and the dynamism, imaginative energy, and riotous variety of Japan's contemporary pop culture forms begin to make sense.[7] Although not all commentators have endorsed Murakami's interpretation – some criticizing it for being overly simplistic, others for exaggerating the lingering power of long-ago traumas[8] – the notion of Japan's pop creativity bursting forth from the horrors of Hiroshima and Nagasaki is convincing historically, appealing intellectually, and compelling emotionally.

Why the world loves Godzilla and Hello Kitty

If Japanese pop culture has emerged from a unique (and a uniquely tortured) history of defeat and subordination, how then has it come to enjoy such remarkable global popularity? What is it about Japan that has apparently placed it just after Hollywood in the ability to create entertainment products that can transcend culture, language, geography, gender, race, and creed? Is there something special about Japan, about Japanese culture, about Japanese aesthetics and sensibilities, some formula that the Japanese have hit on that explains the almost universal global appeal of Japanese animation, films, fashion, video games, and character goods?

One approach to understanding the allure of Japanese pop, at least in North America, is the historical one. Historians of Japanese popular culture's global spread have stressed that a long postwar heritage of cultural interactions between the United States and Japan set the stage for the more recent rise of Japanese pop's prominence in America, and that a well-established stream of postwar entertainment products imported from Japan (beginning with the movie monster Godzilla, whose global debut was in the 1956 feature *Godzilla, King of the Monsters*) conditioned American audiences to the look and feel of Japanese pop. Thus, some scholars argue, we can only understand the contemporary appeal of manga and Hello Kitty by looking back historically and seeing how Godzilla first captured American audiences in the 1950s, followed by the animated Astro Boy (*Tetsuwan Atomu*) in the 1960s, and then Speed Racer (*Mach Go Go Go*), Kikaida, Ultraman, the Mighty Morphin Power Rangers, and the other Japanese serials that made their way across the Pacific and onto American televisions in the subsequent decades. Japan became a part of the American pop culture landscape after World War II almost without anyone noticing it, and its familiarity prepared American audiences (even if only subconsciously) for the waves of Japanese entertainment products that would arrive from the 1980s on.[9]

The role of economic and market considerations on the diffusion of Japanese pop culture products globally, and especially in North America, should also be noted. Through the postwar period, and especially since the rise of television (and then again with the rise of cable TV), the American media industry has desperately needed cheap products of reasonably high quality to fill air time. And, for decades, Japanese movies and television programs, live action and animated, have easily fit that bill. Back in the 1950s and 1960s, Godzilla and other Japanese monster films played this role: US movie theaters needed a constant stream of new films, a demand which even Hollywood could not supply at the time. The celluloid adventures of Godzilla, Mothra, and other monstrous creatures were part of a familiar genre (giant monsters on the loose, on the model of *King Kong*), were very inexpensive to purchase from Japanese studios eager for American dollars, and could be easily transformed into a palatable American entertainment experience with only a small monetary investment in editing and dubbing. Thus Japanese science-fiction pictures became a staple of down-market American theaters – drive-ins, small-town Saturday afternoon double bills – and then later were fodder for late night television and undesirable weekend time slots (when the "Creature Double Feature" would play on so many VHF channels around the country). So, in other words, one reason why, historically, American audiences had access to Japanese popular culture (and thus became conditioned to it over the longer term) was not because it was so polished or engaging or critically acclaimed, but because it was cheap and available.[10]

Theorizing the global appeal of Cool Japan

Other scholars have taken other approaches, needless to say, and often ones that fall quite far from the relatively mundane and accessible realms of history and economics. A time-tested and widely endorsed explanation for the global popularity of Japanese entertainment products was offered in 2000 by Timothy Craig, who edited one of the first scholarly collections on Japanese popular culture, *Japan Pop!* Craig provided a laundry list of why Japanese forms like anime have hit it big internationally and at the top was their reputation for being high quality and innovative. Craig was the first to admit that not all Japanese pop culture rose to such high standards (indeed, there is probably nothing so dreary and derivative as much of Japanese television), but the style, high production values, and creativity of many of Japan's cultural exports certainly are one significant appeal. Next on Craig's list was that Japanese pop "embraces life in all its dimensions" (in other words, that it does not avoid the unpleasant aspects of life or bow to political correctness), that it has a strong strain of idealism, innocence, and romance, and that it is accessible, "close to the ordinary, everyday lives of its audience." Craig also mentions certain themes in Japanese pop which he sees as widespread and appealing globally: an emphasis on human relationships (harmony, cooperation, the group), on the workplace, and on spiritual development and growth. Finally, Craig (like so many other observers) argues that Western audiences have come to embrace anime, manga, video games, and movies from Japan simply because they are so different:

> To the extent that elements that are abundant in Japanese pop culture – complex story and character development; frank portrayals of human nature; dreams and romantic optimism; kids' perspectives; a focus on human relations, work, and mental strength – are scarcer in Western pop culture, Western consumers find that Japan pop enriches their pop culture diet, giving them a fuller range of forms, themes, and viewpoints to enjoy, and perhaps to be influenced by.[11]

In short, Japanese pop is not only different from Western pop culture, but also far more complex and satisfying than the familiar, frequently unchallenging products served up by Hollywood, the television networks, and the marketers of Madison Avenue.

Susan Napier, in her now classic 2001 book *Anime: From Akira to Princess Mononoke*, built upon these ideas. Difference and sophistication, Napier suggested, account for much of the appeal of Japanese animation:

> One salient aspect of anime … is its insistent difference from dominant American popular culture. … What is perhaps most striking about anime, compared to other imported media that have been modified for the American market, is the lack of compromise in making these narratives palatable. … The medium is both different in a way that is appealing to a Western

audience satiated on the predictabilities of American popular culture and also remarkably approachable in its universal themes and images.[12]

But Napier goes even further, arguing that certain themes and characteristics of Japanese animation make it "speak" to twenty-first century Western audiences with unusual relevance. One of these, Napier notes, is a fascination with metamorphosis and transformation:

> Indeed, anime may be the perfect medium to capture what is perhaps the overriding issue of our day, the shifting nature of identity in a constantly changing society. With its rapid shifts of narrative pace and its constantly transforming imagery, the animated medium is superbly positioned to illustrate the atmosphere of change permeating not only Japanese society but also all industrialized or industrializing societies. Moving at rapid – sometimes breakneck – pace and predicated upon the instability of form, animation is both a symptom and a metaphor for a society obsessed with change and spectacle. In particular, animation's emphasis on metamorphosis can be seen as the ideal artistic vehicle for expressing the postmodern obsession with fluctuating identity.[13]

Napier also concludes that a substantial part of anime's appeal is its subversiveness, its reluctance to embrace the Hollywood happy ending that reassures audiences that all is well with the world. Indeed, anime often leaves viewers with the abiding impression that the world is impossibly screwed up and, to many jaded entertainment consumers in a global youth market weaned on sunny Hollywood pablum, such a message is a welcome relief from the predictable narratives of the Magic Kingdom and Steven Spielberg. Napier writes,

> This subversive aspect of anime is a prominent element in comparison with much of American popular culture. Critics such as Douglas Kellner have suggested that in America, "mass culture … articulates social conflicts, contemporary fears, and utopian hopes and attempts at ideological containment and reassurance." While it is certainly true that anime does some of this, much of the best of anime resists any attempt at "ideological containment" and, given the dark tone of many of its most memorable texts, could well be considered a cinema of "de-assurance" rather than one of "reassurance," which … is the dominant tone of most Hollywood films. …[14]

A complementary perspective is provided by the anthropologist Anne Allison, whose 2006 book *Millennial Monsters: Japanese Toys and the Global Imagination* sheds fascinating light on many of the familiar icons of Japanese pop from Pokémon and the Mighty Morphin Power Rangers to Sailor Moon and *tamagotchi* "portable pets." To Allison, the creative inspiration and broad appeal of Japanese popular culture all comes down to "polymorphous perversity" and "animistic technology." The first, she explains, grew out of the crisis of masculinity that gripped Japan in the wake of its 1945 defeat:

> Reflected historically here, amid all the other upheavals experienced by Japan/ese following the war, is the collapse of paternal authority (from the desacralizing of the emperor to the national condemnation of the military leaders who had misled the country into a disastrous war – a discrediting of fathers that trickled down to the male soldiers who returned to the family and household, where adult men no longer commanded ultimate respect). Thus, the dismembering of the nation – physically, psychologically, socially – in wartime and the postwar years helped propel a particular fantasy construction I [term] polymorphous perversity: of unstable and shifting worlds where characters, monstrously wounded by violence and the collapse of authority, reemerge with reconstituted selves.[15]

By animistic technology, which she also tags "techno-animism," Allison means a highly alluring imaginative fusion of the cultural tendency "to see the world as animated by variety of beings, both worldly and otherworldly, that are complex, (inter)changeable, and not graspable by so-called rational (or visible) means alone," with a fixation on technology, on robots and androids, on what the Japanese call "mecha."[16] The result is something undeniably cool: cute, cuddly, and spiritual, yet also appealingly high-tech, sleek, and cutting edge. These qualities, supplemented with other characteristic aspects of twenty-first century Japanese pop – flexibility, portability, miniaturization, global marketing genius – are, at least according to Allison, the secrets of Japan's global popular culture success.

One of the most provocative scholars working on Japanese pop culture today is Iwabuchi Kōichi, who has written numerous essays and an important book, *Recentering Globalization: Popular Culture and Japanese Transnationalism*, that examine Japanese entertainment products in a global context. Iwabuchi's works, which largely deal with the reception of Japanese television, music, and animation in Asia (rather than in the West), revolve around two central propositions. The first is that Japanese pop culture is embraced in Asia because Japan is something of a halfway house between East and West; that is to say, Japan takes the media products of the modern United States and Europe, and it "indigenizes" them, it makes them subtly more "Asian" in sensibility, aesthetics, and content, and thus more palatable to Taiwanese, Singaporean, or even Korean and Chinese audiences.[17] Thus, while Mickey Mouse or CSI might seem too foreign, Pokémon and Japanese television melodramas ring strangely true to East and Southeast Asian media consumers.

Iwabuchi's second intriguing notion regards the *smell* of global pop culture products. In Iwabuchi's telling, all transnational cultural products – movies, cartoons, advertising symbols – have some sort of odor, reflecting the culture and society in which they were made. Many American products, Iwabuchi argues, have a good odor, a fragrance, because they are associated with positive attributes of the American lifestyle and the American dream. Thus Hollywood movies have international buzz because their fragrance carries with them envious yearnings for American wealth, freedom, democracy, leisure, and coolness. Japan, Iwabuchi suggests, doesn't have this kind of pleasant scent in the noses of the world's consumers. Indeed, pop culture products that make people think too readily of their Japanese origins are likely to have a bad odor – a stink – that comes from negative preconceptions of Japan (based on notions of race and inferiority among Western audiences and deriving from Japan's history of imperialism and regional dominance among Asian ones). The only Japanese pop products that have hit it big globally are those that are "culturally odorless," that are slick and sophisticated and creative and well marketed, but which do not smell of Japan to consumers overseas. To Iwabuchi these odorless products, called by other scholars *mukokuseki* (that is, lacking a sense of national origin), are the "3 Cs": consumer technologies (such as VCRs, *karaoke*, and the Walkman), comics and cartoons (that is, manga and anime), and computer/video games. Indeed, Iwabuchi concludes, Japanese goods can only sell internationally if they are scrupulously scrubbed clean of cultural association with Japan, and presented as a kind of placeless, historyless, cultureless, odorless entertainment commodity.[18]

Iwabuchi's ideas are provocative and controversial. His approach may help us explain the popularity of something like Hello Kitty, whose global appeal has generally has been difficult for scholars to comprehend but which seems a perfect example of an odorless global icon. The same might be said of Pokémon or Yu-gi-oh, although in these cases the overarching importance of marketing also needs to be carefully figured in. Some commentators are skeptical of Iwabuchi's notions of smell, questioning just how *mukokuseki* and odorless something like anime is, even if so many of the characters of Japanese animation, with large round eyes, light skin, and blond, pink or blue hair, look anything but Japanese. As Susan Napier's research has revealed, manga and anime are far from *mukokuseki* to their American fans: enthusiasm for Japanese entertainment products and interest in Japanese language and culture are, it seems, frequently intertwined.[19] Such reservations aside, Iwabuchi's ideas are clearly worthy of attention.

One further approach to understanding the global popularity of Cool Japan should at least be mentioned, as it is the latest theory to be advanced and is intellectually appealing, even if rather dubious substantively. In his recent book *Japanamerica*, the journalist Roland Kelts makes the following argument: Japanese pop forms like anime are, as Murakami Takashi has argued, the creative outlet for Japan's unresolved agonizing over the atomic bombings of 1945; the attacks of September 11 are the contemporary equivalent of Hiroshima and Nagasaki, leaving deep scars of fear and horror that Americans have not yet been able to heal or put behind them; thus, Japanese popular culture has "spoken" to US audiences, and especially American youth whose formative life experience was the spectacle of 9/11, because Americans now share the same unresolved tensions that have haunted the Japanese since World War II.[20] Of course, Kelts' theory does not explain Japanese pop's global appeal, well beyond America's borders, nor does it account for the considerable popularity of Japanese anime, manga, films, and video games in the United States even well before the attacks of 2001. And, of course, the very cleverness, elegance, and tidiness of Kelts' story inevitably evokes skepticism in a world of pop culture production and media consumption that is anything but simple, obvious, and neat.

The Japanese state and the limits of soft power

The intrinsic qualities of postwar Japanese popular culture – from its originality, creativity, and subversiveness to its techno-animistic, odorless, and potentially therapeutic appeals – are not the only factors that need to be considered in the global rise of Japanese pop. The role of the Japanese state is well worth exploring, especially considering the profound influence of the Japanese bureaucracy in economic planning and guidance during the postwar "miracle economy" decades, and the fact that, in recent years, a number of governments have invested heavily in cultural and educational programs abroad to build soft power. Not surprisingly, like other nations, Japan has long provided official support for promoting Japanese culture and language around the world. The work of the Japan Foundation and the Center for Global Partnership are good examples of this, as are programs like the Japanese Government (Monbukagakushō) Scholarships that bring overseas youth leaders, educators, undergraduates, and graduate students to Japan. Tokyo's most successful soft power initiative, however, is almost certainly the Japan Exchange and Teaching Program. First established in 1978, JET, which recruits exceptional young people from around the world to teach their native languages in Japanese schools, has created a fund of goodwill for Japan internationally that might even dwarf the impact of icons like Godzilla and Pokémon.[21]

Since the 1950s, the Japanese government has also supported, through lip service, some administrative guidance, and limited financial subsidization, the export of high and popular culture. Until quite recently, when even Japanese bureaucrats could no longer ignore the global popularity (and potential soft power utility) of forms like anime and manga, the state was far more comfortable supporting elite cultural forms than mass entertainments.[22] Under these circumstances, most of the real energy driving Japanese pop's globalization since World War II has come from the private sector; in other words, the international diffusion of Japanese popular culture may have been broadly consistent with postwar public policy, but it was not necessarily guided by official actors so much as by market forces, private organizations, and active fan subcultures. Thus, the global spread of participatory cultural forms from Japan, such as *ikebana* (flower arranging), the tea ceremony, and martial arts like *jūdō* and *aikidō*, have been driven largely by the efforts of Japanese private-sector institutions and the enthusiasm of individual participants. Private philanthropy, from Japanese individuals, corporations, and foundations, has had a significant impact on the development of Japanese studies around the world, especially in universities and in outreach to schools. And, of course, commerce has had an important role: many successful Japanese pop forms – popular cinema, video games, character goods, manga, and anime – have gone global through market mechanisms, merchandised and sold internationally by profit-motivated Japanese firms and their overseas partners. So while government efforts have played a role in the rise of Japanese soft power over the past fifty years, the crucial, even preponderant role of the private sector in the globalization of Japanese popular culture should not be overlooked.

Despite the global ubiquity of products like Hello Kitty and Super Mario, it appears that, so far at least, pop culture has not been a huge profit maker for the Japanese economy. Although entrepreneurial firms like Sony and Nintendo have done well with their soft products internationally, Japan's entertainment industry has not developed into the economic pillar that automobiles, consumer electronics, and even sectors like industrial automation have become. As Roland Kelts notes, Japanese firms have experienced problems in cashing in on the global success of anime, and even the transnational boom surrounding Pokémon ended up accruing more to the benefit of its US distributors than to its Japanese creator, Nintendo.[23]

An instructive case study is a Japanese company called Nikoli and its founder Kaji Maki, who perfected and popularized the number puzzles known as *sudoku*. The game began as an American invention, was tweaked and improved by Kaji and his associates (many of them mathematicians and software designers), and through an unlikely twist of events, became a worldwide craze. Unfortunately for him, Kaji neglected to trademark *sudoku*, so he and Nikoli have gotten no royalties from the more than US$250 million in global *sudoku* revenues to date. As reported in 2007, however, the future looks bright to Kaji, as his firm has developed dozens of new number and logic puzzles which he plans to spring on the world in the not-too-distant future.[24] If indeed companies like Nikoli can manage to capitalize financially on the combination of creativity, the ability to refine and improve products, and the unique pop culture/entertainment sensibility which has evolved in Japan since World War II, then perhaps the future of the Japanese economy will eventually belong to the soft of *sudoku* and animation rather than the hard of automobiles and electronics.

In the end, one cannot help but wonder what the impact of the globalization of Japanese pop culture and the nation's apparently surging soft power will have on Japan's place in the world. Can Japan "cash in" politically on its soft power appeal, for instance in attaining a seat on the United Nations Security Council, gaining international assent to increasing whale harvests, or muting international criticism of rising Japanese nationalism (be it in school textbooks, Yasukuni Shrine visits by government officials, or the public denial of war atrocities)? What benefit will having millions of anime fans and JET alums and Hello Kitty consumers and video game players and *sudoku* puzzlers have for Japan's great power status? This question of the real-world utility of soft power is not just an issue for Japan, but hangs over discussions of soft power more generally. Has, for instance, the ubiquity of Italian food, fashion, and design really had a great impact on Italy's place in the global order? Even in the American case, is it safe to assume that the idiosyncratic view of US life created by Hollywood and Madison Avenue – that mishmash of aspirations and nightmares conjured up by Rambo and Bambi, Starbucks and the Bill of Rights – actually has had a substantive impact on Washington's ability to get its way in the world? Can special effects blockbusters and Tiger Woods really trump the persuasive power of the US nuclear arsenal and the sheer productive (and consumer) power of the American economy?

As scholars continue to debate the sources of Japanese pop culture's creativity and the reasons for its global appeal, policymakers will no doubt continue to work to find ways to translate Japan's swelling "Gross National Cool" into tangible political, economic, or diplomatic benefit. Whether comic books will ever be able to compensate for the military lackings of the Japanese Self-Defense Forces, or the appeal of Japanese fashion among Asian youth somehow counteract the decline of Japanese manufacturing, is dubious at best. Moreover, in today's diverse, complex, and fickle media and entertainment markets, the ability of Japanese pop products to retain their global buzz, especially given challenges like the "Korean Wave" and "Cool Britannia," is questionable as well.[25] Only time will tell if the early twenty-first century globalization of Japanese popular culture will prove a fleeting historical moment, an important turning point, an opportunity lost, or perhaps even the dawn of Japan as the world's first "soft superpower."

Notes

1   Timothy J. Craig, "Introduction" in *Japan Pop! Inside the World of Japanese Popular Culture,* ed. Timothy J. Craig (Armonk, NY: M.E. Sharpe, 2000), 5.
2   Douglas McGray, "Japan's Gross National Cool," *Foreign Policy* (May/June 2002). On the long-term influence of Japan on American culture, see Susan Napier, *From Impressionism to Anime: Japan as Fantasy and Fan Cult in the Mind of the West* (New York: Palgrave Macmillan, 2007).
3   Joseph S. Nye, Jr., *Soft Power: The Means to Success in World Politics* (New York: Public Affairs, 2005), p.x.
4   Geoff Hiscock, "'Soft Power' Part of Balancing Act," CCN.com (September 21, 2006), <http://www.cnn.com/2006/WORLD/asiapcf/09/01/japan.softpower/index.html> (accessed January 16, 2009).
5   Nye, *Soft Power,* 6.
6   Murakami has been memorably described by the journalist Ian Buruma as "a painter of cartoon images, both childlike and sinister, a highly successful designer (of Louis Vuitton bags, among other things), a maker of mildly pornographic dolls, an artistic entrepreneur, a theorist, and a guru, with a studio of protégés that is a cross between a traditional Japanese workshop and Andy Warhol's Factory." Ian Buruma, "Virtual Violence," *The New York Review of Books* 52: 22 (June 23, 2005) <http://www.nybooks.com/articles/18072> (accessed December 20, 2008).
7   Murakami Takashi, ed., *Little Boy: The Arts of Japan's Exploding Subculture* (New York: Japan Society, 2005).
8   See Thomas LaMarre, *"Otaku* Movement" in *Japan After Japan: Social and Cultural Life from the Recessionary 1990s to the Present,* ed. Tomiko Yoda and Harry Harootunian (Durham, NC: Duke University Press, 2006), 358–394; William M. Tsutsui, "Oh No, There Goes Tokyo: Recreational Apocalypse and the City in Postwar Japanese Popular Culture" in *Noir Urbanisms,* ed. Gyan Prakash (Princeton, NJ: Princeton University Press, forthcoming).
9   See William M. Tsutsui, *Godzilla on My Mind: Fifty Years of the King of Monsters* (New York: Palgrave Macmillan, 2004) and William M. Tsutsui and Michiko Ito, eds., *In Godzilla's Footsteps: Japanese Pop Culture Icons on the Global Stage* (New York: Palgrave Macmillan, 2006).
10 Tsutsui, *Godzilla on My Mind,* 115–120.

11 Craig, "Introduction" in *Japan Pop!*, 16–17.
12 Susan J. Napier, *Anime, From Akira to Princess Mononoke: Experiencing Contemporary Japanese Animation* (New York: Palgrave, 2001), 9–10.
13 Napier, *Anime,* 12.
14 Napier, *Anime,* 33.
15 Anne Allison, *Millennial Monsters: Japanese Toys and the Global Imagination* (Berkeley: University of California Press, 2006), 12.
16 Allison, *Millennial Monsters*, 12–13.
17 Iwabuchi Kōichi, *Recentering Globalization: Popular Culture and Japanese Transnationalism* (Durham, NC: Duke University Press, 2002), 11–14; 85–120.
18 Iwabuchi Kōichi, "How 'Japanese' is Pokémon?" in *Pikachu's Global Adventure: The Rise and Fall of Pokémon,* ed. Joseph Tobin (Durham, NC: Duke University Press, 2004), 56–58; Iwabuchi, *Recentering Globalization*, 24–28.
19 Napier, *Anime,* 253–255; Napier, *From Impressionism to Anime,* 169–190.
20 Roland Kelts, *Japanamerica: How Japanese Pop Culture has Invaded the U.S.* (New York: Palgrave Macmillan, 2006), 9–34.
21 See David L. McConnell, *Importing Diversity: Inside Japan's JET Program* (Berkeley: University of California Press, 2000).
22 See, for example, the 2006 speech by Japanese Minister of Foreign Affairs Asō Tarō, "A New Look at Cultural Diplomacy: A Call to Japan's Cultural Practitioners," <http://www.mofa.go.jp/announce/fm/aso/speech0604-2.html> (accessed January 16, 2009).
23 Kelts, *Japanamerica,* especially chapters 3–4.
24 Martin Fackler, "Inside Japan's Puzzle Palace," *The New York Times* (March 21, 2007) <http://www.nytimes.com/2007/03/21/business/worldbusiness/21sudoku.html> (accessed January 16, 2009).
25 Korean Wave is also described as Korean fever and relates to the growing interesting interest in South Korean popular culture and new technologies. Cool Britannia was used commonly in the post-World War II when British rock music and related youth culture elements swept the world.

8 Wakon-Yosai 和魂洋才 and globalization

Norio Ota

Preamble

In the age of globalization, scholars in every country face the issue of dualism; how they acquire new knowledge while maintaining their own cultural identities. The multicultural and multi-racial context in Canada offers us great opportunities to observe this phenomenon. At a personal level, *wakon-yosai* 和魂洋才 also has been an increasingly important and unavoidable issue that begs investigation as to what constitutes my *wakon* 和魂 after so many years of *yosai* 洋才 experience both in Japan and overseas. Yukio Mishima's 三島 由紀夫 suicide in 1970 was a real shocker in Japanese intellectuals' *wakon-yosai* tradition. He tried to resurrect *bushido* 武士道, however anachronistic his action was considered to be by many people. *Bushido* and its Japanese national epic *Chushingura* 忠臣蔵 still seem to touch a chord in many Japanese hearts. Several variations of *wakon-yosai* have been coined. Some scholars claim, for example, that after 1945, Japan adopted *wakon-beisai* 和魂米才 "Japanese spirit, American learning", and now it is *mukon-musai* 無魂無才 "no spirit, no learning". *Wakon-wasai* 和魂和才 "Japanese spirit, Japanese learning" and *wakon-mansai* 和魂満才 "Japanese spirit, all learning" are discussed in a global context.

Background

This chapter is a preliminary probe into a widely accepted concept, *wakon-yosai* 和魂洋才 "Japanese spirit, Western learning", which succeeded the *wakon-kansai* 和魂漢才 "Japanese spirit, Chinese learning" tradition. One of the problems in dealing with the term *wakon-yosai* is that it is overly inclusive, in that even a cursory investigation reveals a wide range of interpretations, approaches and strategies among those who adopted this concept, either consciously or tacitly. Another problem, closely tied to the first one, is that the *wakon* in *wakon-yosai* seems not only unclear, but also varied both synchronically and diachronically. In this paper, *wakon-yosai* is used first as a cover term under the assumption that it was Japan's major strategy for its modernization, so that the issue as to who should be included under this concept is avoided for the preliminary discussion. The concept of *wakon-yosai* has changed according to time and political climate. Some scholars claim that Japan's defeat in World War II was a result of this strategy. Whether or not it is appropriate to compare the first *Kurofune* (black ship) era with the current globalization era, is controversial, it is beneficial to reexamine this tradition through the eyes of some of the early scholars who seem to have questioned the validity of this concept and gone beyond the narrow confines of *wakon-yosai*. Among them are Fukuzawa Yukichi 福沢諭吉, Okakura Tenshin 岡倉天心, Uchimura Kanzo 内村鑑三, Nitobe Inazou 新渡戸稲造, Kuki Shuzo 九鬼周造, and Suzuki Daisetsu 鈴木大拙, who were confronted by Western civilization and probably felt compelled to identify Japanese culture and introduce it to the West. Hopefully, this will shed some light on what wakon 和魂 actually consists of and entails. The next task is to project *wakon-yosai* onto the current global context. Is it still an applicable and viable strategy for Japanese to grapple with the onslaught of globalization process? As a linguist by training, I am also interested in the role of translation and "translation-ism" 翻訳主義. That is, in both *wakon-kansai* and *wakon-yosai* strategies, translation played a major role in learning, new knowledge, and technology. In Maruyama and Kato (1998), Maruyama quotes Ogyuu Sorai 荻生徂徠 in Yakubun-sentei 「訳文荃蹄」 to have shocked 和魂漢才 scholars by stating, "The Rongo 論語 "'Analects of Confucius'" and Moushi 孟子 "'Discourses of Mencius'" that we are reading are written in a foreign language. From ancient times we have been reading them in translation 和臭 "'Japanism'". Ogyuu further claims that if one reads Kanbun 漢文, knowing that it is a translation of Chinese into Japanese, one can understand the structure of Chinese better than Chinese speakers, because it is often the case that native speakers take their own language for granted and do not know about the structure. Maruyama also compares this argument of Ogyuu with Fukuzawa Yukichi's *isshin-nishou* – 身二生 "one body two lives". Fukuzawa contends that people of his generation experienced the feudal system in the first half of their life, and learned Western civilization in the latter half, so if they compare these two lives, they can understand the characteristics of civilization very clearly. They have the advantage over Westerners who have no other means to understand civilization and differences, than to study written documentation about feudal systems which existed several hundred years ago. Their views, although somewhat farfetched, seem to justify "translation-ism 翻訳主義". In reference to Fukuzawa's *isshin-nishou*, Yamamoto states that for Fukuzawa the concept was considered as "diachronic", whereas in the current world it should be regarded as "synchronic" – people live different lives simultaneously. In the present-day context, Karl Löwith's often quoted comment on "no ladder between the second floor (*yosai*) and the first floor (*wakon*)" regarding Japanese scholars still seems quite valid. This research is motivated by a very personal reason as well in that this issue is not only a relevant one, but also a very urgent one for us Japanese scholars.

Wakon-Kansai 和魂漢才 tradition

Wakon-kansai is not the main focus of this paper, and would require an extensive investigation in its own right, but it is absolutely necessary to review several outstanding scholars who excelled in different ways based on the *wakon-kansai* tradition. Ito Jinsai 伊藤仁斎 (1627–1705) and Ogyu Sorai 荻生徂徠 (1966–1728) mastered the teachings of Chu-tzŭ 朱子学 and developed its practical application for in commoners' education and politics, respectively. It is to be noted that they did not accept Chu-tzŭ as a golden rule, but criticized some aspects of it. The tradition of localization and innovation can be found clearly in their work. Ishida Baigan 石田梅岩 (1685–1745) is an excellent example of the enhanced syncretism of Shinto-ism, Buddhism and Confucianism. Tominaga Nakamoto 富永仲基 (1715–1746), on the other hand, argues that each of these traditions must be overcome, and a higher level of understanding must be attained. Naito Torajiro 内藤虎次郎 (1866–1934), Sinologist (1925) admires Tominaga as the first Japanese scholar who established a logical foundation of research, in reference to Tominaga's principles of *kajo*加上 "newer research tends to look at older sources than the previous research" and 異部名字難必和會 "it is impossible to harmonize various theories to get to the one truth". One can see a very healthy critical mind here. Naito in his Nihon-Bunkashi-Kenkyuu 日本文化史研究 gives a persuasive argument for Japanese ingenuity and creativity in adopting new values, ideas, technology in the *wakon-kansai* tradition. It is probably safe to say that, because of this long tradition and experience in the selective adaptation of foreign values, ideas and technology, adaptation to the new environment, localization and innovation were possible in later years. This *wakon-kansai* tradition probably made *wakon-yosai* work for Japan later, whereas the corresponding attempt 中体西用in洋務運動 in China failed. To be sure, there were other factors involved, but China's lack of this tradition due to its super-power position, undoubtedly played a major role. The geographical factor obviously worked to Japan's advantage in comparison with Korea. Three strong trends emerge: localization with innovation, syncretism, and "sublation".

Early wakon-yosai 和魂洋才 tradition

Mori Senzo 森銑三 in Oranda Shogatsu オランダ正月gives a long list of Japanese scientists who were inspired by Western science and technology during the Edo Period, and who made great contributions to society. The list includes:

- Suminokura Ryooi 角倉了以
- Kawamura Zuiken 川村瑞賢
- Tanaka Kyuuguu 田中丘隅
- Aoki Konyoo 青木昆陽
- Yamawaki Tooyoo 山脇東洋
- Maeno Ranka 前野蘭化
- Sugita Genpaku 杉田玄白

- Hiraga Gennai 平賀源内
- Itoo Tadataka 伊藤忠敬
- Katsuragawa Hoshuu 桂川甫周
- Mogami Tokunai 最上徳内
- Ootsuki Bansui 大槻磐水
- Inamura Sanpaku 稲村三伯
- Hoashi Banri 帆足万里
- Mamiya Rinzoo 間宮林蔵
- Takano Chooee 高野長英
- Sakuma Shoozan 佐久間象山

Sakuma Shoozan is considered as the champion of the *wakon-yosai* tradition. He studied the teaching of Chu-zŭ 朱子学 first, which formed his *wakon*, and later learned and developed technology to create canons, *yosai*. This tumultuous period in Japan produced many talented scholars. It is worth repeating that the *wakon-kansai* tradition formed a viable foundation for *wakon-yosai* historically and within each person's life. Seki Takakazu 関孝和 is well known for his unique Japanese arithmetic. This case can be called *wakon-wasai* 和魂和才.

Modern period

Takeda Kiyoko 武田清子 in 「土着と背教」 "Naturalization and Renegation" proposes the following five types of Christianity being naturalized in Japanese society and culture.

1 Acculturation type 埋没型
2 Isolation type 孤立型
3 Renegation type 背教型－有島武郎
4 Competitive or prophetic type 対決型・預言者型－内村鑑三
5 Grafting type 接ぎ木型－新渡戸稲造

Takeda regards the last type as the most successful one. Although Takeda uses these types for classifying Japanese Christians, they seem to be applicable to non-Christians as well. The first three types are not desirable in terms of learning. Uchimura started as a grafting type, but as he was disillusioned by the then state of Christianity in the West, he seemed to have sharpened his criticism and joined the competitive category. Uchimura's effort in understanding *yokon* is indeed remarkable in that most Japanese scholars did not even attempt to understand the religious aspects of the Western culture. He did not revert to Japanese culture even when he was very critical of Western culture. Instead, he considered Japan as a viable home for his "true Christianity". Nitobe, on the other hand, felt the need of explaining Japanese culture (*wakon*) to the West, after he successfully grafted *yosai* to *wakon*. His response was to introduce *bushido* to the West as the essence of *wakon*. While *bushido* focuses on death, Okakura's book on Tea focuses on life. Both Nitobe and Okakura were very fluent in English and they did not have to rely on translation. They were the best candidates who could have introduced *yokon* to Japan, but rather tried to define *wakon* in their own ways. Fukuzawa Yukichi 福沢諭吉 is somewhat different, in that he recommended adopting both *yokon* and *yosai* in order to change Japanese people's traditional values and thinking. His approach was unique among the so-called *wakon-yosai* group. He envisioned the transformation of Japan into a civil and democratic society. Unfortunately, Japan did not follow his lead, as was apparent in the history that followed. Kuki Shuzo 九鬼周造 introduced Japanese culture to the West by defining the concept of *iki*. He was urged to characterize Japanese culture in contrast to Western culture. What is common to these people is that they were looking at Japan only from Japan's perspective. Okakura's slogan, "Asia is one", ended up promoting the narrowest concept of *wakon*, which formed the basis of Japan's ultra-nationalism, imperialism and militarism. Suzuki Daisetsu 鈴木大拙 placed *zen* 禅 in the center of Japanese culture. The slogan of *datsua-nyuuou* 脱亜入欧 "leave Asia and join Europe" was one of the continuing threads of discourse during this period. This issue seems quite relevant now, when we reflect on how we have been dealing with this same issue ourselves.

After WWII

One question which is often asked is how the Japanese could switch from the prewar system to the American-style democratic system. The approach was the same *wakon-yosai*, although the *wakon* was severely criticized and reduced to a minimum level for a long time. In the efforts to maintain *kokutai* 国体 "national polity" before 1945 and after Japan's surrender, one can find various attempts to support a new form of *wakon-yosai*. The negotiations regarding the new constitution reveal an interesting series of events leading up to its official declaration.

As *wakon-beisai* "Japanese spirit, American learning" was coined, American influence was overwhelming in postwar Japan, but the influence of communism and socialism was also widespread. However, under the guise of *yosai*, people lived a dualistic life. *Wakon,* as represented by the *Chushingura* story, continued to undergird the Japanese psyche and value orientation. During the "bubble economy" period, Japan's technological and financial superiority resurrected the "Japan as No.1" mentality. I heard many Japanese saying that we had nothing to learn from the West during that period. The collapse of the communist bloc created a vacuum among intellectuals, and those who "grafted" communism or socialism as *yosai* were totally at a loss. After the bubble burst, the Japanese people lost their confidence and shifted their foci to Asia again.

Era of globalization

It has been a while since Japan's second *sakoku* 鎖国 "national isolation" was discussed. Facing the onslaught of globalization, people are reacting in various ways.

Wakon-yosai seems to be supported by the government. The 9th Central Education Council general meeting 中央教育審議会 warns as follows:

> *Wakon-yosai* is talked about, but in the world of academia *wa* is pushed by *yoo*, and has atrophied. However, the philosophy of *wa,* such as irrationality and transience, is also inevitable …

The Marubeni Corporation exports the *wakon-yosai* approach to South Africa:

> Africans are making renewed efforts to harmonizing their culture with Western culture, at the same time that they are arguing for the necessity of recovering African-ism and self-respect. In those efforts, Japanese culture such as *wakon-yosai* appears very fresh to them, and the role of Japan seems gradually to become clear.

JICA also considers that Japan's accumulated knowledge regarding *wakon-yosai* should be a part of financial cooperation with the recipient countries.

A more eclectic view of *wakon-yosai*, taking good from both, has been promoted by some schools and businesses such as *Shiseido*.

It is also a common approach to try to find evidence to prove that Japanese culture possesses global characteristics. An early example can be found in Hasegawa Nyozekan 長谷川如是閑 (1938), which refers to Keichu 契沖, Kamo no Mabuchi 賀茂真淵 and Motoori Norinaga 本居宣長, who re-examined Japanese characteristics by distinguishing between the influences of Buddhism and Confucianism, in order to find a spiritual basis for a new united nation. Hasegawa discusses the universal nature of Japanese culture, and claims that Japanese national characteristics tend to try to harmonize all conflicting factors based on common denominators. A recent version can be found in Yamazaki Masakazu 山崎正和 (1990) which explores the "universal nature" of Japanese culture, based on the interaction between the "*ie*-system" in the farmer class and the warrior class, and individualism in the merchant class, which have co-existed since the end of the *Muromachi* Era; this dual nature has played an important role throughout the pre-modern and modern periods.

The *wakon-yosai* tradition has a wide spectrum of critics, pros and cons. On the pro side, there are schools and universities which hold this up as their motto. Businesses, for example the Shiseido company, used to advocate this. One can also find promotion of this concept in advertisements for housing. In these cases, the concept is interpreted as eclecticism between Japanese culture and Western culture. As mentioned previously, JICA promotes this as a model strategy for under-developing countries to adopt. On the con side, *wakon-yosai* served to promote Japanese ultra-nationalism, and led Japan to its defeat in WWII. Harsher critics say that in the post-war period, it became *wakon-beisai* 和魂米才 "Japanese spirit, American learning" and now has become *mukon-musa i*無魂無才 "no spirit, no learning". Some advocate *wakon-mansai* "Japanese spirit, all learning" 和魂満才in the era of globalization. In the *anime* and film genre,

Miyazaki Hayao's "Spirited Away", for instance, has many elements derived from Shintoism, Buddhism and Confucianism, which would require a deep understanding of Japanese culture and tradition. Is the movie *The Last Samurai* a case of *beikon-wasai*? In it we can almost see the ghost of the concept of *bushido* Nitobe once introduced to the West. This leads to the question of how scholars in other countries view Japan and Japanese culture. In North America, discussions of Bushido, Zen, Shintoism, Buddhism, Chanoyu, Haiku, Ikebana, Kurosawa Akira 黒澤明, Mishima Yukio 三島由紀夫, Tanizaki Jun'ichiro 谷崎潤一郎, Abe Kobo 阿部公房 seem to be still very popular in Japanese Studies courses. This is a reflection of Western scholars' understanding of *wakon*, which has been recycled among students as well. Is *kakon-wasai* also based on this? Asian scholars from China, Korea, the Philippines, Vietnam and other countries, however, may have quite different understandings of *wakon* and Japan's *wakon-yosai* tradition. The study provides a great opportunity to hear about *chukon-yosai* 中魂洋才 "Chinese spirit, Western learning", *chukon-wasai* 中魂和才 "Chinese spirit, Japanese learning", *kankon-yosai* 韓魂洋才 "Korean spirit, Western learning", *kankon-wasai* 韓魂和才 "Korean spirit, Japanese learning", and so forth. In the Canadian multicultural context, it is a "must" to look into how individuals in each ethnic group, but in particular first-generation immigrants, adopt *kasai* 加才 "Canadian learning" with their cultural spirit, and disseminate their newly created identities through their communities. In Ota (2003) I stated that the *Chushingura* mentality, the essence of *wakon* was still prevalent among Japanese in Japan, and also preserved strongly in more pure form among Japanese Canadians. I cautioned that with that kind of two-dimensional mentality, it would be very difficult to face the onslaught of globalization, the second *kurofune*.

To put this issue into a personal context, like Yamazaki I have been advocating some global nature of Japanese culture, based on my strong criticism of the mistakes Japan made and has been making until now. In my attempt to understand *yokon* as suggested by Fukuzawa, religion is the largest hurdle. This seems to be a common tradition since Arai Hakuseki 新井白石、when he interviewed Giovanni Battista Sidotti in the Edo Era. Kawakita states:

> As a result, we Japanese have lost the ability to comprehend all religious phenomena. Nor are we even trying to understand them.
>
> (Kawakita 1973: 76)

He points out that this is the result of overemphasizing the communalist (group-oriented) tradition over Buddhist tradition (individualism), and suggests that Japanese should reexamine the latter. The *wakon-yosai* tradition seems to have been hampered strongly by Japanese "allergic" reaction to Christianity. Uchimura and Nitobe went far beyond by becoming Christians and probably understood *yokon* more deeply, but that fact could have been one of the reasons why their ideals were not accepted widely. This is, needless to say, very speculative.

Conclusion

Wakon-yosai is not a unique approach for recipient nations of advanced civilization. The problem is, however, that it does not seem to be possible to adopt foreign culture selectively, and still maintain the local spirit intact. *Wakon* has been constantly changing, being influenced by *kansai* or *yosai*.

In the traditional view, *wakon* and *yosai* were separate and not interactive. A more dynamic view is required in an age of globalization. *Yosai* always influences *wakon* because *yosai* comes with *yokon*. Rather than taking a passive view, it is necessary for Japanese scholars to learn *yokon* vigorously, as Fukuzawa suggested, and develop *wakon* as a dynamically and continuously changing entity. Globalization requires *wakon-wasai* and *yokon-yosai* constantly interacting with each other to deepen an understanding of the world with the synergistic effects of both. I am thinking a model something similar to the "reflective model" in education. With given knowledge and through action in reflection, one can gain more experiential knowledge.

References

Bibby, Reginald (1990) *Mosaic Madness*, Toronto, ON: Stoddart.

Doi, Takeo (1990) *Faith and "Amae"*, Tokyo: Shunju-sha.土居健郎 (1990)「信仰と『甘え』」春秋社

Frois, Luis (1991) *European Culture and Japanese Culture,* translated and annotated by Akio Okada, Tokyo: Iwanami. ルイス・フロイス (1991) 「ヨーロッパ文化と日本文化」 （岡田章雄訳注）岩波文庫

Fujisawa, Norio (1997) "Editor's Notes on Western Classical Library", http://www.kyoto-up.or.jp/jp/seiyokoten3.html#fujisawa 藤澤令夫 (1997) 西洋古典叢書編集の辞

Fukuzawa, Yukichi (1942) *Encouragement for Study*, Tokyo: Iwanami. 福沢諭吉 (1942) 「学問のすゝめ」岩波文庫

Hasegawa, Nyozekan (1938) *Unique Characteristics of Japan*, Tokyo: Iwanami. 長谷川如是閑 (1938)「日本的性格」岩波新書

Hattori, Shisou (1963) "Before and After the Black Ship", *Complete Works of Educating about World*, vol. 17, Tokyo: Heibonsha.服部之総 (1963) 「黒船前後」世界教養全集17　平凡社

Irie, Akira (1995) "Japan and Asia – The Weight of the One Hundred Years", February vol., *Sekai*, Tokyo: Iwanami. 入江昭 (1995) 「日本とアジアー百年の重み」世界1995二月号

Kamo, (no), Mabuchi (1941) *Meaning of Words and Meaning of Writing*, ed. by Yoshio Matsuda, Tokyo: Iwanami. 賀茂真淵 (1941) 「語意・書意」 （松田好夫校訂）岩波文庫

Kan, Shochu abd Shun'ya Yoshimi (1999) "Perspective of Globalization – The 1st Article of the Aeries 'A challenge to a hybridized society – seeking a public space in globalization'", *Sekai*, June vol., Tokyo: Iwanami. 姜尚中・吉見俊哉 (1999) 「混成化社会への挑戦－グローバル化のなかの公共空　間をもとめて」第一回「グローバル化の遠近法」世界1999六月号

Kato, Shuichi (1989) "History and People – Thinking of the Showa Era", January vol., *Sekai*, Tokyo: Iwanami. 加藤周一 (1989)「歴史と人間－昭和を考える」世界1989 一月号

Kawahara, Naoto (2004) "On the Transition of Calues in our Country's Medical History", http://www.bioethics.jp/naox_report1-j.html 河原直人 (2004)「我が国の医療史における価値の変遷について」

Kawakita, Jiro (1973) *Exploration of Japanese Culture*, Tokyo: Kodansha. 川喜多二郎 (1973)「日本文化探検」講談社文庫

Koeki, Shoichi (1995) *Birth of the New Constitution*, Tokyo: Chuo-koron. 小関彰一 (1995)「新憲法の誕生」中公文庫

Kuki, Shuzo (1979) *The Structure of Iki*, Tokyo: Iwanami. 九鬼周造 (1979)「『いき』の構造」岩波文庫

Matsuoka, Seigou (2002) A book review of *Genealogy of Wakon-Yosai* by Sukehiro Hirakawa, 1989, Tokyo: New Kawade Shobo. http://www.isis.ne.jp/mnn/senya/senya0686.html
松岡正剛 (2002)書評 平川祐弘(1989)「和魂洋才の系譜」河出書房新社 http://www.isis.ne.jp/mnn/senya/senya0686.html

Maruyama, Masao (1961) *Thoughts of Japan*, Tokyo: Iwanami. 丸山真 (1961)「日本の思想」岩波新書

—— (1998) *Loyalty and Rebellion – Spiritual Phases During the Transitional Period of Japan*, Tokyo: Chikuma.
—— (1998)「忠誠と反逆-転換期日本の精神的位相」ちくま学芸文庫

Maruyama, Masao and Shuichi Kato (1998) *Translation and Modern Times of Japan*, Tokyo: Iwanami. 丸山真男・加藤周一 (1998)「翻訳と日本の近代」岩波新書

Mori, Senzo (1963) "Holland New Year", *Complete Works of Educating about World*, vol. 17, Tokyo: Heibonsha. 森銑三 (1963)「おらんだ正月」世界教養全集17 平凡社

Naito, Torajiro (1925) "Tominaga, Nakamoto, A Commoner scholar in Osaka", http://www.aozora.gr.jp/cards/000284/files/1735_4336.html 内藤虎次郎 (1925)「大阪の町人學者富永仲基」

—— (1963) "Study of Japanese Cultural History", *Complete Works of Educating about World*, vol. 17, Tokyo: Heibonsha.
—— (1963)「日本文化史研究」世界教養全集17平凡社

Natori, Takao (1982) "Japanese Spirit vs. Western Spirit – Agony Among Missionaries in the Meiji Era", http://www5e.biglobe.ne.jp/~jhntakna/wakon.html 名取多嘉雄 (1982)「和魂対洋魂—明治期のおける宣教師たちの苦悩」

Ohtahara, Takaaki (2002) "Uchimura, Kanzo and Nitobe, Inazo", http://socyo.high.hokudai.ac.jp/Journal/J10PDF/No1013.pdf 太田原高昭 (2002)「内村鑑三と新渡戸稲造」

Okakura, Kakuzo (1929) *Book of Tea*, translated by Hiroshi Muraoka, Tokyo: Iwanami. 岡倉覚三 (1929)「茶の本」（村岡博訳）岩波文庫

Ota, Norio (2003) "What is *Chushingura* to current Japan?", a panel presentation, JCCC.

Saeki, Shoichi (1990) *Autobiographies in Modern Japan*, Tokyo: Chuo-koron. 佐伯彰一 (1990)「近代日本の自伝」中央文庫 Shimizu, Masayuki ( ) "History of Sensibility – History of Thoughts re Accepting Science and Technology in Japan", http://www.valdes.titech.ac.jp/~kuwako/kanphi-1-1.pdf 清水正之「感性の来歴－日本での科学技術受容の思想史から」

Shindo, M., T. Sasaki, K. Takeda, S. Kamei and J. Nishikawa (1988) "120th Year After the Meiji Era (began) and 'Globalization' – Past, Present and Near Future of Nationalism" 進藤宗幸・佐々木毅・武田清子・亀井俊介・西川潤 (1988)「明治120年と『国際化』－ナショナリズムの過去・現在・近未来」世界1988四月号

Sugita, Genpaku (1963) "Beginning Dutch Study", *Complete Works of Educating about World*, vol. 17, Tokyo: Heibonsha. 杉田玄白 (1963)「蘭学事始」世界教養全集17 平凡社

Suzuki, Daisetsu (1940) *Zen and Japanese Culture*, translated by Momo'o Kitagawa, Tokyo: Iwanami. 鈴木大拙 (1940)「禅と日本文化」(北川桃雄訳) 岩波新書

Wallace, Michael J. (1991) *Training Foreign Language Teachers: A Reflective Approach*, Cambridge: Cambridge University Press.

Watsuji, Tetsuro (1992) *Study of the History of Japanese Minds*, Tokyo: Iwanami. 和辻哲郎 (1992)「日本精神史研究」岩波文庫

Yamamoto, Hiroshi (2000) "Self-understanding and Lack of a Catalyst – One Way of Reading So's Thesis", 山本博史「自己理解と媒介の不在―曹論文のひとつの読み方―」http://www.res.otemon.ac.jp/~yamamoto/works_2/essay_02.htm

Yamazaki, Masakazu (1990) *Japanese Culture and Individualism*, Tokyo: Chuo-koron. 山崎正和 (1990)「日本文化と個人主義」中央公論社

9　Caught in a "restless dream"

Contemporary Japanese women writers and the era of globalization

Janice Brown

> I am in the midst of a dream, even now, while typing at my word processor ... In the dream I am in the usual place. Even though I say the usual place, I don't know exactly where that is.
>
> (Shōno Yoriko, *Restless Dream.*, Tokyo: Kodansha, 1994, 9)

For some years past, international institutions such as the G7/G8 group, the OECD (Organisation for Economic Co-operation and Development), the World Trade Organization (WTO), as well as numerous other multi-nation blocs such as the North American Free Trade Agreement (NAFTA), Asia Pacific Economic Cooperation (APEC), Association of Southeast Asian Nation (ASEAN), and a host of transnational corporations have placed themselves as front-runners in a race to foster, maintain, and expand the new era of globalization. At the same time, there also appear an even larger number of non-governmental organizations, local civic action groups and associations, and other loosely bound bodies who actively oppose, critique, and struggle to contest what they see as the incursions of a hegemonic global system little different in agenda from that of the former colonizing world powers. As Rey Chow frankly states: "From the perspective of many non-Western cultures, to globalize has meant predominately one thing: to subordinate, derogate, or extinguish one's native language, culture, history, in order to accommodate those of the West" (*PMLA* 2001, 116:1, 69). The tensions generated when these antagonistic forces meet have been amply demonstrated not only in the terrorist attacks in the US and elsewhere, but closer to home on the UBC campus as well as on the streets of Seattle, Quebec City, and Genoa. Although globalization is generally understood as a business or economic-related phenomenon, as seen in these instances, there are also many further implications for peoples and cultures. Such implications are often overlooked in the predominant discourses of globalization. For example, economist Kym Anderson, writing in a recent World Bank publication, defines globalization as "the decline in ... barriers to doing business *or otherwise interacting with people of other nations around the world*" (Anderson, 2000: 9–10, italics mine). Anderson then goes on to discuss the role played by markets, capital, labour, and technology in the globalization process. However, the second half of Anderson's definition, "otherwise interacting with people of other nations around the world," receives short shrift. In fact, it is not addressed in Anderson's article, and we can only surmise what is meant by this phrase. It sounds as if Anderson is referring, however obliquely, to modes of cultural and societal exchange and communication that are inextricably connected in varying degrees with economic factors. Anderson seems only vaguely aware of the interrelatedness of such interchanges, and further, of the implications of complex global/local networks wherein, as Fredric Jameson describes it, "the economic [is] gradually becoming cultural, all the while the cultural [is] gradually becoming economic" (Jameson and Miyoshi, 1998: 70).

The assumption that underlies Anderson's approach, however, is common to many works on globalization, that is, that economic factors subsume all else, and that the financial re-shaping or re-structuring of the world economy is an entirely desirable, even utopic *fait accompli*. This assumption also holds true for many globalization studies on Japan. Accordingly, given the emphasis on economics and business, Japanese cultural production is only beginning to be considered in relation to what we identify and name as globalization. A few recent publications which have ventured into this area of culture and the global with reference to Japan include Roland Robertson's *Globalization: Social Theory and Global Culture* (1992); Rob Wilson and Wimal Dissanayake's *Global/Local: Cultural Production and the Transnational Imaginary* (1996); and John Clammer's "In But Not Of the World? Japan, Globalization and the 'End of History'" in Colin Hay and David Marsh's *Demystifying Globalization* (2000). Lise Skov and Brian Moeran's *Women, Media and Consumption in Japan* (1995) is notable in its exclusive focus on Japan and Japanese women. An important contribution to the definition and application of globalization theory to contemporary Asian culture, focusing on China and Korea but containing no specific Japanese study, is Fredric Jameson and Miyoshi Masao's *The Cultures of Globalization* (1998). I mention these volumes for their excellence as well as for the issues their publication raises with regard to my topic, Japanese women writers and globalization. This chapter will briefly consider selected literary texts of contemporary Japanese women writers which confront the nexus of gender, sexuality, and culture, critical matters which, I will argue, continue to remain at the margins of globalization discourse.

With the exception of Skov and Moeran's work, and one chapter by Karen Kelsky in *Global/Local*, the majority of the above-mentioned texts studiously avoid any substantial treatment of women, gender, gender relations, or sexuality. When the subject of gender is broached, as in Roland Robertson's *Globalization*, the reader is rewarded merely with a "*note* on women and gender" (italics mine), which encompasses three pages out of a 200-plus page text. From works such as these, it would seem that little over half the world's population has small involvement in and even smaller contribution to make to globalization and global culture. This, of course, is far from global reality. Political economist Isabella Bakker is one of many feminist theorists who comment on such exclusionary practices.[1] She finds male-centred globalization discourse effectively "silences" female realities and further, fails "to acknowledge explicitly or implicitly that global restructuring is occurring on a gendered terrain" (Bakker, 1994: 1). As a result, feminist critiques of globalization remain peripheral to and outside the scope of much global theory. Like the "silenced" women it proposes to treat, feminist work on globalization has not yet been accorded a "voice" in mainstream globalization debates. A prominent cultural anthropologist, Sarah Franklin, would also agree, noting that "critical feminist studies have so far had little impact on dominant conceptualizations of the globalization process" (Franklin *et al.*, 2000: 16).

Were women to be fully included in the current globalization debates, we would expect to find prominently placed and fully attended to by all participants in the aforementioned economic and political meetings matters of significant concern which affect women individually and in general, such as factory and sweat shop labour, domestic labour, labour policies and practices in general, emigration ("femigration"), sex trade and prostitution, reproduction and child care, access to education, to name a few.

However, the extent to which gender has been excluded from globalization discourse is a cause for concern. A perusal of two recent major publications on globalization which purport to offer, respectively, according to the book covers, a "striking intervention," and an "essential tool for understanding," provide no significant discussion of gender at all. *Globalization*, edited by one of the foremost globalization theorists, Arjun Appadurai (2001), does not even list "gender" or "sexuality" in the index, even though one of the contributors to the volume treats Chinese women and issues of gender and sexuality in some detail. The other, *Globalization: The Reader*, edited by John Beynon and David Dunkerley (2000), mentions gender twice, and provides one selection on "virtual sex." Male bias in globalization studies and the unchallenged assumptions that underlie such bias would seem to call for a bit more "intervention" and "understanding" than is offered by these texts.

When scholars like Arjun Appadurai do address gender, they tend to do so in perfunctory and stereotypical fashion. Even in "Disjuncture and Difference in the Global Cultural Economy," in which Appadurai puts forward his well-known idea of global cultural flow in terms of "scapes" (e.g., ethnoscapes, mediascapes, technoscapes, finanscapes, ideoscapes) (Appadurai, 1990: 6–7), he has little to say about women, unless they are prostitutes, domestic workers, household managers, or something called "airline stewardesses" (Appadurai, 1990: 13; 18–19; 12). All Appadurai's primary examples are concerned with men; his imaginary formulations which purport to be gender-neutral are, in fact, male-dominant. For Appadurai, there seems to be no possibility of a "genderscape."

Even Jameson and Miyoshi, whose collection of essays on globalization offers substantial critical food for thought, completely misses the gender issue. A graduate student questions this oversight. In a comment appended to the end of the text "In Place of a Conclusion," the student notes that none of the contributors explored feminism or sexuality-based critiques. She wonders why pro-globalization discourse as well as the "critiques of globalization (such as represented by Jameson and Masao's volume) [do not] address issues of gender and sexuality as central concerns ..." (Jameson and Miyoshi, 1998: 377). Neither Jameson nor Miyoshi provide an answer to her question; in fact, they are uncharacteristically silent. That the female graduate student's comment is simply tacked on at the end of the volume underlines further not only the marginal position occupied by feminist critique in globalization discourse but also the complicity of male scholars and theorists in maintaining the status quo. Being silenced, however, does not necessarily mean that female voices do not speak, only that they are unheard. One such group of voices that speaks volubly and well on a variety of topics, including globalization, is modern and contemporary Japanese women writers. Despite attempts by a male dominant literary establishment to position female writers in a literary "ghetto," women writers in Japan have challenged and continue to challenge such stereotyping, forging for themselves with varying degrees of success a place on the global/local cultural stage.

Reading/writing women in modern and contemporary Japanese literature

Women's writing in modern Japan, despite its celebrated ancient tradition, has experienced many vicissitudes in its relatively short history. When Japan went "global" in modern times in 1867, opportunities for women burgeoned. Participation in the new literary order, fed in part by translations that poured in from abroad, brought women into the forefront of literary production. Although both women and men faced discrimination from a society that tended to look down on professional writers, it was women who suffered most in the conservative backlash of 1880s Japan. Under pressure from government and social theorists, women were declared fit only for the role of "good wife, wise mother," and were effectively barred from literary and public life. By the Taishō era, women had again managed to put forward their own writing through the Bluestocking group, or Seitō, as both the group and its eponymous magazine were called. Flourishing off and on from 1911 through 1916, *Seitō*, too, was eventually quashed by the authorities, yet writing by women had become difficult to dismiss completely. The 1920s saw another brief efflorescence of female authors before the eclipse of modern Japanese literature and culture under the militarist regime of the 1930s and 40s. By the 1950s Japanese women writers were again seeking fora for their voices. It was not until the feminist movements of the 1970s, one hundred years after the first attempt by modern Japanese women to enter literary occupations, that women writers began to be heard in a more significant way within Japan and within the Japanese literary establishment. As for global recognition, however, we must look to the bubble and post-bubble eras of the 1980s and 90s for the voices of Japanese women writers to be heard around the world. Through the endeavours of translators, journalists, and scholars no less than the efforts of the writers themselves, Japanese women writers have only recently succeeded in securing for themselves a small portion of international literary recognition and acclaim.

New directions: the *shōjo* phenomenon

One of the most successful of these new bubble/post-bubble voices is Yoshimoto Banana (b. 1964),[2] known primarily for her immensely popular and best-selling *Kitchen*. Appearing in Japanese in 1988, and in translation in 1993, *Kitchen* may be considered one of the defining moments in contemporary Japanese literature. Things have never been quite the same since. Breaking away from the entrenched forms and themes of the dominant and dominating masculinist literary culture, Banana succeeded in creating a new type of novel. Fusing the style and language of the popular *shōjo manga* (girls' comics) with the *shōsetsu* form, Banana breathed a breath of fresh air into the Japanese literary world. She also, in the best bubble fashion, made a lot of money. Banana's literary and financial success is comparable in some respects to that of Hayashi Fumiko in the 1920s. Like Banana, Fumiko achieved both fame and fortune as a young writer with her *Hōrōki* ([*Diary of a Vagabond*] 1928–1930), which even today represents such a departure from Japanese mainstream fiction as to remain literally unclassifiable. The comparison must stop there, however, for unlike Banana, Fumiko's text remains one of a kind; no matter how revolutionary, it did not lead the literary world in new directions. Banana's writing on the other hand seems to have ushered in a whole new genre and to have encouraged a host of new female writers, the so-called *shōjo shōsetsu* writers, such as Yamamoto Fumio and Iwai Shimako, who in their turn have also captured top literary prizes, similar to Banana; Yamamoto received the Naoki Prize in 2001 for *Puranaria* ([*Planaria*] 2000) and Iwai a number of other awards in 1999 and 2000. These writers, and others like them, have continued to explore the psychology of young women, like Banana, and to promote new ideas and areas, such as fantasy and horror fiction, in mainstream literature.

Another important female writer who developed out of what we might call *shōjo manga* romance fiction is Yamada Eimi (b. 1959). In comparison to Banana, Eimi is much less innovative with regard to gender and gender relations. While both Banana and Eimi's narratives may be classed as *shōjo* romance, Banana's writings tend to problematize gender, focusing on romantic entanglements that conjure up brother/sister rather than girlfriend/boyfriend, or on the other hand, openly challenging traditional male/female roles, as in the case of the transsexual father/mother figure, Eriko, in *Kitchen*. By way of contrast, Yamada Eimi's stories and novels are not gender-benders. For Eimi, the heterosexual love relationship is of prime concern. Her female protagonists are always searching for a "good man." What fascinated and scandalized many early readers of Eimi's first published work, *Beddotaimu aizu* ([*Bedtime Eyes*] 1985), was not the female protagonist's struggle with gender relationships per se, but the fact that the main love interest was an African-American GI stationed at a US military base near Tokyo. Eimi's fascination with African-American men in particular and with black culture in the US in general resonated with the "burakku" (black) trend that swept Japan in the late 1980s and early 90s, Eimi being one of the main proponents of this domestic craze. It led Eimi to continue to write a number of stories and novels that feature young Japanese women intimately involved with this exotic "Other."

Many of these works, like her debut piece, have transliterated English titles (for example, *Sōru myūjikku rabāzu onrī* [*For Soul-Music Lovers Only*] and *Hāremu wārudo* [*Harlem World*], both 1987); English words and phrases, mostly slang and obscenities, are skillfully integrated into the Japanese text. Although Yamada Eimi has been successful in introducing some aspects of African-American experience to Japanese readers, her work reads as a kind of reverse "Orientalism" (or more simply, perhaps, as "Occidentalism"?). In Yamada's stories, African-Americans are often romanticized as being "slovenly ... feeling-oriented ... with an insatiable appetite for love" (Mulhern, 1994: 462). Some critics have harsh criticisms, such as Karen Kelsky, who notes: "(Yamada's) works themselves are nothing more than soft-core pornographic novels which capitalize on the very worst racist notions of black male sexuality and racial inferiority ..." (Kelsky, 1996: 180). Locked into such essentialist agenda, it becomes difficult for Eimi to maintain her role of sympathetic solidarity with black culture except only insofar as she wishes to lose herself in the hedonism she identifies within the culture of this exotic Other. Further, relations between men and women in Eimi's texts, in spite of the unconventional background, remain surprisingly conventional, even to the point of pathology. In *Trash* (*Torasshu*, 1991, tr. 1994), Eimi tells the story of a young Japanese woman living in the US with her abusive, alcoholic, African-American boyfriend. The female protagonist stays with him because "there isn't a woman alive who can love Rick the way I do" (*Trash*: 7). Eventually, she leaves Rick but only after she has managed to secure another male lover. Eimi's dependent love-sick females resonate not only with the typical *shōjo* romance but also with the long-suffering, perennially waiting women of classical Japanese literature. In terms of *shōjo* romance fiction, however, we find in Yoshimoto Banana's writings an attempt to de-construct traditional images of Japan and create new visions of romance and family, while Yamada Eimi's passionate pursuit of African-American males may be read as an escape from Japan rather than an engagement with real issues in either culture. In spite of her apparently radical chic, Eimi's refusal to question standard gender dichotomies results in a re-confirmation of repressive familial and societal norms. At the same time, however, her work also foregrounds atypical notions of cross-cultural, contemporary global interaction.

Despite their success, writers of *shōjo shōsetsu*, like Yoshimoto Banana and Yamada Eimi, have been criticized frequently for literary production that caters to the whims of mass culture. Their very popularity brings with it a commodification that mitigates against "serious" consideration by certain (mostly middle-aged male) elements within the literary establishment.[3] Nonetheless, despite accusations of "over-wrought sentimentality," "banality," and so on (Treat, WMCJ: 287), the *shōjo* writers have been eminently successful in changing what is deemed suitable both as form and as subject matter in contemporary Japanese literature. As John Treat points out in his work on Banana, her fictions are viewed by readers as "easy to understand," and written in a style that evokes the "real" (Treat, CJPC: 279). Although Banana's literary creation of alternate families and trans-gender mother/fathers is not necessarily identifiable as a common experience for Japanese (or global) readers, Treat points out that what is meant by the "real" is less an evocation of quotidian reality than the fact that Banana's "emerging sub-genre of fiction positively affords readers the power to imagine themselves and their place as other than the constraints of everyday life otherwise dictate" (Treat, CJPC: 285). In retrospect, this imaginative appeal of Japanese *shōjo* fiction may be identified as a major factor in its exponential spread beyond the boundary of its origins.

Treat's articles on Banana Yoshimoto constituted an attempt to provide an explication of Japanese popular literary culture of the 1980s and 90s. However, by the 00s, many if not most of his observations have become increasingly relevant on the global literary stage. In particular, Treat's observations – that the *shōjo* may be understood as "a master-sign for economic consumption"; and that "in some sense, anyone who consumes in Japan today is to that extent a shōjo" (Treat, CJPC: 281) – are no longer applicable only to Japan. Consumers of *shōjo* fiction continue to proliferate worldwide. Given the enormous popularity of *shōjo* fiction and *shōjo*-inspired literary and cultural productions, including manga, anime, and a host of concomitant artifacts and commodities, it is clear that Banana and the *shōjo* are today part of a vast global phenomenon. The global appeal of *shōjo* fiction, however, is the result not only of economic factors but also of a shared recognition among consumers that her works "function both as a corroboration of consumer culture … and as a corrective imaginary …" (Treat, CJPC: 304).

For all their appeal, works of *shōjo* fiction in general remain largely unconcerned with matters that go beyond the immediately personal or in producing a coherent critique of Japanese culture and society. For some of the most sustained, even virulent social critiques of and by women in the new global order as well as the process of globalization itself, we must look not to the *shōjo* writers but to what may be termed "dream" fiction by contemporary Japanese women writers.

"Dream" fiction: breaking the bounds of global "reality"

Somewhat less known outside of Japan than either Banana or Eimi, anti-realist, "dream" fiction writers have just begun to receive a great deal of critical attention. Many are beginning to be translated.[4] Some of these writers, like Ogino Anna (b. 1956) and Matsuura Rieko (b. 1958), construct wildly humourous and improbable worlds filled with freaks and the grotesque. The protagonist of Matsuura Rieko's *Oyayubi P no shugyō jidai* ([*The Apprenticeship of Big Toe P*] 1993), for example, wakes up one day with a huge penis in place of her big toe. The author proceeds to deconstruct the categories of "male," "female," "lesbian," "gay," "bisexual," etc. as viable descriptors of human beings in what one critic, Tatsumi Takayuki, has labelled "slipstream literature" (*JLT*, 1995: 70).[5] By this term, Tatsumi seems to imply that Matsuura's crazily transforming gender regimes have somehow violated the stable category of literature itself, sweeping it away in the wake of her bold experiment.

Other female anti-realist writers like Tawada Yōko (b. 1960) and Shōno Yoriko (b. 1956) move beyond such Rabelaisian rebellion into other dimensions, creating bizarre dreamscapes in which female protagonists find themselves stranded in distant foreign lands, unable to fully demarcate self or other, as in Tawada Yōko's "Missing Heels" ("Kakato wo nakushite", 1992; tr. 1998, Margaret Mitsutani in *The Bridegroom Was a Dog*) or "The Gotthard Railway" ("Gotthard tetsudō", 1996; tr. 1998, ibid.). In Shōno Yoriko's writing, female figures wander alone through a post-industrial, alien Japan, as for example, in "Timewarp Complex" ("Taimu surippu kombināto," 1994, tr. 1995, Fulford, Takahashi, and Itō in *JLT*: 20) or find themselves under attack by zombies in a dangerous role-playing computer game, as in *Resutoresu dorīmu* ([*Restless Dream*] 1994). Unsettling and disturbing, these works seem as typical of the 90s and 00s just as the upbeat writings of Yoshimoto Banana and Yamada Eimi were of the 1980s bubble era.

Unlike the writers of *shōjo* romance fiction, the writers of "dream" narrative rely on distortion of reality, the bending and re-working of accepted boundaries of space and time, and the incorporation of deterritorialized, technological, and/or electronic environments in their texts. For these writers, the dream is less a state of consciousness, than a site of writing, or word processing, as Shōno Yoriko would have it, where the boundaries between author and protagonist, global and local, real and virtual, overlap, intersect, fuse. Ever cognizant of the new opportunities offered by the compressed/collapsed space-time of a borderless, globalized world as well as its disjunctures and biases, these writers are not "swept away" in the slipstream, as Tatsumi would have it. In fact, they remain alert and critical, fully aware of the inequities, contradictions, and ironies of their situation. In line with comparatist Reingard Nethersole's observation that globalization has meant not only the erasure of distinctions and boundaries, but also the "redrawing" of new boundaries and borders (Nethersole, 2001: 644–646), writers like Tawada and Shōno are eager to explore these new dimensions, at the same time extending limits and adding their own designs.

I would like to examine briefly three examples of "dream" fiction by these two writers: "Missing Heels" by Tawada Yōko, and "Timewarp Complex" and *Restless Dream* by Shōno Yoriko. In all three narratives, dream plays a major role, yet does not function as romantic device, as is the case in the *shōjo* romance; neither does it operate at the level of elegant philosophical musing as in the indigenous tradition.[6] Instead, dream is the trope through which these writers describe and interrogate the contemporary environment, discovering in this discursive space a de-humanizing yet fantastic arena in which "reality" shifts continually between dream and nightmare. Besides the resonance with certain types of science fiction and fantasy texts, the approach of these Japanese women "dream" fictionists may also be compared to the "magical realism" of such Latin American authors as Jorge Luis Borges (1899–1986), or with the fiction of Franz Kafka (1883–1924). While it is beyond the scope of this essay to explore these relationships fully, one major point of connection between these forms of writing can be seen in the lack of distinction between the "dream" world and the real world. Dreams do not appear to be any more or less frightening or absurd than waking consciousness; and whether dreaming or awake, the protagonists in all cases experience worlds that are macabre and/or hyper-real. The dream, in fact, offers a critical perspective through which writers may explore ideas, situations, and events that are disturbing, frightening, unsettling.

In "Missing Heels," for example, Tawada Yōko introduces a young mail-order bride who arrives in an unspecified European country presumably from the impoverished third world. Thrown unceremoniously off the train "like a canvas mailbag" (Tawada: 65) at her destination, the young bride has to make her way alone through the city in search of her husband. What follows is a *cauchemar* of the monstrous as the migrant bride navigates a culture-shock scenario of violent crime, rampant nationalism, xenophobia, and obscure yet enigmatic examples of patriarchal control and manipulation, each event imbued with a hallucinatory quality. The sense of dream-like absurdity is ever-present. At one point, soon after her arrival, she watches a billboard being stripped of its signage so that new advertising can be put into place. The workman "tore away the stomach of a woman in blue tights, [then] a breakfast eggcup and teapot appeared, then a whale off to one side, another layer down" (Tawada: 65–66). This peeling away of layers in which the commodified female body reveals first eggs and then a sea creature beneath its surface is to be re-enacted as if in a distorting mirror by the bride herself during the course of the story.

These three elements – female body, eggs, and aquatic animal – are re-positioned and interchanged with dream-like randomness as the global Alice in Wonderland experiences an ever-increasing sense of dis-ease and dislocation. In the main instance, the bride is forced to share a large house with a mysterious husband she never meets, except in her dreams. Nonetheless, he manages to leave a freshly boiled egg for her breakfast every morning. Overcome with curiosity, the bride eventually hires a locksmith to open her husband's room, although she has been told never to enter his quarters. The room proves to be empty, except for a small blob on the floor which, on closer examination, turns out to be a dead squid.

Recalling fairytales of Bluebeard, or Japanese folktales of non-human husbands, the dead squid-husband is a much less potent figure than male figures in the anterior tales. His actual presence is relatively unnecessary to the bride; even as a foreigner, she is able to go about her daily business without his aid or assistance. The husband's existence need be invoked only on occasion, such as when the bride attempts to gain the respect of institutions and officials by declaring, "I'm married." The oblique naming of the husband in this way and its effect on teachers, doctors, nurses, policemen, and other representatives of the alien first world society demonstrates not only the unquestioned power of patriarchal law but also suggests, given that the husband in question is a mere squid (and eventually a dead one at that), the impotence that masquerades behind the façade of power.

The bride herself, however, is by no means blameless; she is also implicated in the deception – in a very corporeal way. In spite of her attempt to marshall respect by invoking the patriarchal husband, she finds herself laughed at repeatedly by the people of the city. She is shocked to discover that her body seems to share a physiology similar to that of her mysterious partner; like a squid, she has no heels.[7] The significance of such disfigurement is linked to her status as a migrant female in a series of episodes that problematize the absurd, dream-like narrative with jarring intrusions of political and economic realities. For example, at one point, the teacher at the language school makes it clear that the bride has no claim to equality; she is at most a second- or third-class citizen, a woman of "an inferior sort" who, like many others, has been "brought into the country from poorer parts of the world" as cheap, domestic labour (Tawada, 104). The teacher's complaint is that "since far too many men here were interested in [these women], marriage opportunities for her more liberated countrywomen were more and more limited" (Tawada: 104). The young bride protests that she is not like those women; she came to this country of her own free will. The teacher replies: "Poor people have no will of their own … whatever they do, they have no choice in the matter – poverty drives them to it" (Tawada: 104). The teacher's superior attitude is shared by all with whom the bride comes into contact, even the nurse at the hospital who gives the bride a pamphlet entitled: "The Heel and Other Cultures: A Socio-medical Study" (Tawada: 120). Clearly, the bride from the poor country is seen as something less than human – an exotic specimen, her body inscribed by the dominant discourse as immigrant, poor, uneducated, culturally backward. She is essentially unemployable, good only for "marriage," that is, domestic servitude. Nonetheless, the bride manages to find some consolation in her deformity. While working at a job tearing the ears off squid in a street stall, the bride comes to admire the legs of these creatures because they have no heels and "can go whichever way they please … backward as well as forward" (Tawada: 73). Without doubt, migrant women, such as the heelless bride, do find opportunity and advantage in their bid for a better life. According to one European political economist, Brigitte Young, globalization has provided some opportunities for women, and "should not be looked upon only as a negative phenomenon for gender relations," (Young: 45) nor as "only a nightmarish scenario" (Young: 46). Nonetheless, Tawada's text seems to challenge any such positivist notions; the bride's situation is far from opportune; her heels are missing, and so, of course, is her squid-husband. Thus, the possibility that a poor, underclass, non-European woman might be able to move, like the heel-less squid, in "any direction she wishes" by making her way to a rich, first world nation, is undercut even as the success of such undertaking is denied by the trope of the missing heels.

In this story, Tawada Yōko treats the experiences of a migrant, non-European female in the brave new global world as a frustratingly ridiculous chimera. The most the heelless bride can expect is a life of servitude and dependence and, despite the promise of a desired traditional domestic arrangement, she finds herself inhabiting a realm of nightmare rather than dream-come-true. While migrant women now number in the millions[8] and are indispensable in maintaining diverse global systems, not to mention the process of globalization itself, their contribution and participation in the on-going "fundamental realignment of the social, economic, and political" spheres (Brodie: 58), like that of the heelless bride, remains largely unacknowledged and unrecognized by male globalization theorists.

The approach to gender and globalization issues through "dream" fiction is developed from a more "glocal" perspective by Shōno Yoriko in her writings of the 1990s. In "Timewarp Complex," Shōno, similar to Tawada, also describes a dream romance. Instead of a squid, however, the female protagonist in "Timewarp Complex" claims to be in love with a tuna. She pursues this dream lover by train and on foot through the badlands of post-industrial Japan, which she describes as the "aftermath of the devastation of the industrial dream, the scene of what's left after everything is over" (Shōno: 26–27). In its bleakness and unrelieved absurdity, the view from the window of the train confirms the protagonist's angst:

> Past Tokyo, narrow canals enter my field of vision. Apartment houses peep out between buildings drab as the back of a cat's tail ... Amid a succession of low-rise apartments and high-rise condominiums, only factory names and signboards stand out. Galle Omori Stainless Processing, Asahi Glass, Asahi Cardboard, a somber giant crane, Japan Electron ... Vietnamese cuisine. A sign for Egg Calcium 50, PALIO – what the heck's that?
>
> (Shōno: 32)

The fellow passengers she comes into contact with are equally beyond her understanding. She notices two fashionably dressed young women seated next to her:

> [T]hey've been speaking in oddly quiet voices ever since I boarded the train: Ri-te-ne." "Shi-te-ne." "Ri-te-ne." "Shi-te-ni-ne." ... "Ri-te-ne ki-u-i-shi-te shi-te-ni. Ah, fukiyo, Express." "Ni-neri-shi-te-ni. Ni-neri-shi-te-ni ..." Their hands move along to the words. Both have their hands over at an angle to the right, fingertips together and up at eye level, poised it seems to deliver a slap. ... Maintaining the slapping pose, the women stand up, then go for their bags. I expect them to start delivering theatre handbills or pamphlets for a new religion, then out come big packs of generic Sweetened Jumbo Corn just like the ones they sell at Family Mart.
>
> (Shōno: 32–33)

Not only is the female protagonist unable to comprehend the meaning of the advertising signs she sees, the gestures and language of her fellow passengers are also unfathomable. The Japanese language spoken by the two fashionable *shōjo* is nothing more than gibberish – an ironic comment that points not only to a critique of *shōjo* culture in particular but also to the breakdown of meaningful communication in a consumerist world bound almost entirely by factory signs and brand names.

Literary scholar Yonaha Keiko views Shōno's work as that of a writer who is engaged in a "radical war with words" (Yonaha: 196) and indeed, as in the above quotation, Shōno's antagonism seems directed as much at language as at the industrial wasteland or feather-brained *shōjo*. In this regard, the above passage is preceded by the protagonist admitting she knows nothing of the "real" world. She states that, for her, politics and economics are even "more incomprehensible than a foreign language" (Shōno: 26). Being unable to understand the major discourses of a globalizing world, that is, politics and economics, the protagonist finds herself at a decided disadvantage. The entry of the consumer-adept *shōjo*, who seem able to operate easily within the "real-world" system and thus able to communicate volubly with each other, if not with the protagonist, further serves to heighten and confirm the female protagonist's already acute sense of linguistic disorientation and dislocation. The "timewarp" of the title thus seems to be a kind of "space-time trap" whereby the protagonist finds herself caught up in a glocalized world, but is unable to construct meaning, or secure for herself a suitable niche. As well, time itself proves to be problematic.

After several missed trains and false trails, the protagonist reaches her destination. But it is too late. The tuna is not there. Instead, she finds a Tōshiba factory where her mother worked for half a year as an engineer over forty years ago. The mother was forced to leave her job because her fellow workers resented her trying to earn the same wages as a man. After she left the factory, she went to work in a food product company where she was assigned simple, repetitive tasks. As the female protagonist calls up this memory, she peers between the boards of the train platform at the ocean in which she discovers a resemblance to the sea of her dream. Yet it is "[t]he sea of the dream minus the tuna of the dream" (Shōno: 48). Like Urashima Tarō, Shōno's female traveller, too, has received the call of the ocean and the promise of love from the deep, but in the end meets only desolation and unhappy memory. On the factory wall a sign catches her attention: "Together with the factory let's advance without limit towards the twenty-first century" (Shōno: 48). Past, present, and future, as well as the protagonist's dreamtime telescope into a disappointing, even menacing, reality. If, as Roland Robertson maintains, globalization emphasizes "the scope and depth of consciousness of the world as single place" (Robertson: 113), then Shōno's global vision is decidedly disturbing. As her protagonist declares: "Outside it's *Blade Runner*; inside it's *Star Wars*; I'm a replicant; and Mad Max may be out there somewhere as well" (Shōno: 46). Clearly, the protagonist's narrative encapsulates a single female space beset by exploitative, masculinist forces operating on a global/local stage without restraint. In Shōno's post-bubble imaginary, the position of women seems to have taken a downward spiral. This dismaying dream-tale of a journey to nowhere in search of a non-human dream-lover who never materializes shares parallels with "Missing Heels" and the plight of the immigrant bride. Yet in its evocation of local specificity, Shōno's dream narrative both delineates as well as indigenizes the deranged socio-economic "genderscape" of globalization.

Shōno Yoriko's exploration of a neo-liberal, post-human world is found not only in "Timewarp Complex." In *Restless Dream* (1994), such concerns reach a "virtual" crescendo. In this longer fiction, the female protagonist is trapped in a computer game world she can enter only as a role-playing dreamer. Throughout the novel, the female dreamer occasionally "wakes up," and finds herself back in her own room, tapping at her word-processor, keeping a dream-diary. Despite her attempt to make sense of the dream, she is unable to control it or escape it;

neither is she able to define her point of entry into it. There seems to be no way to keep the two realms separate as game/dream unexpectedly become reality, and vice versa. Shōno's continually transforming text reads as literary recognition and representation of the fears of globalization of critics like Paul Virilio who writes: "To my mind, this is one of the most crucial aspects of the development of the new technologies of digital imagery and of the symbolic vision offered by electron optics; the relative *fusion/confusion* of the factual … and the virtual …" (Virilio: 60, italics mine). Not only is the protagonist ensnared in a Virilian cyber-nightmare, she is also forced to return to the game again and again, and to repeat the same actions over and over, a prisoner of whatever role the game deems she must play. As in "Timewarp Complex," the dream both motivates and directs the protagonist's actions; yet in *Restless Dream*, the dream is intensified as computer operated, in control of the production of the text just as it is of the protagonist's "reality."

Somewhat different from the geo-specific indigenous wasteland in "Timewarp Complex," Shōno's game/dream comprises non-geographical, yet gendered sites of battle and contestation, infinite and ever-escalating. The digital world and its virtual images thus comprise a powerful new "virtuality" which the protagonist must navigate in order to insure her own survival. The numerous interactive environments in which she finds herself are inhabited by deadly insects, killer zombies, and other hideous beings. In this violent *otaku*-esque dreamland, the only escape is to move on to the next level. At the end of the narrative, the female protagonist does manage to extricate herself from the game, but only by destroying her role-playing alter-ego. At one point, having survived an attack of killer-zombies, the protagonist finds herself in a "Hell for Stupid Women." In this level of the game, the world consists of a madly swirling escalator of words. As the female gamer attempts to escape the dizzying maze by climbing the stairs, each step lets loose with a barrage of verbal abuse: "It's the stupid woman." "Stupid woman's here." "Kill the stupid woman." "It's that stupid woman who annoys men." "Where's that stupid woman?" "I said stupid woman." "Hey, I'm no stupid woman." "Stupid woman" (Shōno: 56).

Although the Hell for Stupid Women is purported to exist only in digital space with no basis in "reality," its misogynist agenda is not unfamiliar in the real world. Shōno's interplay of virtual/actual in *Restless Dream* points to the new digital technologies as front-runners in the globalization of the entertainment and communication media, and thus to the stereotypes broadcast and disseminated through such media production. In *Restless Dream*, the stereotypical representations generated by the computer, such as the stupid woman, have the power to destroy, both virtually and actually. If we now inhabit a "teletopian reality," and are on the verge of moving into a "reality" that is actually an interactive virtual environment where we will end up, due to new advances in computer technology, "acting instantaneously in a geographical environment that has itself become virtual" (Virilio, quoted in Beynon and Dunkerley, 2000: 35), then all stereotypes, such as the "stupid woman," and their digital representations are as dangerous as Shōno would have us believe.

In "Timewarp Complex," the dream intrudes into and affects the real while in *Restless Dream*, the dream world is a virtual dystopia, a digital space overlapping with actual place. In both narratives, the protagonist, caught up in the dream, has great difficulty processing reality without reference to the dream. Similar to what Mitsuhiro Yoshimoto calls "the entanglement of the global and the local," (Yoshimoto: 109), Shōno's dream fiction constructs a textual space in which dream and reality, the virtual and the actual, global and local, are inextricably enmeshed. As her female protagonists attempt to find a "place" within this all-encompassing, all-consuming "net-scape," they move into seemingly borderless dimensions and yet at the same time are forced to accept old limitations as they discover/create new boundaries. Thus, in *Restless Dream*, Shōno's protagonist locates herself "in a dream" at the same time that she finds herself "typing at [her] word processor." Intertwining the movement of dream with the fluidity of virtual creation, Shōno's fiction cannot help but be other than always on the move, compelling, contestatory, "restless."

Conclusion

Both Tawada Yōko and Shōno Yoriko explore the outer limits of what they see as a new global "reality." This reality, described and demarcated through the unsettling trope of the dream/nightmare, reveals disempowered female protagonists who occupy central but insignificant roles. No matter what action they undertake, their situation remains problematic; their connections to reality tenuous and contingent. Recent findings by feminist scholars and critics in Japan tend to echo, albeit in different language, the observations of the dream fiction writers; one prominent scholar, Kano Keiko, writes: "… despite institutionalized reform and restructuring of sexual divisions of labor, the subordinate position in which women are placed has not changed" (Kano: 3). Kano's remark is specific to Japan, but could easily be applied to a global context, and in varying degrees to entrenched attitudes that still persist within the new global order. In spite of the so-called breakdown of traditional boundaries, the pale of gender has yet to be effectively breached.

Although the dream fiction writers offer no solutions, their writings reveal a new awareness among contemporary Japanese women writers, one seldom seen in the past, which reaches out to a fragmented, contentious, yet integrally interconnected planet and attempts to construct a mode of response to the injustices and inequities that they perceive. This new fiction provides a fresh literary approach that readily acknowledges the new realities even as it offers scathing critique. Rather than the empowered consumerist women of Yoshimoto Banana and Yamada Eimi's *shōjo* texts, the powerless, uncertain female figures of Tawada Yōko and Shōno Yoriko's contemporary dream fiction speak vividly and earnestly to the uncomfortable realities of a globalized world.

Notes

1 Many feminist scholars comment on this blindness to gender issues. Inderpal Grewal and Caren Kaplan state unequivocally that "[a]s feminists who note the absence of gender issues in all of these world-system theories, we have no choice but to challenge what we see ..." See *Scattered Hegemonies: Postmodernity and Transnational Feminist Practices*, Inderpal Grewal and Caren Kaplan, eds., Minneapolis MN, London: University of Minnesota Press, 1994, 13.

2 When Japanese writers assume pen names, e.g., Natsume Sōseki, Hayashi Fumiko, Yoshimoto Banana, the general practice is to refer to these writers not by their surnames but by their pen names – that is, as Sōseki, Fumiko, Banana, etc.

3 See John Whittier Treat, "Yoshimoto Banana's *Kitchen*, or the Cultural Logic of Japanese Consumerism" in *Women, Media and Consumption in Japan*, Lise Skov and Brian Moeran, eds., Honolulu: University of Hawaii Press, 1995 (herein WMCJ). This book chapter has appeared in two other publication formats (a kind of prequel and sequel?) with some changes in title and contents. See "Yoshimoto Banana Writes Home: Shōjo Culture and the Nostalgic Subject" in *Journal of Japanese Studies*, 19:2, 1993; and "Yoshimoto Banana Writes Home: The Shōjo in Japanese Popular Culture," in *Contemporary Japan and Popular Culture*, John Whittier Treat, ed. Honolulu: University of Hawaii Press, 1996 (herein CJPC).

4 Some recent translations include Matsuura Rieko's *The Apprenticeship of Big Toe P*, trans. Michael Emmerich, Tokyo: Kodansha, set for release in 2010, as well as a number of works by Tawada Yōko, including *The Naked Eye*, trans from German by Susan Bernofsky, New York: New Directions, 2009; *Facing the Bridge*, trans. Margaret Mitsutani, New York: New Directions, 2007; and *Where Europe Begins*, trans. from German and Japanese by Susan Bernofsky and Yumi Selden, New York: New Directions, 2002.

5 The term "slipstream fiction" or "slipstream literature" was coined by science-fiction writer, Bruce Sterling in 1989. See Bruce Sterling, "Catscan 5," in *Science Fiction Eye* 1, no. 5 (July 1989): 77–78. I am indebted to Brad Ambury for this information.

6 One of the most famous "dream" poems in pre-modern literature is found in the *Ise monogatari* (*The Tales of Ise*) where the Ise Virgin sends this reply to her lover: "kimi ya koshi / ware ya yukikemu / omoezu / yumeka utsutsuka / eteka sameteka? Did you come to me? / Was it I who went to you? / I am beyond knowing. / Was it a dream or reality? / Was I sleeping or awake?" See Steven D. Carter, trans., *Traditional Japanese Poetry: An Anthology*, Stanford University Press, 1991, 79.

7 See Reiko Tachibana, "Tawada Yōko's Quest for Exophony" in *Yōko Tawada: Voices from Everywhere*, ed. Doug Slaymaker (Lanham, MD, 2007), 163, for a further discussion of "missing heels" as an indicator of foreignness.

8 The Philippines, for example, has an exceedingly large outflow of workers. Non-governmental organizations in that country calculate that "there are approximately 6.5 million Filipino migrants," and over half of these are women. See Rhacel Salazar Perreñas, *Servants of Globalization: Women, Migration, and Domestic Work* (Stanford, CA: University Press, 2001), p.1. Although migrant women have yet to make a political impact on the global labour force, the political mobilization of women proceeds apace in many so-called third world countries. See Valentine M. Moghadam, "Gender and the Global Economy" in *Revisioning Gender*, Myra Marx Ferree et al., eds., Thousand Oaks, CA, London, New Delhi: Sage Publications, 1999. Moghadam comments: "... if there is a spectre haunting the global economy, it may very well be that of its 'Other,' a global women's movement" (153).

References

Anderson, Kym. "Towards a global financial architecture for the 21st century." In *Local Dynamics in an Era of Globalization*. Shahid Yusuf, Weiping Wu, and Simon Everett, eds. Oxford: Oxford University Press, 2000.

Appadurai, Arjun. "Disjuncture and Difference in the Global Cultural Economy." *Public Culture*, Spring 1990, 2:2, 1–24.

—— ed. *Globalization*. Durham and London: Duke University Press, 2000.

Bakker, Isabella. "Introduction: Engendering Macro-economic Policy Reform in the Era of Global Restructuring and Adjustment." In *The Strategic Silence: Gender and Economic Policy*. Isabella Bakker, ed. London: Zed Books, 1994, 1–29.

Beynon, John and David Dunkerley, eds. *Globalization: The Reader*. New York: Routledge, 2000.

Brodie, Janine. "Shifting the Boundaries: Gender and the Politics of Restructuring." In *The Strategic Silence: Gender and Economic Policy*. Isabella Bakker, ed. London: Zed Books, 1994, 46–60.

Carter, Steven D., tr. *Traditional Japanese Poetry: An Anthology*. Stanford, CA: Stanford University Press, 1991.

Chow, Rey. "How (the) Inscrutable Chinese Led to Globalized Theory." *PMLA*, 116:1 [January 2001], 69–74.

Clammer, John. "In But Not Of the World? Japan, Globalization and the 'End of History.'" In *Demystifying Globalization*. Colin Hay and David March, eds. Hampshire, England and New York: Palgrave, 2000.

Ferree, Myra Max, Judith Lorber, Beth B. Hess, eds. *Revisioning Gender*. Thousand Oaks CA, London, New Delhi: Sage Publications, 1999.

Franklin, Sarah, Celia Lury, Jackie Stacey, eds. *Global Nature, Global Culture*. Thousand Oaks, CA, London, New Delhi: Sage Publications, 2000.

Grewal, Inderpal and Caren Kaplan, eds., *Scattered Hegemonies: Postmodernity and Transnational Feminist Practices*. Minneapolis, London: University of Minnesota Press, 1994.

Jameson, Fredric and Masao Miyoshi, eds. *The Cultures of Globalization*. Durham and London: Duke University Press, 1998.

Kano Keiko, *Gender Studies and Modern Japanese Literature*, Kurume daigaku bungakubu kiyō, 17–18 [2001]: 1–13.

Kelly, Rita Mae, Jane H. Bayes, Mary E. Hawkesworth, Brigitte Young, eds. *Gender, Globalization, and Democratization*. Lanham, MD, Boulder, CO, New York, Oxford: Rowman and Littlefield, 2001.

Kelsky, Karen. "Flirting with the Foreign: Interracial Sex in Japan's 'International' Age." In *Global/Local: Cultural Production and the Transnational Imaginary*. Durham and London: Duke University Press, 1996.

Matsuura Rieko. *Oyayubi P no shugyō jidai* (*The Apprenticeship of Big Toe P*). Tokyo: Kawade shobō shinsha, 1993.

Mulhern, Chieko. *Japanese Women Writers: a bio-critical sourcebook*. Westport, CT: Greenwood Press, 1994.

Nethersole, Reingard. "Models of Globalization." *PMLA*, 116:3 [May 2001]: 638–649.

Parreñas, Rhacel Salazar. *Servants of Globalization: Women, Migration, and Domestic Work*. Stanford, CA: Stanford University Press, 2001.

Robertson, Roland. *Globalization: Social Theory and Global Culture*. Thousand Oaks, CA, London, New Delhi: Sage Publications, 1992.

Shōno Yoriko. *Resutoresu doriimu* (*Restless Dream*). Tokyo: Kodansha, 1994.

—— "Taimu surippu kombinaato: Timewarp Complex." Trans. Adam Fulford, Takahashi Yuriko, and Itō Nobuji. *Japanese Literature Today*, 20 [1995]: 19–49.

Skov, Lise and Brian Moeran, eds. *Women, Media and Consumption in Japan*. Honolulu: University of Hawaii Press, 1995.

Tachibana Reiko. In "Tawada Yōko's Quest for Exophony" in *Yōko Tawada: Voices from Everywhere*. Doug Slaymaker, ed. Lanham, MD: Lexington Books, 2007, 153–168.

Takayuki Tatsumi. "*Oyayubi P no shugyō jidai* (The Apprenticeship of Big Toe P): a novel by Matsuura Rieko." *Japanese Literature Today*, 20 [1995]: 68–73.

Tawada Yōko, "Missing Heels" in *The Bridegroom Was a Dog*, trans. Margaret Mitsutani. Tokyo: Kodansha International, 63–128.

—— *The Naked Eye*. Susan Bernofsky, trans. New York: New Directions, 2009.

—— *Facing the Bridge*, Margaret Mitsutani, trans. New York: New Directions, 2007.

—— *Where Europe Begins*, Susan Bernofsky and Yumi Selden, trans. New York: New Directions, 2002.

Treat, John Whittier. "Yoshimoto Banana's *Kitchen*, or the Cultural Logic of Japanese Consumerism." In *Women, Media and Consumption in Japan*, Lise Skov and Brian Moeran, eds. Honolulu, HI: University of Hawaii Press, 1995.

—— "Yoshimoto Banana Writes Home: Shōjo Culture and the Nostalgic Subject" in *Journal of Japanese Studies*, 19:2 [1993]: 353–397.

—— "Yoshimoto Banana Writes Home: The Shōjo in Japanese Popular Culture," in *Contemporary Japan and Popular Culture*, John Whittier Treat, ed. Honolulu: University of Hawaii Press, 1996.

Virilio, Paul. *The Vision Machine*. Julie Rose, trans. Bloomington and Indianapolis: Indiana University Press, 1994.

Wilson, Rob and Wimal Dissanayake, eds. *Global/Local: Cultural Production and the Transnational Imaginary*. Durham and London: Duke University Press, 1996.

Yamada Eimi. *Trash*. Trans. Sonja Johnson. New York: Kodansha International, 1994.

Yonaha Keiko. "Gendai sakka." ("*Modern Writers*"). In *Josei bungaku o manabu hito no tame ni* (*For People Who Teach Women's Literature*). Watanabe Sumiko, ed. Kyoto: Sekaishisōshi, 2000, 192–198.

Yoshimoto, Mitsuhiro. "Real Virtuality." In *Global/Local: Cultural Production and the Transnational Imaginary*. Rob Wilson and Wimal Dissanayake, eds. Durham and London: Duke University Press, 1996, 107–118.

Young, Brigitte. "Globalization and Gender: A European Perspective." In *Gender, Globalization, and Democratization*. Rita Mae Kelly, Jane H. Bayes, and Mary E. Hawkesworth, Brigitte Young, eds. Lanham, MD, Boulder, CO, New York, Oxford: Rowman and Littlefield, 2001, 27–47.

10 Japan and the Cold War frontiers in East Asia in the era of globalism[1]

Kimie Hara

Accelerating globalization since the end of the twentieth century has made many parts of the world closer connected and deepened their mutual dependencies at an unprecedented pace. While the world is becoming "border-less" in many ways, however, the issues of border demarcation and territorial sovereignty, which are classical components of international relations, still keep providing sources of conflict and remain significant issues of international concern. These two phenomena seem to have opposite directions in their nature, but have important relevance in the world we live in. As the world has become more interdependent and people's interests are interwoven in more complex manners, to secure a safe and stable environment is significant to any level of international actors. East Asia is the region, where these contrasting two phenomena are most prominently seen – countries and peoples are getting intimately connected in various aspects of their society, e.g. economics and culture, but still deeply divided over political and security issues, including those of border demarcation and territorial sovereignty. This chapter considers issues of the latter category, particularly those derived from the post-World War II territorial settlement with Japan.

Many regional conflicts in East Asia have a common foundation in the postwar Japanese disposition of Japan, particularly the San Francisco Peace Treaty. In September 1951 Japan signed a peace treaty with 48 countries in San Francisco. The peace treaty should have been a clear settlement to end the Pacific War and start a "postwar" period. However, this treaty fell far short of settling outstanding issues at the end of the War or facilitating a clean start for the "postwar" period. Rather, various aspects of the settlement were left equivocal. The treaty's handling of territorial disposition was not an exception. Close examination of treaty drafts reveals key links between the regional Cold War that was unfolding in 1951 and equivocal language about the designation of territory, which can be related to several contentious frontier problems in contemporary East Asia. More than half a century later, the so-called Acheson Line and Containment Line still divide countries and peoples of the region, part of a legacy of unresolved problems. The global shift to the post-Cold War, and/or globalization, era does not negate the significance of the Cold War origins of these problems. In fact, it is appropriate to pinpoint their common origin and consider solutions in a multilateral context.

The San Francisco Peace Treaty's legacy of unresolved problems

Postwar East Asia has been plagued by numerous conflicts involving major regional players. These include the conflict over the divided Korean Peninsula, the cross-Taiwan Strait problem, and the sovereignty disputes over the "Northern Territories"/Southern Kuriles, Takeshima/Tokdo, the Senkaku/Diaoyu Islands, and the Spratly/Nansha Islands. These and other disputes, such as the Okinawa problem pivoting on the large US military presence in the region, are divisive issues that continue to stir conflict throughout East Asia.

Japan's defeat in the Pacific War led to the dismantling of a vast empire acquired over the previous half-century. In Article 2 of the San Francisco Peace Treaty, Japan renounced territories ranging from the Kurile Islands to Antarctica and from Micronesia to the Spratlys. The treaty did not specify to which country or government Japan renounced these territories, however; nor did it define their precise borders. This ambiguity would engender various unresolved problems throughout the region.[2] Previous studies have tended to treat these regional problems separately, or as unrelated, neglecting their common origin in postwar peace arrangements with Japan.[3] Examination of the treaty provisions, however, provides a means for grasping common features of numerous outstanding disputes, which continue to affect the regional security environment.[4]

The wide-ranging and interconnected strands of the San Francisco treaty make it difficult to solve particular problems bilaterally, or through negotiations confined to the countries directly involved in disputes. In fact, many of the disputes may be irresolvable so long as they remain within bilateral frameworks. The Allies' documents – particularly those of the USA, the main drafter of the treaty – are important sources for learning how these unresolved problems were created. The documents make clear that the regional Cold War, linkages among territorial disputes, and the disputes' origin in multilateral negotiations are critical aspects of all of the frontier problems.

Regional Cold War

Prior to the final draft of the San Francisco Peace Treaty, which was completed in 1951, six years after the war ended, several treaty drafts were prepared. As a whole, earlier US drafts were long and detailed, providing clear border demarcation. They not only delineated new Japanese borders, specifying latitude and longitude, but also indicated the names of small islands along these borders. Such an approach promised to minimize territorial conflicts in the future. However, the drafts went through various changes and eventually became shorter and "simpler." For example, early drafts specified that Takeshima/Tokdo (Liancourt Rocks in English) was Korean territory, then transferred ownership to Japan (1949), then omitted any designation of this area (1950). China was specified as the recipient of Taiwan for some time, but this designation also vanished (1950). Similarly, the USSR was initially specified as the recipient of

THE SAN FRANCISCO PEACE TREATY OF 1951
CHAPTER II
Territory
Article 2
(a) Japan, recognizing the independence of Korea, renounces all right, title and claim to Korea, including the islands of Quelpart, Port Hamilton and Dagelet.
(b) Japan renounces all right, title and claim to Formosa and the Pescadores.
(c) Japan renounces all right, title and claim to the Kurile Islands, and to that portion of Sakhalin and the islands adjacent to it over which Japan acquired sovereignty as a consequence of the Treaty of Portsmouth of September 5, 1905.
(d) Japan renounces all right, title and claim in connection with the League of Nations Mandate System, and accepts the action of the United Nations Security Council of April 2, 1947, extending the trusteeship system to the Pacific Islands formerly under mandate to Japan.
(e) Japan renounces all claim to any right or title to or interest in connection with any part of the Antarctic area, whether deriving from the activities of Japanese nationals or otherwise.
(f) Japan renounces all right, title and claim to the Spratly Islands and to the Paracel Islands.

Article 3
Japan will concur in any proposal of the United States to the United Nations to place under its trusteeship system, with the United States as the sole administering authority, Nansei Shoto south of 29° north latitude (including the Ryukyu Islands and the Daito Islands), Nanpo Shoto south of Sofu Gan (including the Bonin Islands, Rosario Island and the Volcano Islands) and Parece Vela and Marcus Island. Pending the making of such a proposal and affirmative action thereon, the United States will have the right to exercise all and any powers of administration, legislation and jurisdiction over the territory and inhabitants of these islands, including their territorial waters.

Source: *Conference for the Conclusion and Signature of the Treaty of Peace with Japan, San Francisco, California, September 4–8, 1951, Record of Proceedings*, Department of State Publication 4392, International Organization and Conference Series II, Far Eastern 3, December 1951, Division of Publications, Office of Public Affairs, p. 314.

Table 10.1 San Francisco Peace Treaty and regional problems in the Asia-Pacific[5]

San Francisco Peace Treaty	Relevant regional problems	Concerned states
Article 2		
(a) Korea	Reunification of Korea	DPRK - ROK
	Takeshima/Tokdo Dispute	Japan - ROK
(b) Formosa (Taiwan)	Cross-Taiwan Strait Problem	PRC - ROC
	Senkaku/Diaoyu dispute	Japan – PRC, ROC
(c) South Sakhalin, Kuriles	"Northern Territories"/South Kuriles Dispute	Japan – Russia (USSR)
(d) Micronesia	Status	USA – FSM, RMI, ROP, CNMI
(e) Antarctica	Antarctic Sovereignty Dispute	UK, Norway, France, Australia,
	[Frozen by the Antarctic Treaty]	New Zealand, Argentina, Chile
(f) Spratlys, Paracels	Spratlys and Paracels Disputes	PRC, ROC, Vietnam,
	Philippines, Malaysia, Brunei	
Article 3		
Okinawa, Bonin, Amami Is.	Status (Okinawa)	USA – Japan (Okinawa)
	Senkaku/Diaoyu Dispute	Japan – PRC, ROC

the Kurile Islands, but this specification disappeared in the final stage of treaty drafting (1951).[6]

The equivocal wording of the treaty was neither coincidence nor error; it followed careful deliberation and multiple revisions. Various issues were deliberately left unresolved due to the regional Cold War. Earlier drafts were, as a whole, based on US wartime studies and were consistent with the "punitive peace" plan and the Yalta spirit of inter-Allied cooperation. However, with the emergence of the Cold War in the immediate postwar years, Japan was given central status in the US Asia strategy, and the peace terms changed from punitive to generous as US strategic thinking focused on securing Japan within the Western bloc and assuring a long-term US military presence in Japan, particularly in Okinawa.

After the establishment of communist regimes in North Korea and mainland China, the so-called "Acheson Line" was proclaimed in January 1950. It included Japan and the Philippines in the US defense area of the western Pacific, but it left Taiwan and Korea outside, suggesting that the loss of these areas was considered acceptable. In June 1950, US policy toward Korea and China hardened with the outbreak of the Korean War; the US soon placed an embargo on China and met it on the battlefield in Korea. With war underway, the "Containment Line" was fixed at the 38th parallel in Korea and in the Taiwan Strait. In response to the above events, drafts of the Japanese peace treaty were "simplified," and intended recipients for Takeshima, Taiwan (Formosa), the Kuriles and other territories disappeared from the treaty's text. In this way, the treaty sowed the seeds of future disputes.

As for the Spratlys, while Chinese possession was considered during US wartime preparations for a postwar settlement, final disposition was not specified in the peace treaty, not simply because rightful ownership was unclear, but in order to make sure that none of the islands would fall into the hands of China.

The territorial problem between Japan and China originally focused on Okinawa. Chiang Kai-shek's Republic of China had expressed interest in "recovering" Okinawa, which had been occupied by the US military since 1945. However, Article 3 of the peace treaty neither specified Japanese renunciation nor recognized Japanese sovereignty over these islands; their final disposition was left equivocal. John Foster Dulles, who represented the US at the San Francisco Peace Conference in 1951, suggested Japanese possession of "residual sovereignty" over Okinawa. Nevertheless, he would threaten not to return the islands to Japan in his famous warning of 1956 – delivered when his Japanese counterpart, Foreign Minister Shigemitsu Mamoru, was about to reach a compromise over the "Northern Territories" and sign a peace treaty with the USSR – thus showing how the US position could shift depending on political conditions. After the reversion of administrative rights in Okinawa to Japan in 1972, the focus of the sovereignty dispute shifted to the Senkakus. Meanwhile the US military retained its large stake in Okinawa, and problems associated with the bases continue to this day.

The territorial dispositions of the San Francisco Peace Treaty ultimately created regional Cold War frontiers in East Asia, many of which remain intact. From north to southwest along the Acheson Line, territorial problems were left to be worked out between Japan and its communist (or partially communist) neighbors – the "Northern Territories"/Southern Kuriles with the USSR, Takeshima/Tokdo with a divided Korea, and Senkaku/Diaoyu with China/Taiwan. These problems lined up like wedges securing Japan in the Western bloc, or like walls dividing it from the communist sphere of influence. On the southwestern end of the Acheson Line, the Spratlys were left disputed between China and its Southeast Asian neighbors, including the Philippines and other claimants. Furthermore, the Containment Line came to be fixed along the 38th parallel and the Taiwan Strait, dividing Korea and China respectively to this day.

Except for the demise of the USSR, the regional Cold War structure essentially remains intact in East Asia. In addition to the frontier problems, the communist and authoritarian regimes continue to exist and constitute potential threats to their neighbors. The US maintains its military presence through bilateral security arrangements, i.e., the so-called San Francisco Alliance System. US military withdrawal (*tettai*) from Okinawa became a nationwide issue in Japan in the mid-1990s, but it has somehow slipped into discussion of transfer (*iten*) of troops on and around the island.

Tensions have relaxed at times, but, unlike in Europe, this has not resulted in the demolition of the Cold War structure. In fact, while post-Cold War eastward expansion of NATO has proved possible, there is little sign of fundamental shift in the Asia-Pacific's basic security framework from bilateral to multilateral alliances. The inauguration and development of the ASEAN Regional Forum (ARF), as well as other formal (Track I) and informal (Track II) multilateral frameworks, has shown that multilateral security dialogue and cooperation have been actively pursued in this region since the 1990s – just as in Europe with the Conference on Security and Cooperation in Europe (CSCE) after the 1970s' détente.[7] However, the countries of the region do not yet have relations of sufficient mutual trust to form an alliance. Meanwhile, the remaining structure of the confrontation continues to produce tensions and divide countries in the region.

Linkages among disputes

Japanese territorial issues were related to, or linked with, other territorial dispositions or political issues that were addressed in postwar occupation policy, in the peace treaty, or by subsequent arrangement. Various linkages were in fact recognized in US government studies and negotiations with the other Allies prior to the peace conference.[8] For example, the "Northern Territories" were used as a bargaining chip not only to secure US occupation of the southern half of the Korean Peninsula, but also to assure US trusteeship of Micronesia. The UN resolution formula once emerged as a disposition plan for Korea, and affected disposition plans for Taiwan and the Kuriles.[9] That plan was dropped, however, when the Korean War developed to the disadvantage of the UN (i.e., US-led) side.

Differences emerged even among the Western Allies in their policies toward this region, which in turn affected the treaty. In particular, the US–UK differences over China deeply affected the Japanese peace settlement, including the disposition of Taiwan. China itself was ultimately not specified in the treaty.[10] This affected other decisions; most importantly, the treaty does not specify the final destination of any territories.

The Kuriles and Okinawa were most carefully examined in the US preparation for postwar territorial disposition of Japan. Their linkage became clear in the 1956 "Dulles' Warning" during the Japan–USSR peace negotiations. Okinawa was necessary for US Cold War strategy in Asia, and so was an unresolved dispute over the "Northern Territories". Thus, it was not coincidental that Japan and the USSR held another summit and peace negotiations in 1973, a year after the reversion of Okinawa. However, US forces remained stationed on the returned Okinawa, and no fundamental rapprochement (i.e., territorial settlement and signing of a peace treaty) was achieved in the Soviet–Japanese negotiations.

Multilateral origins

Although the San Francisco Peace Treaty was signed between Japan and forty-eight other countries, there was no consensus among the states that would be directly involved in the great regional conflicts that ensued. In particular, states such as Korea, China and the USSR were not parties to the treaty. Countries such as Great Britain, France and Canada that did participate became "concerned states" with a stake in the disposal of the disputed territories.

The Taiwan Strait and the divided Korean Peninsula were international issues even before the peace treaty was signed, with the US playing a direct role as both occupying force and provider of aid and diplomatic backing for the Republic of China (ROC) and the Republic of Korea (ROK), led respectively by Chiang Kai-shek and Syngman Rhee, both of whom were eager to re-unify their countries. The outbreak of the Korean War in particular prompted vigorous US intervention, resulting in the international involvement desired by both Chiang and Rhee.

The US, together with the UK, finalized the treaty drafts by adopting certain ideas from other "concerned states." For example, countries such as Canada – which became concerned about a possible accusation of unequal treatment of different territories – proposed not to specify the final devolution of any territory after the allocation of Taiwan (to China) vanished from the treaty drafts, while the recipient of the Kuriles (the USSR) was still specified. The eventual adoption of this proposal proved convenient for the US Cold War strategy as well, for example in preventing rapprochement among the countries of the region.[11]

Thus the regional conflicts were created multilaterally, but left to be settled bilaterally or by countries directly involved in the disputes.

History and the future

Today, East Asia is one of the most dynamic regions in the world. Most of the regional states are engaging their different economic stages of development well within their deepened mutual interdependence. Various efforts to develop multilateral cooperation and integration have been actively attempted centering in the area of economy in this region as well. However, as indicated earlier, significant political differences still remain between the major neighboring states and keep sending political headwind to such a movement, preventing confidence-building, and providing political instability in the region.

An important condition for peace is removal of the sources of conflict. Even though relaxation of tensions occurs and/or conflict management works at times, as long as the sources of the conflicts remain unchanged, there are always the possibilities that tensions resurge and conflicts escalate. Furthermore, where difference remains, there also remains a possibility of political exploitation, both domestically and internationally. Clearly agreed borders make good neighbors, and they should be established while the relations among the disputants are relatively good.

History of the last half century indicates that, so long as many of these issues are addressed exclusively within bilateral frameworks or frameworks confined to the countries directly involved in the disputes, they are likely to defy solution. Thus, the possibility of settlement within a multilateral framework needs to be investigated. In particular, it is worth remembering their common origin in the postwar peace settlements with Japan, and considering future solutions that involve re-linking them in a multilateral context.

Then, what kind of multilateral framework is suitable? Existing frameworks may be used, or new ones created. Alternatively, an international conference may be held by "concerned states" that share historical responsibility or national interests in this region. Such frameworks may be used to discuss, endorse, or legitimatize a settlement. Yet, for concrete dispute settlements, instead of "arbitration" using international platforms or formal multilateral organization, it will be more appropriate to aim for a political resolution created through multilateral negotiation. For example, in dealing with international disputes, International Court of Justice (ICJ) became available after the World War II and its decisions are supposed to be internationally respected. However, it would be extremely difficult to bring the East Asian disputes into this kind of framework. Through over half a century of disputes, most of the disputants' positions are widely known, and mutually exclusive. In such a case any settlement produced by an international organization, even within a multilateral framework, would likely be viewed as a win–lose situation, with a danger of international loss of face. When the disputants are two parties with confronting positions, settlement by third-party arbitration runs the same risk of having any settlement viewed as a "win–lose" situation and potential loss of face.

If the issue were placed within a multilateral framework along with a number of other outstanding issues and their disputant states, however, then the circumstances would be different. Mutually acceptable solutions not achievable within a bilateral framework may be found in multilateral negotiations by creatively combining conditions. In addition, this would blunt domestic criticism of a zero-sum kind, such as of "too large concessions" or "defeat by negotiating partner," which tend to follow bilateral negotiations, thus saving both governments' face.

A settlement to several regional issues, therefore, may be pursued together, within a multilateral framework that reflects the historical background and present reality of international relations. In other words, several "unresolved problems" should be negotiated together, using a framework comprising the major disputants and "concerned states" that were involved in the original disposition and still have strong influence and deep interests in the region. The countries involved, including Japan, may have to review or revise policies solidified during the Cold War era. Yet it seems worth investigating the area of contribution, or of possible linkages to other disputes, just as was the case when most of those disputes were created.

Such an approach could include a combination of mutual concessions involving more than one territorial dispute and/or the resolution of other unresolved problems. For example, linkage could be made among the conflicts over the "Northern Territories"/Southern Kuriles, Takeshima/Tokdo, Senkaku/Diaoyu, and the South China Sea islands. Also, it might be possible to link these problems with other political, economic, military, or non-conventional security agendas of the involved states. Solution of one problem may lead to solution of others, as their origins show them to be mutually related in one way or another.

In the past few decades, non-disputant states, particularly most of those outside East Asia have kept distance from, and coolly observed, regional political disputes such as territorial and border issues that often throw cold water on neighboring state's relations, as if they are someone else's affairs. However, many of these states were in fact the "concerned states" that played important roles in creating, or leaving seeds for, the major postwar regional conflicts. Reconsidering their historical involvement and responsibility, and also current national interests in the region, such "concerned states", including Canada, could well play far more constructive roles in solving those dispute, which will eventually contribute to peace and stability of East Asia.

Multilateral international agreements tend to be more durable than bilateral ones. The more participating states there are, the stronger restraint tends to be, and the greater the possibility that a country in breach will be internationally isolated. It is therefore desirable to obtain wide international recognition for agreements concerning the settlement of these disputes, including specific conditions attached to it (e.g., demilitarization, neutralization, autonomy etc.), in other words, to install international recognition from the concerned states that participate in such multilateral negotiations, and/or a rather large framework like the UN, along with bilateral consensus on the issue. Some arrangements for international monitoring and reporting may be made for some cases.

There would seem to be multiple possibilities for solution that have not yet been explored.

Notes

1 This chapter is largely drawn from Kimie Hara, *The Cold War Frontiers in the Asia-Pacific: Divided Territories and the San Francisco System* (Routledge, 2007). An earlier version of this paper appeared at *The Asia-Pacific Journal: Japan Focus,* September 4, 2006.

2 The peace treaty left the status of Taiwan undecided, with options for its future including possession by the People's Republic of China (PRC), possession by the Republic of China (ROC), or even independence. The treaty did stipulate Japanese recognition of Korean independence, but it did not specify to which government or state "Korea" was renounced. There was then, and is still, no state or country called Korea. Rather, there are two states, the Republic of Korea (ROK) in the south and the Democratic People's Republic of Korea (DPRK) in the north. "Korea" was not a country name but a geographical area.

3 Linkages among the various disputes appear to have been ignored for reasons such as limitations on access to materials – in many countries, official documents are generally closed to public scrutiny for at least thirty years – and the different ways in which the Cold War and certain disputes developed in the region. Furthermore, some of the problems (such as those involving the Senkakus and the Spratlys) received little attention until the disputes escalated, over issues such as natural resources or introduction of the United Nations Convention on Law of the Sea (UNCLOS). In the meantime, the common foundation of the disputes was forgotten. These frontier problems have never been examined in the larger context of the Cold War.

4 For details, see Hara (2007).

5 Hara (2007), pp. 186.

6 *Ibid.*

7 Organization for Security and Co-Operation in Europe (OSCE) since December 1994.
8 *Ibid.*
9 The UN resolution formula concerning Japanese recognition of Korean independence was adopted in the August and September 1950 drafts. Because the Korean War was fought under UN auspices, to equate Korea's future with a UN decision was undoubtedly advantageous to the US and its allies. Thus, "Korea" in this text meant the Republic of Korea. A similar approach was adopted to decide the future of Taiwan, the Kuriles and Southern Sakhalin in the same drafts.
10 Britain soon recognized the People's Republic of China, whereas the US continued to support Chiang Kai-shek's Republic of China.
11 For details, see Hara (2007).

11 National mobilization and global engagement

Understanding Japan's response to global climate change initiatives

Carin Holroyd

The growing consensus about the reality of global climate change presents both national governments and global governance institutions with a formidable chall-enge. The task of balancing national economic development and environmental considerations has proven difficult for all countries; the need to mobilize governments and citizens to address an issue that is truly global in origin and impact has so far eluded diplomats and politicians. The Kyoto Protocol, an amendment to the United Nations Framework Convention on Climate Change signed in 1997 and in force as of 2005, became the symbol of the new era of international environmentalism.[1] The Protocol called on signatory nations – close to 170 in total – to make significant reductions in greenhouse gas emissions and to thus reduce the trajectory of human-created climate change. But that accord has stalled, stymied by the refusal of the United States of America, China and India to embrace the process and, equally, by the inability of those nations which signed the agreement to meet the targets outlined in the Kyoto Protocol. The Government of Japan, as the former host of the critical Kyoto negotiations, has repeatedly declared its intention to honour its commitment.

In the years after the Kyoto agreement, government leaders sought ways of reconciling national imperatives and global responsibilities. At the 2007 APEC Summit in Sydney, Asia Pacific leaders offered another attempt to move beyond the Kyoto Protocol and yet provide a manageable strategy for ecological preservation:

> The APEC region has a major stake in global responses to the challenges of climate change, energy security and clean development. Economic growth and technology development are indispensable elements of our future agreed approach. The scale of these challenges demands new and innovative forms of international co-operation. We, the APEC Leaders, reaffirm our commitment to work with all members of the international community for an enduring global solution to climate change.[2]

Japan was singled out for playing a role in bringing APEC to a modest consensus by developing a workable compromise on regional environmental plans.[3]

In 2006, Japan began to put itself on a self-appointed path for global leadership on national environmental strategies, but turmoil in domestic politics shifted the government off focus fairly quickly. At an Asian leaders' meeting in May 2007 and again at the G8 Summit in June 2007, former Japanese Prime Minister Shinzo Abe[4] announced a "Cool Earth 50" initiative, declaring a commitment to cut Japan's emissions in half by 2050 and proposing steps that would leverage the Japanese programme into a global initiative. At a United Nations plenary session on climate change in August of the same year, Ambassador Koji Tsuruoka offered his country's plan as the foundation for a global strategy: "As a responsible member of the international community and the host country of the negotiations that led to the Kyoto Protocol, Japan is striving to take the lead in tackling global warming."[5] Japan's promising environmental image after the 2007 meetings, however, suffered a significant public relations set-back during the December 2007 Bali Conference on global climate change. In this instance, Japan sided with the United States and Canada in favouring a more limited – supporters would say pragmatic – approach to controlling greenhouse gas emissions. In particular, the unpopular triumvirate, argued that developing countries had to agree to reduce their emissions before the industrial world agreed to a scaling back in pollution. Without the active participation of China and India, they argued, major initiatives by the rest of the world would be largely without meaning.

In their 2006 study, *Global Environmental Politics*, Pamela Chasek, David Downie and Janet Welsh Brown make it clear that formidable barriers lie between the identification of an environmental challenge and the creation of a national consensus to address the issue. Their review makes it clear that international solutions are significantly more difficult than national initiatives, particularly if compliance with a specific agenda puts their country at an economic disadvantage vis-à-vis other nations.[6] The authors argue that the dynamics of national politics, the challenges of maintaining public interest, and administrative responsibilities and other structural barriers can impede the implementation of a successful national environmental regime.[7]

Assessing Japan's response to the Kyoto Protocol and to the general environmental challenges of the twenty-first century against these well-known evaluative standards reveals the difficulty associated with moving from the appreciation of the problem to the implementation of an effective and sustainable environmental regime. In this regard, Japan shares many characteristics with other industrial nations, with a significant gap emerging between public rhetoric, stated national positions, and practical policy implementation. As an overview of "Green Japan" initiatives demonstrates, Japanese officials have attempted to tackle the issue by stimulating a national debate, by seeking a consensus about the urgency of the issue, by identifying regulatory instruments and compliance mechanisms. In this regard, Japan follows a well-established international pattern, albeit one that has delivered unspectacular results in the years following the Kyoto Protocol.

In the case of Japan, however, one specific factor – the search for technological solutions to environmental issues – has assumed considerable primacy in terms of public policy. This issue has long been identified as a key element in global environmentalism. As Adam Jaffe and Robert Stavins argued, "The effect of public policies on the process of technological change may, in the long run, be among the most significant determinants of success and failure in environmental protection."[8] Japanese leaders have endeavoured to mobilize the country's scientists to seek scientific, administrative and technological measures to offset or prevent environmental change. Following on the well-established "triple helix" approach of coordinating the work of government, the universities and the private sector, Japanese authorities have likewise tried to connect environmental change with national research and development activities and to thereby secure a significant place for the country in the growing international environmental business sector. Rene Kemp's detailed study, *Environmental Policy and Technical Change*, argues that "The reason why some technologies and designs are dominant depends not just on engineering and imagination but also on the accumulated knowledge, cost efficiencies achieved in certain designs, the infrastructure around a technology, and the embedment of technologies in the economic systems and people's way of life."[9] It is this connection between sociological and technological factors, between national goals and science-based solutions that describes the central approach in Japanese environmental policy. Within Japanese science and technology policy, investigating climate change and developing energy sources that do not release carbon dioxide and exploring sustainable material cycles and waste disposal systems are key priorities.[10]

Japan, therefore, faces the same political and administrative challenges as other major industrial nations in its search for environmental solutions in the age of global climate change. The political and civil service leadership struggle to accommodate the rhetoric and urgency of the Kyoto Protocols and the broader debate about ecological sustainability within the much more restricted framework of national policy and politics. In facing the central challenge of twenty-first century national and global politics, Japanese leaders are able to draw on some crucial experiences and accomplishments from earlier decades. The country's rapid economic growth after the mid-1950s created a near-environmental crisis in Japan. Stories about mercury and cadmium poisoning made cities like Yokkaichi and Minamata global icons of environmental degradation and human suffering.[11] As one commentator wrote, "Probably no other country had come to feel the consequences of unrestrained industrial growth as early and as painfully as Japan. Critical observers from other countries even saw Japan as doomed to commit 'ecological hara-kiri' (or seppuku, the proper Japanese word)." A wave of local protests and the growing success of left-wing and environmentalist politicians jarred government and business leaders into action. Japan righted itself, due in part to the willingness of judges to hold companies and decision-makers accountable for egregious acts of pollution. With remarkable speed, "Japan did not only shed her image as a 'pollution nation'; in some respects she now stood out as a paragon of effective anti-pollution policy."[12]

The country became increasingly energy conscious following the oil shocks of the 1970s which underscored its energy vulnerability. Japan's image as an innovator in environmental protection strengthened as the country's record for new approaches to environmental protection continued to attract international attention.[13] Japan's shift to greater reliance on clean energy, particularly nuclear power, cleared the skies over the major cities and was bolstered by a number of major reclamation projects and conservation measures. While the nuclear energy sector suffered numerous setbacks with the most recent being reports of radiation leakages at a power plant near Niigata in July 2007, the country has nonetheless made major strides over the past thirty years in responding to the ecological challenges of this generation.

The rhetoric and public commitment to environmental issues quieted down in the 1990s. This was due, in part, to the long-established practice of mixing partisan politics and regional economic development, one result of which has been the largely unrestrained development of rural and coastal areas, despite mounting criticism about the aesthetic and environmental impact of such projects.[14] Through the 1990s, the Japanese public was not extensively engaged in environmental initiatives and appeared to be less confident about the effectiveness of community-level action in protecting the environment.[15] The country remained more science-friendly and preoccupied primarily by personal and community health concerns than with waging major internal battles over environmental issues.[16]

Japan has, in both political commentary and government policy, taken its commitments under the Kyoto Accord more seriously than many nations. Not always deeply engaged in issues of global governance and international engagement, the Japanese authorities have responded somewhat differently on the environmental front. Japan, like other nations, has wrestled with the process and structures for internalizing international agreements, such as the Kyoto Accord, and used them as a foundation for concerted government actions. International protocols, accords and treaties are the primary currency of global governance. Intense and time-consuming discussions, with political leaders often building atop of years of research, planning and strategizing by professional staff, lead to the negotiation and ratification of international agreements. Over the past decades, accords as varied as the Geneva Convention, the founding documents of the United Nations and the World Trade Organizations, new frameworks for international trade, the International Covenant on Economic, Social and Cultural Rights, and the International Covenant on Civil and Political Rights have been implemented. In the process, governments have sought the political and legal means of connecting national policy and practice with international agreements, strengthening the legitimacy of international governance and providing global standards for the assessment of the practices of individual countries.

Managing environmental behaviour has presented a particularly formidable challenge for both national governments and international institutions. Slowing the use of pollutants and requiring stronger ecological protection have immediate and often significant economic and social benefits and costs. Even many among the most prosperous nations, signatories to the Kyoto Protocol and strong public defenders of global environmental management, have nonetheless concluded that imposing the precise terms of a controversial international accord would have devastating economic effects and, even more, would generate a strong political backlash against environmental regulation generally. This has clearly been the case for Canada, where the national calculus of environmental versus economic trade-offs suggested major job and business losses if the Kyoto Protocol were to be adopted, and for Australia, a heavy energy-consuming nation, which refused to ratify the Kyoto agreement until the next Prime Minister, Kevin Rudd, ratified it at the Bali conference. The challenge of responding to a global environmental accord is substantial, for governments must regulate business activity related to energy use and environmental preservation while also changing citizens' behaviours and expectations related to resource use, consumption, and personal responsibility for ecological change.

The expansion of Japanese environmentalism

Japan provides a useful case of the evaluation of efforts to coordinate global ecological accords and national action. Japan made important changes to its industrial and pollution control strategies as the environmental consequences of rapid economic expansion became evident in the 1960s and 1970s. Indeed, Japan's successful rehabilitation of urban air quality, recovery of major waterways, and advanced industrial controls has often been touted as a model of contemporary developing nations.[17] The assertive, often aggressive, environmental movement in the country attracted far more attention than subtle changes in industrial regulations and corporate strategies, but the latter possibly contributed as much as the former to the creation of a new environmental mindset in the country.[18]

Academic studies of emergent Japanese environmentalism document a lengthy struggle between grass roots movements and the "top actors in the major institutions, government, party and business – the Ruling Triad".[19] Political and commercial leaders, it seems, reacted slowly to emerging threats and growing public concern:

> From 1955 until the early 1990s, this pattern of elite communitarianism held. When challenged by the wave of grassroots pollution protests and local victories by opposition parties, members of the triad responded with two tactics: pre-emptive policy compromise and soft social control. Their facility at enacting preemptive pollution control policies speaks to the effectiveness of the horizontal, relatively egalitarian networks among members of the triad. The soft social control, however, reveals the presence of "inverted V" type vertical networks between elites and ordinary citizens. The triad made substantive policy compromises in order to preserve regime stability. When the electoral threat declined, however, the triad gradually reasserted capital accumulation as its central principle. This prevented the pollution regulation principles behind Japan's "pollution miracle" from generalizing and making all production follow environmental principles.[20]

Concluding his detailed study of pre-1995 environmentalism in Japan, Jeffrey Broadbent concluded that convincing government and business to adhere to environmental policies "seems to depend upon their ability to link environmentalist values to pocketbook and health-related demands. Only then can environmentalists forge a voting constituency powerful enough to threaten pro-growth elites with political defeat, and thereby jog the elites into taking steps to repair environmental degradation, contrary to their immediate economic interests."[21]

Over the past decade, pressures have increased on Japanese leaders to respond even more aggressively on environmental issues. Like several European nations, Japan has taken the Kyoto Protocol very seriously and has endeavoured to bring its national policies and citizens' behaviour in line with global priorities. As the Kyoto Protocol was signed on Japanese soil, the Japanese government feels a strong obligation to honour its 1997 pledge to reduce greenhouse gas emissions to six percent below 1990 levels between 2008 and 2012. "We are determined to exert all efforts by the entire nation to ensure that Japan achieves its commitment to reduce emissions by 6 percent," said former Prime Minister Abe.[22] The Japanese government has introduced a range of initiatives designed to cut greenhouse gas emissions, encourage the production and use of low emission technologies, increase recycling, promote green products and generally encourage citizens, governments and business to adopt a more environmentally friendly lifestyle.

With pressure and incentives from the government, and with growing public awareness of environmental considerations, corporate environmental activism has also expanded. Beyond actions and processes decreed by government, many Japanese companies are competing to demonstrate their green credentials. There has been a surge of interest in environmental reporting, encouraged by a series of government guidance papers, and company reports now proudly extol the range of environmentally friendly actions the corporation has undertaken.[23] More than 80 companies offer goods or services as prizes as part of a government campaign against global warming. In September 2007, for example, McDonald's Japan offered customers a half price Big Mac if they demonstrated a commitment to global warming by signing an online form from the Ministry of Environment that outlined 39 measures individuals could take to fight global warming. The day after the McDonald's campaign started, the government website crashed from the deluge of hits.[24] Such unorthodox initiatives had more symbolic than practical impact, but did serve to keep environmental issues in the public sphere.

The Japanese domestic commitment has also had external elements. As mentioned, at a dinner with Asian leaders in late May 2007, and reiterated two weeks later at the G8 summit in Germany, then Prime Minister Shinzo Abe invited the world to participate with Japan in "Cool Earth 50", a three pillar strategy aimed at the global reduction of greenhouse gas emissions.[25] Prime Minister Abe challenged the world to cut global emissions by half the current level by 2050, thus matching industrial output with the capacity of the earth to absorb carbon dioxide naturally. This would involve the development of innovative technologies, which will allow for economic growth and the reduction of greenhouse gas emissions to occur simultaneously, and by building a "low carbon" society centred on those technologies. The Prime Minister cited research on eliminating carbon dioxide emissions from coal fired power generation (which accounts for almost one-third of global carbon dioxide emissions), on the development of safe and reliable nuclear power generation technologies and on efficient solar power generation, fuel cells and low emission vehicles. Japan, he said, committed itself to making significant contributions to this research.

The second part of the Prime Minister's proposal called for the development of an international framework for addressing global warming from 2013 onward. This framework, he argued, must include all major carbon dioxide emitters, be flexible and diverse and reach a balance between economic growth and environmental protection. Japan, Prime Minister Abe announced, would financially support developing countries trying to reduce their greenhouse gas emissions. Japan would also try to get the support of other industrialized countries and international organizations, like the World Bank and the United Nations, to do the same.

The government of Japan clearly believed that its policies and initiatives could be replicated outside the country and could provide a foundation for concerted global action. To build the low carbon society that Cool Earth 50 envisions, the Japanese plan indicated, all nations must encourage their people to reduce their carbon dioxide emissions. Prime Minister Abe said, "The amount of carbon dioxide emissions by GDP of Japan is the least among major industrialized countries in the world, and public transportation accounts for 47 percent of all movement of people in Japan – by far the highest among industrialized countries. We will demonstrate the "Japan model" in the world."[26] Japan, he pledged, would redouble its efforts to achieve its Kyoto protocol commitment. Abe's Cool Earth 50 also included an aggressive strategy for citizen mobilization. Japan's National Campaign for Achieving the Kyoto Protocol Target said simply: "With the motto of '1 person, 1 day, 1 kg' for reducing greenhouse gases, we will call upon the people to reexamine lifestyles and call for efforts and creative ideas at home and workplace."[27] Unfortunately, not long after this pledge, Prime Minister Abe resigned suddenly and domestic political considerations engulfed Japan's leadership.

Japan faces a formidable challenge in seeking to achieve its Kyoto Protocol targets. The country's greenhouse gas emissions have grown over 8% since 1990. To achieve its newly announced goal, Japan will need to reduce its emissions 14% between 2007 and 2012. Japan plans to achieve almost nine percentage points of its reduction through domestic measures with the remainder made up by sinks (the removal of gases from the atmosphere that occurs naturally through forests, oceans and the soil) and Kyoto mechanisms.[28] Kyoto mechanisms include Clean Development Mechanisms (the funding of projects to reduce emissions in developing countries), Joint Implementation (the funding of projects to reduce emissions in industrialized countries which have made reduction commitments), or Emissions Trading. Achieving a 9% reduction through domestic measures alone over the next five years will be a test for Japan, particularly as compared to other industrialized nations as its emissions are already relatively low (on a per capita basis).

The success of Japan's first steps at leadership on global warming is not assured.[29] Cool Earth 50 could mark Japan's emergence as a leader on the world stage, but this will depend, among other things, on its ability to deliver on its pledges. Further, it is not clear whether Japanese initiatives will work outside the country. With a homogenous population and a deep-seated acceptance of technological innovation, Japan is atypical on the global scene. The various environmental initiatives described below have been developed, proposed and promoted by the national government. That there has been substantial acceptance by both corporate Japan and the general public is at least partly due to a much greater acceptance of governmental leadership than is seen in much of the industrialized world. Whether that kind of leadership and/or the expectation of placing the collective ahead of individual needs and desires that some of these initiatives require will work outside Japan is debatable.

However, the urgency of the challenge of global warming that confronts the world may mean that many citizens in many countries are ready to embrace leadership from wherever and however it comes. Whether Japan or any nation is able to provide the necessary leadership remains to be seen. At the Group of Eight summit held in July 2008 at Lake Toya in Hokkaido, Japan, global warming and the sharing of energy efficient technologies with developing countries were key topics of discussion. As the host nation, Japan wanted to ensure that there are convincing proposals to replace the Kyoto Protocol which expires in 2012. The meeting attracted little global attention and produced no striking international consensus on coping with climate change. The communiqué outlined a pragmatic, compromise approach to environmental protection, based more on adaptation, technological innovation and country-specific responses than a uniform and enforceable plan for dealing with environmental issues.[30]

The policies of combating climate change

In recent years, the Government of Japan has launched a complex series of initiatives designed to address the challenges and needs of environmental sustainability. A review of several of the more prominent examples demonstrates the government's determination to produce a web of public mobilization, environmental business initiatives, government regulation and scientific innovation. The Japanese strategy calls on the wide-ranging mobilization of national resources and energy to address global climate change. The partnership of government, business, the academy and the general public replicates the Japan Inc. approach and the collaborative ethos has long characterized the Japanese strategy for rapid national change.

Team minus 6% national project

In April 2005, the government launched a national campaign designed to encourage every citizen and business organization to make efforts to combat global warming.[31] A number of Japan's domestic initiatives fall under the Team Minus 6% National Project. Led by the Ministry of the Environment, and called Team Minus 6%, in reference to the amount of greenhouse gases that under the Kyoto Protocol Japan had pledged to cut,[32] everyone in the "team", meaning the country, has been encouraged to take six actions:

- limit their use of air conditioners
- reduce water consumption
- stop idling cars
- buy environmentally friendly products
- refuse extra wrapping of purchases, and
- unplug unused appliances.

By May 2008, over 2.2 million individuals had signed up and over 20,200 companies were part of the rapidly expanding programme.[33] As part of Team Minus 6%, the government started a Cool Biz campaign in the summer of 2005 with the aim of conserving energy during the summer. With the catch phrase "No Necktie, No Jacket", the Cool Biz campaign (which now runs from 1 June to 30 September annually) advises all offices to set their air conditioners to turn on only when the temperature reaches 28 degrees Celsius. All government offices immediately complied and, gradually, Japanese companies, large and small, began to follow suit. Many of Japan's largest companies including Sharp, Toyota, Hitachi, Matsushita, Canon, Toshiba, Nissin, Daiei and Tokyo Gas implemented Cool Biz. In October 2006, the Ministry of the Environment announced its household "stop global warming" campaign. Entitled Uchi-Eco (uchi means house), its aim is to promote ways that individuals can save energy at home and in their own lives.

For much of the last decade, the government of Japan has identified scientific and technology innovation as being the key element in defining the country's long-term economic prospects and responding to domestic and international pressures. Japan's consistently high investments in scientific and technology research have provided the country's universities, government research laboratories and corporations with the resources and incentives necessary to invest heavily in products, services and processes that contribute to national priorities in such areas as nanotechnology, biotechnology, and information technology. Through this period of research intensiveness, green technologies have featured prominently in Japanese high technology efforts, receiving a global showcase during the 2005 Aichi World Fair. This "Love the Earth" exposition emphasized the imperative of ecological co-existence and highlighted Japanese contributions in renewable technologies and environmental protection.[34] The development of commercially viable low emission technologies has been a central element in Japan's initiative to address ecological issues through science and technology. Japanese companies and corporate and government laboratories are particularly active in researching clean energy vehicles, inorganic light emitting diodes, residential fuel cell cogeneration systems and photovoltaic power.

A lack of landfill capacity and a densely populated urban environment combined with a desire to reach its Kyoto targets, spurred the Japanese government (primarily the Ministry of the Environment and METI) to begin enacting laws to promote recycling and resource conservation. Beginning with the Basic Law for Establishing the Recycling-Based Society, which went into effect in 2000, the government established a framework for both recycling generally (source reduction or waste prevention, reuse, recycling, energy recovery, appropriate disposal) and extended producer responsibility (EPR) for the recycling of the products and services they produce. The general idea of EPR is to shift responsibility for recycling, physically and/or economically, from municipalities toward the producers. This, in contrast to the polluter pays principal, is particularly suitable when the product itself is in need of recycling after a number of years of use.[35]

The Container and Packaging Recycling Law, enacted in 1997 initially for PET (polyethylene terephtalate) bottles and glass, expanded to paper and plastic containers and packaging in 2000. The Home Appliance Recycling Law was enacted in 1998 and went into effect in April 2001. Japan's 44 million households dispose of 100 million appliances annually and landfills were running out of room. Before the law was passed, approximately 70% of scrapped home appliances were waste with the remainder exported or resold.[36] Japan's Home Appliance Recycling Law stipulates that manufacturers and retailers of home appliances, specifically air conditioners, refrigerators, televisions and washing machines, are obligated to take back and recycle them. The manufacturers are responsible for financing the recycling of their own products but consumers who dispose of used home appliances are charged a fee to offset those costs.[37] Electrical retailers are required to take back used appliances from consumers – either with a proof of purchase receipt or when a new appliance is purchased.[38] The goals are to create a "closed loop" economy, where used materials become new products, and to divert waste from rapidly filling up landfills.

The Construction Material Recycling Law (2000) requires that contractors constructing or demolishing buildings are required to have a plan for the recycling of construction and demolition waste and to recycle what cannot be reused. The Food Waste Recycling Law (2001) sets out guidelines for all food related businesses. This sector, which includes food manufacturers, retailers, and restaurants that generate more than 100 tons of food waste had to reduce their food waste by 2006. An amendment introduced in 2007 established rules to promote food recycling in the retail and restaurant industries and provided more administrative guidance for companies seeking to comply with the regulations. The End of Life Vehicle Recycling Law (2002) established a national automobile recycling law.[39] About 5 million ELV are generated annually in Japan. Over 1 million are exported for reuse in other countries, leaving 4 million to be recycled within Japan. The law makes auto manufacturers and importers responsible for receiving and recycling automobile shredder residue (ASR), fluorocarbons and airbags which had not to this point been recycled. All of these waste products are hazardous and have significant environmental impacts. The other parts of the car are recycled by existing recyclers, including difficult to dispose of items like batteries and tires.

The Eco Town Program is an initiative of the Ministry of Economy, Trade and Industry (METI) to promote local economic development through the creation of environmentally oriented businesses and community recycling and waste elimination systems.[40] Local governments submit an EcoTown Plan to METI and the Ministry of the Environment. If approved, the local government, working with private organizations, receives support to implement the recycling projects. Since the programme's inception in 1997, over 25 EcoTowns have been created.[41] Kitakyushu, on the northern tip of Kyushu island, one of the first EcoTowns to be approved, now has recycling facilities for PET bottles, home electric appliances, office automation equipment, automobiles, fluorescent tubes and pachinko machines. It also has a manufacturing facility for making construction material from waste timber and plastic and for producing an anti-foaming agent used in iron making.[42]

Government, business and technological responses

Implicit in the government's agenda for environmental sustainability has long been a belief that scientific and technological solutions are essential. Through a series of major investments in university and government research, and using a wide range of incentives, subsidies and regulatory steps, the Government of Japan has endeavoured to promote greater engagement in environmental products, services and processes.

For much of the last decade, the government of Japan has identified scientific and technology innovation as being the key element in defining the country's long-term economic prospects and responding to domestic and international pressures. Japan's consistently high investments in scientific and technology research have provided the country's universities, government research laboratories and corporations with the resources and incentives necessary to invest heavily in products, services and processes that contribute to national priorities in such areas as nanotechnology, biotechnology and information technology. Through this period of research intensiveness, green technologies also featured prominently in Japanese high technology efforts, receiving a global showcase during the 2005 Aichi World Fair. This "Love the Earth" exposition emphasized the imperative of ecological co-existence and highlighted Japanese contributions in renewable technologies and environmental protection. The development of commercially viable low emission technologies has been a central element in Japan's initiative to address ecological issues through science and technology.

Clean energy vehicles

Toyota developed the Prius, the world's first practical hybrid vehicle. Under the Kyoto Protocol Target Achievement Plan, by 2010 the aim was to have introduced 2.33 million hybrid vehicles. This goal was designed to reduce CO_2 emissions by 3 million tons.[43] Japanese auto manufacturers are researching and developing a range of clean energy vehicles including those that use liquid petroleum gas, methanol, fuel cells, compressed natural gas, electricity and solar power. Many of these have been developed to the prototype stage. Work continues to make these sources of energy less expensive and/or able to sustain a vehicle over longer distances.[44] One example of the importance of government leadership on environmental issues comes from the fact that as early as 2004, all official government vehicles were replaced by low emission vehicles.[45]

Inorganic light emitting diodes

In 1998, the Ministry of Economy, Trade and Industry asked the New Energy and Industrial Technology Development Organization (NEDO) to begin a new research project entitled "The Light for the Twenty-First Century" to develop low energy lighting systems. The goal was to create LED lamps with lights that last longer and are more energy efficient than conventional fluorescent lights. Thirteen companies and two universities participated in the research programme. A number of Japanese companies are now working on everything from LED lighting applications on signboards (Nippon Paint) and streetlights (Iwasaki Electric) to traffic lights, automotive instrument panels, mobile phone handset lights and others.[46]

Fuel cell technologies

The Japanese government has been funding a national strategy to support the commercialization of fuel cells.[47] The strategy aims to have 5 million fuel cell vehicles and be generating 10 GW of electricity from fuel cells by 2020. In early 2008, fuel cells were identified as one of 21 innovative technologies that could aid Japan in its goal to halve greenhouse gas emissions by 2050. Japan has the potential to become the first mass market for fuel cell technologies in the world.

Japan has also encouraged the development of new residential cogeneration energy systems designed to replace hot water supply heaters with much more energy efficient approaches. The systems produce electricity to run household appliances and use the heat generated by the power source to heat water for the home. The first of these systems in the world were developed and implemented by Tokyo Gas, Ebara Ballard and Matsushita. Japan hopes to have 1 million systems in residential use by 2010. The Japanese Prime Minister's official residence was one of the first homes to install a cogeneration fuel cell system.

Photovoltaics

Photovoltaic research is an area where the Japanese commitment to science-based innovation was matched with the socio-political priority of reducing dependence on imported oil. In the 1990s, the Japanese government made major efforts to convince homeowners to commit the US$20,000 needed to install a proper system. In 1993, it started the New Sunshine Project, a series of national and local subsidies, which started at 50% of the costs in 1994 and declined gradually over the next decade. The Project provided incentives to 300,000 homeowners willing to use photovoltaic electricity. By the early twenty-first century, Japan was recognized as an international leader in the field of domestic photovoltaic systems and had convinced thousands of consumers and, importantly, many of the leading residential construction companies in the country to use the new system. Japanese firms quickly grew to dominate the world market until an upsurge in foreign competition, particularly from Germany, in 2006.[48] Sharp accounted for almost one quarter of the world's production, dropping to 17% in 2006; the next three largest Japanese firms, Kyocera, Sanyo and Mitsubishi Electric produced another 24%. Tokuyama dominates an important part of this sector, producing 20% of the total supply of the silicon needed for the panels. Until last year, Japanese firms controlled almost half of the world's market and produced about four times the number of photovoltaic modules as the US Increased foreign competition led Japanese solar panel makers to encourage the government to consider another consumer subsidy programme. Germany offers homeowners who use solar panels fifty cents for each kilowatt hour they generate through solar power for the next two decades.[49] Japanese officials are studying this programme and a similar one in California.

Green Purchasing Law

The Law on Promoting Green Purchasing took effect in 2002. Its goal was to promote environmentally friendly products and services by promoting green purchasing by public organizations and increasing awareness of environmentally friendly goods and services among the general public. The law was passed to make a market for eco-friendly products so that the government would purchase the goods first, ensuring a market and thereby creating more opportunities for consumers to purchase these goods. Under this law, the national government has been promoting the procurement of eco-friendly products by designating a number of items as green products (after they meet certain criteria) and then encouraging the purchase of those items. By last year, 214 items had been designated as green products. Over 90% of office paper and over 95% of office equipment meets the green standard.[50] The government is also working not only on shifting to eco-friendly products but is also re-evaluating the necessity of its purchasing decisions.[51]

The prospects for a Green Japan

Explaining the nature and depth of contemporary Japanese environmentalism requires an appreciation of the complexity of domestic and international political economy. Environmental concerns, while prominent in Japan, have not entered the national consciousness to the same degree as they have in North America and Europe. The government's new policies do not reflect a buckling to the wishes of a strident or powerful environmental movement, although one does exist in the country. Rather, Green Japan appears to be rooted in a series of interlocking developments. The country's leaders appear intrigued with the possibility of global leadership on an issue of world-wide importance and high political profile. There are limits to this engagement, as the country's interventions in Bali demonstrate, but Japan appears to be pushing forward cautiously in the environmental realm.

It can do so, in part, because of the Japanese track record in tackling major environmental issues on the domestic front and its willingness to take the lead through technology transfer and aid for the developing world.

There are pressures from below for political change, of course. Japan has many examples of effective political action, particularly at the local and regional level, designed to improve environmental conditions and to mobilize public support for substantial change in the approach to industrial and domestic activities. There is also widespread realization that eco-business or green business might well hold a key to Japan's continued prosperity; in this regard, Japan is being prepared and presented as a test-bed for valuable, exportable products and services that will re-enforce domestic economic strength.[52] Finally, the nation's confidence in scientific and technological solutions remains very strong. The application of research-based solutions to environmental challenges is a logical outgrowth of a nation-wide commitment to capitalizing on Japan's strengths in basic and applied science. All of these factors are underscored by a strong desire to reach the targets promised in the Kyoto Protocol, an international agreement that will always be linked to Japan.

Japan, like many other industrial nations, wishes to coordinate its international commitments with domestic policies, regulations and priorities. The country appears committed to achieving the goals in the Kyoto Protocol, perhaps more than most industrial nations. More importantly, the country's leaders, though weakened by a series of domestic political scandals and crises, hopes to assume a prominent global role on this issue. Other nations are also pursuing climate change and environmental protection initiatives; in selected areas, their policies, regulations and plans are more aggressive and effective than the Japanese activities. What does stand out in Japan is the country's desire to mobilize public support and the willingness of the government to impose tough restrictions on government and business. The central thrust of the Japanese plans appears to be the desire to make each Japanese family, company, agency, city and leader factor environmental questions and responses into their daily lives and operations. Clearly, having the nation internalize the values and principles of global environmentalism is the ultimate goal, reaching beyond the Kyoto accord and holding the potential, if not the promise, of a sustainable approach to environmental protection.

Rene Kemp's analysis of the connection between environmental policies and emerging technologies concluded with this observation about energy regimes in the age of environmentalism:

> One of the things it implies are special science and technology programmes for promising energy technologies with long-term benefits. Policy makers should also engage in experimentation with new technologies to learn more about their economic costs, technical feasibility and social acceptance. One way of doing this is through the creation of niche markets through government procurement, regulation, tax policies, subsidy schemes, etc. Other policies are the creation of networks of technology suppliers, research organizations and users, and the coordination of energy technology and environmental policies

with other policies: agricultural policies, transport policies, land-use policies, land-use planning, and industrial policies. This does not mean that carbon taxes or tradable quotas have no role to play in greenhouse policies; they do, but only as elements of a comprehensive energy technology policy aimed at making a transition towards a more sustainable energy system.[53]

The Green Japan approach suggests that the country has taken significant, but as yet not transformative steps, along the path that Kemp and others have suggested. It is too soon to tell if individual initiatives will be maintained over time or if significant changes in lifestyle and commercial and administrative processes have actually been institutionalized. Given the global urgency currently attached to ecological matters, and given the challenges facing industrialized nations the world over in meeting Kyoto targets, the Japanese experiences merit attention if only as one set of examples of how a country has taken a broad international agreement and brought the objectives and methods of addressing the protocol's objectives into the daily lives of citizens, communities, corporations and government agencies. Not all of the programmes will prove effective in the long run and the ambitious targets for specific initiatives may be missed. There is little question, however, but that the Government of Japan hopes to change personal and collective behaviour and ameliorate environmental change in the process.

Among the key developments in Japan are the following.

- The Japanese government has been a key adopter of new technologies and has tried to be something of an exemplar in responding to Kyoto and other environmental imperatives. The leadership role played by government, and something as simple as the Prime Minister not wearing a suit jacket and tie in the summer months and the regulation of heating and cooling in buildings, should not be under-estimated as a means of encouraging collective action.
- The Japanese model has, as in other areas, encouraged product, service and process development by the private sector, believing that the engagement and mobilization of business is crucial both to the attainment of national objectives and the creation of economic opportunities in an emerging sector.
- The government of Japan has been willing to use commercial and producers' subsidies to spark innovation, as with the photovoltaic initiatives, but with the understanding that direct support to businesses and consumers should come off quickly to avoid dependency and false economies in these key sectors.
- Scientific and technological innovation sits at the centre of Japanese attempts to meet the Kyoto targets and to become a truly "green" country. The mobilization of academic, government and commercial research scientists is deemed to be an essential element in tackling environmental challenges in a productive, cost-effective manner, with the potential side-benefit of producing a national or international business opportunity in the process.

- Sustainable environmental change, the Japanese authorities clearly believe, requires both clear national leadership and commitment to public engagement. Rather than focusing on punitive restrictions and tough and costly regulations, Japan has emphasized fundamental changes in behaviour and actions that can be taken by every person, family, company and community. In this manner, Japan has tried to make the whole country responsible for meeting the targets agreed to by the national government.

The Japan lesson works on the concept of connected action, with government policies and legislation connected to changes in basic domestic behaviour and business operations. It seeks, more generally, to create an environment where citizens watch, monitor, support and cajole each other, thus sharing the burden and mobilizing the nation in tackling a matter of great urgency and global importance. This approach, however, is likely only one piece of the necessary response to climate change. Current efforts focus on carbon emissions trading and caps, new technologies, and economic incentives. There are some who argue that the world requires a fundamentally different approach to the global economy.

If one lesson stands out from the Japanese experience – and the time involved is too short to determine the long-term effectiveness of actions to date – it is the manner in which the government of Japan has combined directions to the country at large with self-regulation and changes in government behaviour. Most observers agree that meeting the challenge of the Kyoto Accord will require effective and collective action on an almost unprecedented scale, the ecological equivalent of a war-time footing. The building blocks of Kyoto rest within nation-states, for no global solution will be found without the mobilization and transformation of individual countries. Japan has clearly made important strides toward meeting a key international goal; it remains to be seen if the Japanese model works within the country and, even more, if it can become an effective model for other nations seeking to bring their citizen's and business community's environmental behaviour in line with the requirements for global ecological preservation.

Climate change is the ultimate challenge of the age of globalization. Japan has, from the signing of the Kyoto Protocol, been symbolically associated with the effort to slow the pace of human-induced climate change. More importantly, Japan assumed national responsibility for getting its environmental house in order, particularly by mobilizing science, technology and business in the interest of environmental responsiveness and responsibility. The combination of regulatory action, technological innovation and the commercialization of environmental solutions (such as solar panels) has not solved all of Japan's ecological challenges, let alone those of the rest of the world. The Green Japan movement, however, captures the essence of Japan's response to the environmental aspects of globalization and demonstrates the country's clear understanding that it is, politically, economically and ecologically, very much a part of an interconnected world.

Notes

1 Details on the Kyoto Protocol can be found at http://unfccc.int/kyoto_protocol/items/2830.php

2 Sydney APEC Leaders' Declaration on Climate Change, Energy Security and Clean Development, 9 September 2007,   http://www.apec.org/etc/medialib/apec_media_library/downloads/news_uploads/2007aelm.Par.0001.File.tmp/07_aelm_ClimateChangeEnergySec.pdf

3 Ibid.

4 Prime Minister Abe resigned unexpectedly on September 12 and was replaced by Yasuo Fukuda on 25 September 2007.

5 "Japan recommends removing ties, jackets, turning AC down at U.N." *Japan Today,* 2 August 2007 – http://www.japantoday.com/jp/news/414010

6 Pamela Chasek, David Downie, Janet Welsh Brown, *Global Environmental Politics,* 4th Edition (Boulder, CO: Westview Press, 2006), 198–199.

7 Ibid., pp. 230–231. In this very helpful survey of global environmental politics, Pamela Chasek, David Downie and Janet Welsh Brown identified three fundamental elements in measuring the effectiveness of an environmental regime:

- **Regime Design** – the manner in which a country or international organization identifies the environmental threat and develops systems for monitoring, reporting, assisting and compelling compliance
- **Implementation** – the degree to which the core objectives are codified in legislation and regulations
- **Compliance** – the extent to which participants adhere to the rules, goals and expectations laid out in the regime.

8 Adam Jaffe and Robert Stavins, "Evaluating the Relative Effectiveness of Economic Incentives and Direct Regulation for Environmental Protection: Impacts on the Diffusion of Technology", paper for the WRI/OECD Symposium Towards 2000: Environment, Technology and the New Century, 13–15 June 1990. Quoted in Rene Kemp, *Environmental Policy and Technical Change: A Comparison of the Technological Impact of Policy Instruments* (Cheltenham: Edward Elgar, 1997), 19.

9 Rene Kemp, *Environmental Policy and Technical Change: A Comparison of the Technological Impact of Policy Instruments* (Cheltenham: Edward Elgar, 1997), 326–327.

10 National Institute of Advanced Industrial Science and Technology (AIST) publications (http://www.aist.go.jp) and the National Institute for Environmental Studies (NIES), Outline of the Second Five Year Plan (2006–2010) – http://www.nies.go.jp

11 For an interesting perspective on the political response to Minamata, see H. Funabashi, "Minamata Disease and Environmental Governance", *International Journal of Japanese Sociology*, Vol. 15, Issue 1 (November 2006), 7–25.

12 "Preface", in S. Tsuru and H. Weidner, eds., *Environmental Policy in Japan* (Berlin: Sigma Nohn, 1989), 9.

13 This issue is reviewed in H. Weidner, "Japanese Environmental Policy in an International Perspective: Lessons for a Preventive Approach", in Tsuru and Weidner, eds., *Environmental Policy in Japan,* 479–552.

14 Perhaps the most impassionate critique is Alex Kerr, *Dogs and Demons: Tales from the Dark Side of Japan* (New York: Hill and Wang, 2001).

15 Robert Mason, "Whither Japan's Environmental Movement?: An Assessment of Problems and Prospects at the National Level", *Pacific Affairs,* Vol. 72 (2) (1999), 187–207.

16 On the science-friendly nature of Japan, see Carin Holroyd and Ken Coates, *Innovation Nation: Science and Technology in 21st Century Japan* (London: Plagrave Macmillan, 2007). On the priorities of the pre-1990 environmental movement, see

J. Pierce et al, "Vanguards and Rearguards in Environmental Politics", *Comparative Political Studies,* Vol. 18, No. 4 (1986), 419–447.

17 See T. Terao and K. Otsuka, eds., *Development of Environmental Policy in Japan and Asian Countries* (London: Palgrave Macmillan, 2007).

18 One of the best studies of grass roots environmental mobilization in Japan is Lam Peng-Er, *Green Politics in Japan* (New York: Routledge, 1999).

19 Jeffrey Broadbent, *Environmental Politics in Japan* (Cambridge: Cambridge University Press, 1998), 345.

20 Broadbent, p. 355.

21 Broadbent, p. 367.

22 "Invitation to 'Cool Earth 50' – Three Proposals, 3 Principles", Speeches and Statements by Prime Minister – http://www.kantei.go.jp/foreign/abespeech/2007/05/24speech_e.html

23 Chris Knight and Paul Scott, "Japanese Disclosure Sets the Pace", *Environmental Finance,* July–August 2001.

24 "Half-price Big Mac to Fight Global Warming Proves Big Hit in Japan", 5 September 2007 – http://green.yahoo.com/omdex.php?q=node/1508

25 "Invitation to 'Cool Earth 50' – Three Proposals, 3 Principles", Speeches and Statements by Prime Minister – http://www.kantei.go.jp/foreign/abespeech/2007/05/24speech_e.html

26 Ibid.

27 Ibid.

28 Miki Baba, "Government Purchased emission credits for 12.2 billion yen" Nikkei Business Online http://business.nikkeibp.co.jp/article.tech April 17, 2007; Hideki Minamikawa, Japanese Ministry of the Environment, Speech to the Air Resources Board, Sacremento, California, 17 January 2007; Team -6% Official Website http://wwwteam-6.jp

29 Yasuo Fukuda replaced Shinzo Abe as prime minister in late September 2007. It is not yet clear how high the environment will be on his agenda.

30 The G8 Hokkaido communiqué from 9 July 2008 can be found at http://www.g7.utoronto.ca/summit/2008hokkaido/2008-mem.html

31 A more detailed description of the various Japanese global warming initiatives is described in CIGI Technical Paper #3, Green Japan.

32 "Japan's Eco Market Takes Root" *JETRO Japan Economic Monthly,* September 2005.

33 Team -6% Official Website http://www.team-6.jp. For updates on the impact of the programme, see http://www.team-6.jp/english/result.html

34 http://www.expo2005.or.jp/en/

35 Mitsutsune Yamaguchi, "Extended Producer Responsibility in Japan", ECP (Environmentally Conscious Products) Newsletter of the Japan Environmental Management Association for Industry, No. 19, 2002.

36 Steve Karpel, "Recycling Japan", *Metal Bulletin Monthly, London,* April 2006, Iss. 424, 33–34.

37 Kiyoshi Ueno, "Current Status of Home Appliance Recycling in Japan", Environmentally Conscious Products (ECP) Newsletter of the Japan Environmental Management Association for Industry, No. 18. 2002.

38 The consumer pays a national recycling fee plus transportation costs (4,600 yen for a fridge, 3,500 yen for an air conditioner, 2,700 yen for a cathode ray television and 2,400 yen for a washing machine). If consumers do not remember from where they bought the appliance or they don't have a receipt or the shop is too far away, then collectors will pick up the item. Televisions, for example, are picked up by the Post Office.

39 For the political contest of this law, see K. Togawa, "Background of the automotive recycling law enactment in Japan", *Environmental Economics and Policy Studies,* Vol. 6, No. 4 (2006), 271–284.

40 For examples of community mobilization on environmental issues, see S. Shin, "East Asian Environmental Cooperation: Central Pessimism, Local Optimism", *Pacific Affairs,* Vol. 80p, No. 1 (Spring 2007), 9–26.

41 Ministry of Economy, Trade and Industry website – http://www.meti.go.jp/policy/recycle/main/English/3r_policy/ecotown.html; http:www.env.go.jp/en/press/2005/0916a-01.html

42 http://www.env.go.jp/en/press/2005/0916a-01.html; Video made by the City of Kitakyushu, June 2006.

43 Speech by Yuriko Koike, Minster of the Environment of Japan, "Japan on the Move: Japan's Innovative Technologies for Tackling Climate Change" Montreal, Canada, 7 December 2005. http://www.env.go.jp/earth/cop/cop11/climate_c.pdf

44 Research and Development of Clean-Energy Vehicles: the Need for More Environment Friendly automotive Technologies: Japan Automobile Manufacturers Brochure – http://www/njkk.com/library/bro-enviroFriendly/enviro_3.htm

45 Speech by Yuriko Koike, Minster of the Environment in Japan, "Japan on the Move: Japan's Innovative Technologies for Tackling Climate Change" Montreal, Canada, 7 December 2005. http://www.env.go.jp/earth/cop/cop11/climate_c.pdf; Kazuyuki Harada, Ministry of the Environment, Japan "The Green Purchasing Law, and Promoting Green Procurement in Japan", a presentation on 23 March 2006.

46 Paul Johnson and Tadashi Shirai, British Embassy, Tokyo and Philip White, DTI Global Watch Service, "Inorganic Light Emitting Diode (LED) Development and Applications in Japan".

47 Fuel cells, viewed briefly as a key to energy sustainability, are designed to provide self-rejuvenating energy and storage systems. See also OECD, *Innovation in energy technology: comparing national innovation systems at the sectoral level,* Chapter 6: Japan: Fuel Cells (Paris: OECD, 2006).

48 Jochen Legewie, "Foreign Competition Begins to Overshadow Japan's Solar Industry", *The Japan Times,* 30 July 2007.

49 Ibid.

50 Kazuyuki Harada, Ministry of the Environment, Japan "The Green Purchasing Law, and Promoting Green Procurement in Japan", a presentation on 23 March 2006.

51 "The Law on Promoting Green Purchasing Five Years Later – Progress and Future Tasks", *Japan Sustainability Newsletter* #058, June 2007.

52 An insightful study of the commercial approach to environmental certification demonstrates that corporate interest in new standards reflects both a realization of the financial benefits attached to an eco-business approach and support for environmental considerations among leading managers. See M. Nakamura et al., "Why Japanese Firms Choose to Certify: A Study of managerial Responses to Environmental Issues", *Journal of Environmental Economics and Management",* No. 42 (2001), 23–52.

53 Rene Kemp, *Environmental Policy and Technical Change: A Comparison of the Technological Impact of Policy Instruments* (Cheltenham: Edward Elgar 1997), 327.

Conclusion

Japan in the age of twenty-first-century globalization

Carin Holroyd and Ken Coates

Japan has experienced successive waves of globalization in the past 75 years: the turmoil of global war, the tension of the Cold War, the global impact of rapid industrialization and economic growth, the period when Japan and the other Asian Tigers appeared destined for global dominance, the cultural–political globalization of the late twentieth century, and the collective collapse and global angst of 2008–2009. At times, globalization has been defined in simple terms, tied to the rise (and fall) of dominant states and economic systems, collective demographic or environmental calamities, the global reach of Western popular culture, and the pernicious and often hidden ties of the global financial system. At other times, it has been viewed as a hydra-headed monster, a multifaceted, centreless force with the power to recast societies and restructure economies. For most observers, globalization is now viewed as being much more than one thing, one process, one threat or one opportunity.

Instead, and this is key to understanding the effects of globalization in Japan, the concept defines a broad set of characteristics that link a nation to large, undirected international influences. There was a time – and pre-Meiji Japan is as much as exemplar of this tradition as contemporary Burma/Myanmar – when nations and cultures operated largely in isolation from the rest of the world, controlling contact with outsiders and determining the nature and flow of trade, culture and political influences in and out of the country. The prospect of true isolation withered over time, largely due to the powerful reach of international trade and the increasing complexity of international politics and warfare. No nation could remain a total island in such environments, even though hermit states like Albania and Bhutan struggled purposefully to keep the forces of global integration at bay.

By the late twentieth century, the combined forces of economic ties, environmental interconnectedness, technological linkages, cultural flows and political entanglements ensured that all nations of earth – Japan very much among them – were caught in global nets. In political and public conversations, globalization tended to be reduced to a single dominant thread – typically economic connections, often fear of Western cultural influences, and latterly concern about collective environmental challenges – and usually associated with a major and serious global danger. Globalization has generally been viewed as a threat. On occasion, nations have seen the elimination of barriers to trade, politics and culture to be an opportunity. At all times, however, it is seen as a matter to be monitored closely. Implicit in the debates over globalization are two assumptions: that vigilance was required to protect the country from significant loss as a consequence of global influences and that, properly handled, globalization could be managed for national benefit.

The subtleties and perniciousness of globalization are now much better understood. The economic turmoil of 2008–2009 – blindingly fast in impact and distressingly broad in reach – demonstrated the deep interdependence of the world's economies; the slow and uneven recovery from the global recession provided ample evidence of the interconnected of economies and societies around the globe. But as analysts, including the contributors to this collection, broadened the investigation of globalization it became increasingly clear that this crucial phenomenon operated and operates in a very complex manner.

Globalization, in Japan as elsewhere, is not a contemporary phenomenon and, indeed, has substantial roots in the past. Jay Goulding illustrates that, at the level of the philosophical insights and values that define a society, international influences have long shaped Japanese thought. It is important to recognize that, from early times, external ideas and concepts featured significantly in the evolution of Japanese thinking. Japanese corporate histories, a potentially valuable source for understanding the emergence of post-war Japan, as Jeff Alexander shows, outlines how Japanese firms sought to position themselves in the international realm. He shows that Japanese corporations have been reluctant to integrate their wartime experience into their narrative, seeking to downplay unfavourable associations with of World War II. Dawn Grimes-McClellan, in turn, documents the changing understanding of childhood in Japan, linking the expectations of childhood to both a global debate on this subject and to imported views of how children should behave and be treated.

For many observers, globalization is a force that is at once very contemporary and largely economic in origins and impact. The contributions from Beason *et al.* and Nakamura describe the corporate effects of the post-bubble effort to Westernize Japanese business practices, an era ironically which came on the heels of several decades of Western companies attempting to replicate Japan's manufacturing and corporate achievements. In the business world, clearly, globalization has been running in multiple directions, and Japan has been both a sender and a recipient of commercial influences. Coates and Holroyd show that the seemingly old-fashioned forces of nationalism and loyalty to country shape the quintessential late twentieth century global race, especially in an area of growing importance like the commercialization of science and technology. Japan, they argue, manages to combine a global outlook with a strong commitment to the nation, thus ensuring that the top scientists, entrepreneurs and companies stayed in Japan to develop their commercial innovations.

Globalization is, of course, much more than an economic phenomenon. Indeed, there is ample evidence of the multi-directional and pervasive cultural influences of globalization. In Japan's case, as William Tsutsui demonstrates, the pathways of cultural globalization go in multiple directions. Japan's contributions to popular culture – from anime to Hello Kitty – are as widespread and influential outside the country as KFC and Major League Baseball are evident inside. Much is made in Japan, as Norio Ota demonstrates, of the complex linguistic interactions between English and Japanese. Fear of the growing dominance of English and the sweeping impact of Western popular culture has been prevalent in Japan and other Asia countries for generations. At both the official level, particularly evident in national educational policies and curriculum, and in the broader cultural and nationalistic debates about Japan's future, concern about the invasive effects of foreign cultural forms, values and content remains widespread. Many people in Japan wrestle with the forms and content of cultural globalization, seeking to find both authentic Japanese voices and to understand how foreign influences are reaching into Japan. Janice Brown demonstrates these creative tensions in her study of Japanese women writers, who themselves struggle with the interplay of the local and global, the Japanese and the international.

The multiple forces of globalization raise significant questions about Japan's place in the world and about the interactions between national priorities and global influences. This struggle is clearly evident in many aspects of Japan's foreign relations. Kimie Hara uses the debates about the Cold War and Japan's changing role in East Asia to illustrate the interplay of Japanese security concerns, and to show how Cold War problems require multi-lateral solutions appropriate for a globalized political environment. Japan's diplomacy and defence arrangements have long been strongly influenced by geopolitical struggles originating far outside the country. The ongoing debate about climate change, forever linked to Japan by the signing of the Kyoto Accord, provides another example of the interplay of global and domestic forces. As Carin Holroyd argues, Japan's political and commercial response to the realities of climate change reflected both its international commitments and national imperatives tied to a growing concern about quality of life and the preservation of the natural environment. Japan's innovative commercial environment is also producing lessons, ideas and products for the rest of the world.

Globalization is multi-directional, multisectoral, highly integrated, and extremely difficult to track. At one time, globalization was something of a code word for Westernization, a more polite way of decrying the cultural influences of the United States on countries like Japan. It is now abundantly clear that all countries are affected by global influences, that all countries contribute to the ebb and flow of ideas, business, political actions, and that cultural influences spread around the world. The realities of globalization present opportunities for trading nations – Japan being one of the best – to extend their reach and thereby improve prosperity. It presents challenges in terms of new ideas, values and cultural forms, some of which strike at the heart of national assumptions and preferences. And, perhaps most importantly, globalization defines the central truism of the twenty-first century – that countries share a common humanity and, in all likelihood, a common destiny, one linked inextricably by the powerful forces of environmental change and defined by the triumvirate of politics, business and culture.

Japan has moved uneasily in the first decade of the twenty-first century. Much of the world's focus – and fear – has shifted from Japan to China, the fearsome Asian superpower that has assumed Japan's mantle as the greatest threat to Western economic and political dominance. The country pulled itself out of a long recession, only to be slammed hard by the economic debacle of 2008–2009. The remarkable sight of the leadership of Toyota Corporation apologizing profusely for the company's failure to respond properly to the economic meltdown will stand for some time as a mark of Japan's acknowledged vulnerability to the realities for globalization. Japan has taken tentative steps toward greater global engagement, forever linked at least by name to the Kyoto Accord on climate change, making small steps toward international peace-keeping, and seeking to use international organizations to contain the greatest threat to its security.

There have been growing signs of Japanese awareness about international perceptions of the country, especially in Asia, and evidence of an increased commitment to regional security and economic integration in East Asia. Japanese popular culture has found increasing favour around the world, particularly through anime and video games, and a stronger presence throughout East Asia. At the same time, there is increased interest in Korean, Chinese and Western popular culture inside Japan, and considerable concern about the loss of Japanese values in the surge of Western movies, television, music and literature. Japan even, in the summer 2009 elections, experimented with that most Western-style political tradition of alternating political parties, with the Democratic Party ousting the long-serving Liberal Democratic Party from office. This latter, however, was tied much more to domestic realities than to any identifiable Western forces taking over national politics in Japan.

Globalization will spark endless debate, inside Japan and around the world. As in Japan, people will identify commercial opportunities and threats. They will argue about the best means of shaping the education system to respond to the new realities. There will, invariably, be nativistic responses against creeping foreign influences, and these will likely be stronger in Japan than in most countries. Other nations, it must be said, will rail against growing Japanese influences in their midst, from increased Japanese control of manufacturing and trade to the continued spread of Japanese popular culture. Japan, like other countries but with a particularly twist around the international engagement of the Japanese military, will debate its role in political hotspots such as Afghanistan. There will be, as a result of growing awareness of the intricate interconnections of the environment, pollution, trade and finance, increased attention to each country's place within these global systems. Globalization is no longer a force, an influence or a phenomenon. It is a reality of the twenty-first century, and will remain so into the foreseeable future.

In most countries, the most passionate debates about globalization focus on language and culture, typically with a condemnatory emphasis on Western television, movies, music, popular literature and the Internet, the latter being among the fastest and more pervasive threat. Japan is no exception. A current debate about changes in the Japanese language captures the intensity and diversity of opinion on the issues of globalization. Minae Mizumura, a highly regarded Japanese novelist, published a provocative book, *The Fall of Japanese in the Age of English* (*Nihongo ga Horobiru Toki – Eigo no Seiki no Nakade*).[1] Mizumura argued that the Internet was a primary culprit, holding the capacity to render languages such as Japanese into only "local" languages of no compelling international interest. She argued, further, that the Japanese education system was complicit in the decline, for more time was spent learning English than Japanese. This, in turn, she suggests, is stripping Japanese of its richness and diversity, with the decline in the language certain to accelerate as younger, Internet-savvy Japanese assume more of a role in society.

Not everyone agrees, of course. Other Japanese embrace or accept the substantial changes that are occurring. Famed novelist Haruki Murakami argued, "My personal view on the Japanese language (or any language) is, 'If it wants to change, let it change.' Any language is alive just like a human being, just like you or me. And if it's alive, it will change. Nobody can stop it." There is no such thing as simplification of language, he added. "It just changes for better or worse (and nobody can tell if it is better or worse)."[2] With English usage and access becoming more pervasive, and with new technologies emerging as increasingly important mediating tools for language and culture, it is obvious that the debate will continue. But suggestions of the imminent demise of the Japanese language through the spread of English and cultural globalization are extremely premature. Readership of Japanese language books and newspapers remains extremely high, as are national literacy rates. The Japanese language is not going anywhere soon – although changes are occurring and will continue in the future.

Globalization is a crucial part of the new realities, for Japan and all other countries. The past thirty years has seen a crucial confluence of events and developments: the end of the Cold War, the opening of China, liberalized international trade, the expansion of global financial networks, the destruction of distance and time through new technologies, the spread of popular culture through television, movies and the Internet, and the demise of cultural myopia that has opened people around the world to products, services, ideas and values from other lands. No land, no people, no culture and no economy really stand aloof from these influences (with the exception of truly totalitarian states like North Korea and Burma). Government policies and regulatory regimes, particularly in areas related to culture, can slow but rarely stop the infiltration of foreign influences.

Japan, among only a handful of nations, plays a formidable role at both ends of the globalization chain, feeling the effects of various international forces while at the same time spreading its ideas, values, products, services and approaches to countries around the world. As both a recipient and leader of globalization, Japan will clearly continue to be shaped dramatically by the forces of change and the opportunities for outreach and integration. The essays in this collection make a consistent point: Japan and the Japanese people are aware of the rapidly changing nature of the world order and are being affected by the shifts in politics, business, government, culture, language and values. Moreover, the influences of globalization are not new, but have featured prominently in Japanese life for many generations, providing the country with an opportunity to learn the dangers and opportunities of engagement with the broader world.

The academic challenges of studying globalization in Japan and Japan's impact on the world at large are formidable. The traditional approaches in most disciplines assume the primacy of the nation-state and focus on the nuances and characteristics of the national setting. Globalization, while quite clear at a macro level and obviously pervasive, is also quite an elusive force. Figuring out the flow of trade in and out of a country or the net effects of immigration and emigration is relatively straightforward; determining the exchange of ideas and values around business management, childhood education or literature is an all-together different challenge. Similarly, academics are well practiced at understanding literary debates and influences within a national body of literature; teasing out the intellectual, social and cultural factors that originate outside the country is a unique academic enterprise. *Japan in the Age of Globalization* was designed as a multi-disciplinary exploration into the nature of globalization. The contributors to this volume have demonstrated, in a variety of different ways, the significant intellectual contributions to be found from situating Japan in a global context and seeking to identify the ways in which global influences are changing Japan and how Japanese influences are changing the world. As the pace and impact of globalization picks up, it will rest with the scholarly community to continue to push the boundaries of the academic study, for Japan and elsewhere, of globalization. The world has become remarkably interconnected in the twenty-first century. Determining how global influences interact with local and national realities will remain one of the primary intellectual challenges of this age.

Notes

1 Minae Mizumura, *Nihongo ga Horobiru Toki – Eigo no Seiki no Nakade* (Tokyo: Chikuma Shobo, 2008).
2 Emily Parker, "Is Technology Dumbing Down Japanese?," *New York Times, Sunday Book Review*, 5 November 2009.

Index